ALWAYS ANOTHER
HORIZON

ALWAYS ANOTHER HORIZON

A JOURNEY AROUND THE WORLD

Tina Olton

To Stephanie —

Fair winds ; calm seas!

Tina

iUniverse Star

New York Lincoln Shanghai

Always Another Horizon
A Journey Around the World

Copyright © 2005, 2007 by Tina Olton

iUniverse Star
an iUniverse, Inc. imprint

iUniverse books may be ordered through booksellers or by contacting:

iUniverse
2021 Pine Lake Road, Suite 100
Lincoln, NE 68512
www.iuniverse.com
1-800-Authors (1-800-288-4677)

ISBN-13: 978-1-58348-473-9 (pbk)
ISBN-13: 978-0-595-86325-9 (ebk)
ISBN-10: 1-58348-473-6 (pbk)
ISBN-10: 0-595-86325-6 (ebk)

Printed in the United States of America

For Stephen,
my love and companion on this voyage,
and in all of life.

Contents

Prelude

The world is constantly revolving—and evolving. It astounds me how much the world has changed since we returned from the voyage described in these pages. My husband, Stephen, and I often say to one another how lucky we are to have traveled here or there when we did. Would we sail up the Red Sea today, we wonder? Would we visit Israel today? Sri Lanka? Yemen? Egypt? Would we stop in Bali—or anywhere in Indonesia? It is very difficult to say without being closer to these places and having a clearer picture of the risks or dangers and the micropolitical climate—that is to say, how the local people in our anchorage would feel about who we are. Governments, wars, politicians, and extremists are one thing. Local people minding their own business, tending their property, and living their lives day to day are quite another. The reader will discover, for instance, that we visited the Sudan at a time many would have thought foolish. Yet our visit to Sudan was not only satisfying, but illuminating—and quite possibly the most complete experience of the voyage.

This story is, by necessity, a hop, skip, and jump through our experiences. Some subjects receive minute attention; others are breezed over. The reader may be frustrated by my superficial treatment of some place, or bored by the long description of some other. I can't exactly predict which stories will amuse, which will disappoint, which will illuminate, or which will annoy. I have written them the way I think about them. If the geography is scant, I send you to your atlas. If the history is full of holes, your encyclopedia may fill in the gaps. If the cultural background is meager, I hope readers will comb their library, avail themselves of their local bookshop, or surf the Internet for more information. This is what world exploration is all about: searching the avenues of the globe.

Sailing around the world is to sailors what climbing Mt. Everest must be to mountaineers: the ultimate challenge. There are more difficult sailing challenges—a passage around Cape Horn through the "roaring sixties" might be one—just as there are more difficult mountains than Everest to climb, but circumnavigating the world has the cachet of conquering Everest. It is not just sailing around the world, however, but experiencing the world as you go that makes such a voyage more than a challenge. It's an education, and more than that, it tests the very mettle of your life. This was more than a trip, or even a voyage, and God knows it was *not* an extended vacation, as so many well-meaning souls have said to me. It was our *way of life* for eight years.

Paul Theroux once wrote, "You have to be supremely confident to be a traveler." I don't pretend to have been supremely confident all of the seven years and nine months it took us to go around the world, nor would I suggest that I am particularly courageous, but if I'm not, I must be nuts. Who in their right mind would head out to sea *knowing* it will be weeks before you sight land, let alone civilization, again? But wait! Isn't that the romance of it, you ask?

You think it romantic that your husband is so seasick he is puking all over the cockpit? You think it romantic that half the waves in the ocean have washed over the boat and everything on it, including you? You think it romantic that you are fifty, and you don't know if you're having a hot flash or it's just too damn hot, period? You think it romantic that the Eritrean navy starts after you with their guns aimed low? Ah, but I get ahead of myself....

Let the reader proceed.

Beginnings

I don't remember the exact moment when we decided to sail around the world. Did Stephen and I say to one another on some foggy evening by the fire in our Berkeley home, "Okay, let's do it?" I don't think so. It grew out of years of sailing together, thinking about sailing the oceans, securing our anchor in remote tropical islands, discovering new cultures, and meeting the people of new countries. And, indeed, we tried it out one year. We took leaves from our jobs, cajoled our youngest daughter, Holly, into leaving her teenage friends, and sailed from San Francisco to the South Pacific and back. That was the Trial Run.

Soon after that adventure our thoughts wandered to wider horizons. Why not make the ultimate sailing voyage—a circumnavigation? The first voyage had merely whetted our appetites. We yearned for more.

Although it is possible to retire and just say you are going to sail around the world, it usually requires some experience. And if you are going to do it with a mate, it usually requires a mate who is willing, at the very least, but preferably able as well. Stephen was lucky in me. I was very willing, and as it happens, I was able too.

Stephen loves telling his family joke about how he met me. It was in Houston, Texas. He owned a 25-foot wooden sloop, and he loved sailing. We met at a party and discussed the possibility of my joining him for an afternoon on Galveston Bay. He asked, as he had learned to do, what my previous sailing experience had been. And I replied, "Oh, only on very small boats," which he interpreted to mean something like a board boat—a Sailfish or Sunfish. On the appointed day, Stephen relished his role as captain and hopped around showing me how to hoist the sails, pull in the sheets, cleat down the lines.

"By the end of the day," he says now, "I began to smell a rat. I watched her move around the boat, and saw that she knew more than she was letting on." He eventually pulled out of me that I had been sailing since childhood, I had been a sailing instructor on Martha's Vineyard for years, and I even had a few silver trophies on my mantel that said things like "First Place, Edgartown Regatta." Well, they *had* been small boats—smaller than 25 feet—so I didn't think I had lied. But perhaps I had misled him; I am never one to lay down all my cards at once.

There was a day, in fact, when I resisted sailing. My father had the sailing bug as a youth too, but with no outlet until he had established a career, corralled a wife, and gathered a family around him. In our leisure time, he announced, we would go sailing.

He purchased a lovely, open-cockpit day-sailer that we could sail in and around Boston Harbor. I was five. On my maiden voyage the wind became "sprightly," and our course became confused. *Our* family joke was that if there was a rock or shoal to be discovered, our father would find it—by hitting it— which he did on the morning of my first sail. With the sails crashing, the lines slatting, my father yelling, my mother weeping, what could a five-year-old conclude? Sailing was not fun.

I remember awakening on Saturday mornings and lying in bed, looking out my window at the trees—looking, looking for a single leaf quivering, thus indicating *wind*. Of course we lived fifteen miles from the shore and any flipping leaf in our backyard would scarcely indicate the coastal weather. But what five-year-old knows this? If I felt there was any breeze, I looked for alternatives.

Our neighbor remembers many Saturday mornings when I appeared on their doorstep begging to remain with them for the day—perhaps to take care of their cat, or play with their baby—if only I did not have to go sailing.

Our family's sailing phase didn't last long. My mother's disinclination to the activity, my teenage siblings' other interests, and my stubborn refusal soon had my father putting the lovely boat up for sale.

But in my teenage years I spent a number of summers at a Girl Scout sailing camp on Martha's Vineyard. I learned to sail and learned well. I was good, hence the silver "First Place, Edgartown Regatta." After those years, however, as I floundered around looking for a future in the Midwest, sailing was eclipsed— until I met Stephen.

The boat he owned was a well-found craft, a Cheoy Lee Frisco Flyer—25 feet of wood molded into classical yacht lines. Stephen adored her. I thought she was grand, but lacking in some of the essentials: the toilet, for instance. Oh, there was one, but you had to back down on it, stooped over, unbuckling your britches as you went, hoping to land, bare-bucked, at the right moment. There were two narrow berths in the salon, on which a really good night's sleep was not possible. There was no stove, no fresh water, no room to stand up—nothing to suggest a comfortable time on the seas.

"Let's ditch this thing ... ah, this *beauty*," I declared, "and find a seaworthy yacht that we can sail without getting drenched on the first wave." And so began our cruising life together. Every five years we upgraded our yacht by five feet—25 to 30, then 35, and finally 40. The first boat we purchased together—the 30-footer—was named *Horizon*. During our courtship Stephen had given me a photo torn from a Sunday newspaper magazine. It showed a man on the deck of a sailboat, looking forward to the bow where the sails were full and pulling with the wind. The caption to this photo read: "When all that holds us is the horizon, that will be our freedom." Too many boats are named *Freedom*, so we named ours *Horizon*—only slightly fewer of them around.

The 35-footer was named *Horizon Too,* and our daughter, Holly, suggested *New Horizon* for that first 40-footer. This was the boat we purchased to make the Trial Run. By then we had moved ourselves from Texas to the San Francisco Bay Area.

New Horizon was a Valiant 40, acquired after months of research, reading, discussing, looking, and, when we could, sailing various possibilities while we talked vaguely of sailing the vast oceans.

The essential issue at this time was our nearly teenage daughter. Holly was adamant about any long-term voyage: "Not with me on board." But when we began to talk about a voyage that had a beginning, a middle, and an end, and for *only* six months, she began to acquiesce. Her ears were pricked; she was listening, assimilating what this might mean to her. It would be something none of her peers had done, something no one else knew about, something unique. For a teenager that was either glory or death. Holly chose glory.

If she were going, however, she said the boat had to have a "cabin" for her, with a door that she could close or slam, depending on her mood, for privacy. *New Horizon* had a stateroom aft near the crux of things (steps to the cockpit, navigation station, galley, and so forth) for the captain and mate, and a forepeak (up front in the bow of the boat)—with a door—that could be Holly's den.

We made our Trial Run in seven months: San Francisco to French Polynesia to the northernmost Cook Island (Penrhyn), then to Palmyra, to Hawaii, and home. Nine thousand miles in seven months, almost as if we were racing, when in fact we were trying out the "cruising lifestyle." We were captivated. This was it for our retirement years.

So now that we had the experience, we needed to do a bit of planning.

*   *   *   *   *

It took three years to put together the campaign for this venture. The timing was opportune. In three years Holly would begin college, and Stephen would turn sixty and could decently retire early. At ten years his junior, I could quit my job and leave my friends, my family, and my home—everything that had been our life for the last twenty years. It would be a prodigious undertaking.

Financial spreadsheets were churned out on the computer. We calculated our pensions, with Social Security kicking in at the appropriate years, and income from this, that, or the other retirement plan, investments, and bits and pieces of things we had haphazardly thrown into the bank over the years. Strategic plans were designed that would get us to the point of casting off the dock lines for the last time. This was like starting up a new business—strategic and financial plans.

Meanwhile, we visited colleges with Holly, discussing the pros and cons of East Coast or West Coast, large or small, state or private, and women only or coed. It was hard for Stephen and me to concentrate as we simultaneously visited boat shows and clambered over numerous decks, caressing hulls, kicking keels, sitting in cockpits, and dreaming of how it would be. As capable as *New Horizon* was, the old dear that had taken us to the South Pacific once was probably not up to the stress of a round-the-world venture without considerable overhauling. We needed the security of a newer yacht, so we sold the house to buy *Another Horizon*. And we applied to colleges. We looked again at those spreadsheets, and we hoped for the best. The world was already spinning in my head as the pace of the predeparture marathon picked up.

*   *   *   *   *

About this time I looked at the keys on my key ring. There was a whole bunch: three for the house (front, back, and basement), two for my work (front door and the door to my office), two for my car (ignition and trunk), and one for Stephen's car. There was a key for the mailbox at the mail service center, one for the safe-deposit box at the bank, and one for the gym locker. There was one for the neighbor's house, in case of an emergency, and one for the marina gate where we kept *Another Horizon* berthed. Keys to all the trappings of my life, including one key whose purpose I no longer remembered. Perhaps that key said more about what our lives had become, and why this venture was coming none too soon. The keys to the house were the first to be discarded.

Divesting ourselves of possessions was easier than I thought possible. The intensity of our new goal made it easy to say yea, nay, keep, sell, Salvation Army, or throw away. In the end there were twenty-four cartons of various sizes that contained the precious things from our twenty years together. Onto *Another Horizon* went our pared-down wardrobes (lots of shorts, T-shirts, and bathing suits; no more pin stripes, career suits, or silk blouses), our CD collection, and all the books for which we could find space. In two weeks we sold the house and everything in it—lock, stock, and piano—and moved onto the boat.

With some regret, we returned the key to our neighbor's house, with good-byes to the old neighborhood. A marina on the estuary between Oakland and Alameda became our neighborhood for the next year. During that period we combined the end of our careers with readying the boat for long-term voyaging, while making arrangements for a thread of our shore lives to continue. Although we would have no house, no cars, no material possessions of any kind left in the Bay Area, we did need an address for mail and a bank account for depositing pension checks.

We were fortunate to find that our tax accountant's assistant was willing to look after our financial affairs—the occasional Visa bill, our checking account—and our mail. This arrangement also kept our financial records in one place, ready for April 15. The contents of the safe-deposit box went into a fireproof box in their office. Another key down.

When asked where she hailed from, one cruising friend halfway around the world said, "The rest of my life, what there is of it, is stored in Seattle, so that must be where I'm from." Another said, "My mailbox is Tallahassee; that's as close as I get to 'being from.'" We would keep a permanent mailing address in the Bay Area, and our twenty-four cartons would be stored with friends and family. We would continue to "hail" from Berkeley—it said so on the stern of our boat—but our home was our boat, wherever in the world that craft was.

The gym membership came up for annual renewal, but there was no point in renewing; I was getting enough exercise running errands up and down the docks. I turned in the key to the gym locker.

At the beginning of June, Stephen officially retired. At the end of June, I said farewell to my career as a publishing house financial officer. The personnel manager took my office keys with a hug. It was two months to departure day.

We began an intense period of finishing the preparation of the boat and bringing our shore life to a close. We kept thinking of things that absolutely needed to be done. The ham (amateur shortwave) radio had to be installed, jacklines for deck safety made, cockpit leecloths sewn, warm-weather rain gear purchased. It wasn't long before the list was divided into categories: "Absolutely needs to be done," "Would be better if it were done," "Can be done after departure," and "If it never gets done, so be it." We were counting days now, instead of weeks or months.

*   *   *   *   *

The college applications were successful and my "one and only" got her wish—a women's college near Boston, where there was family to whom she could turn if she needed help. Seeing Holly off on the plane for college put one of the last steps to our leave-taking into place. What was happening, I suddenly realized, was real. And I realized too late that she wasn't leaving us, we were leaving her—and everyone and everything else that had been our lives for twenty years. I was shocked to realize that I had underestimated how I would feel about that.

But there was no time to ruminate about my feelings. We dashed from the airport to the grocery store for the last provisions, and turned the last of my keys—to my car—over to the friends who had bought it. We clambered aboard *Another Horizon* to await the dawning of the next day and the ritual casting off of the dock lines. In the gray of the morning there were friends on dock to watch, wave, and call out good wishes. It was thrilling, scary, exciting—and final.

El Nuevo Mundo

California and Mexico

We sailed under the Golden Gate Bridge with a high fog obscuring the tops of the bridge towers. The wind was boisterous and cool for the 4th of September.

"*Another Horizon, Another Horizon,*" came a call on our VHF radio, "this is *JayDee.* Do you copy?"

We scrambled for the microphone. "*JayDee!* This is *Another Horizon.* Where are you?"

"Approaching the San Francisco ship channel." Only a few miles away.

We had first met *JayDee,* a cutter-rigged Valiant 40 (the same design as *Another Horizon),* in French Polynesia three years earlier during the Trial Run. *JayDee* was now sailing for San Francisco after a 49-day passage from Japan.

"We heard other boats calling you, wishing you well," remarked Jerry. "It sounds like you're under way again." Indeed we were.

We crossed paths with *JayDee* one mile outside San Francisco Bay. It was an auspicious omen. How could they have crossed more than 5,000 miles of ocean to sail into San Francisco at the very hour we were sailing out? As the wakes of our hulls intermingled, we waved and shouted good wishes. It was a poignant moment: they were finishing their five-year voyage, and ours was but five hours old.

⋆ ⋆ ⋆ ⋆ ⋆

As we sailed between Santa Cruz and Morro Bay, the wind was near gale force, the seas were high, the engine was overheating, Stephen was seasick, the autopilot had stopped working, and it was a very dark night. There was dense fog. It made the night darker than dark; there was no ambient light from the shore or from the sky. It was impossible to discern a horizon. We couldn't see where we were going, where we'd come from, or if the next wave would swamp us or slip under the hull. It's not unusual to have these conditions—high winds and seas, dense fog—along the California coast, but they are not conditions anyone would wish for, certainly not me. I hated all of it.

We were both on deck grappling with the sails to reef them. It was my watch, and I had waited too long to wake Stephen to get his help with this task. The wind was whistling and it was difficult getting the sails under control. We were being flung from side to side by the confused seas. In the dark we couldn't anticipate the wave action and were readily thrown off-balance. With no horizon to focus on, it was easy to become disoriented, although with all the sea action flinging us about, it was pretty hard to focus on anything.

And then the foghorn boomed off our starboard side. Oh, man! He was close, he was big, he was going fast, and no doubt he hadn't any notion that we were out there with him. We blew our own horn, a puny, tinny sound. I rushed to the radar to watch his blip marching closer and closer to our path. Stephen called on the radio: "Ship traveling south at about latitude 35 degrees 52 minutes north, longitude 121 degrees 39 minutes west, off Cape San Martin, this is the sailing vessel *Another Horizon* off your port bow. Do you copy?" No answer. We had little time to decide on an evasion plan. Our usual policy was to assume nothing, and get out of the way of anything bigger than we were. This ship was definitely bigger; we could tell by the deep tone of his horn. It was possible he was blasting away because he *did* know we were out there (our radar reflector produced a pretty good blip too), but unless we could raise him on the radio to confirm that, we had to steer clear.

We turned into the seas. The sails slatted and crashed, the bow pumped up and down, and the waves rolled over the deck. We were drenched by seawater and at a near standstill. We watched his radar blip slide past us as we floundered in the troughs and crashed through the crests of the waves. We never saw even a shadow of his hull. Oh, how I hated this!

The next morning the wind had abated some, but the fog continued to swirl around the rigging in wet tendrils as we approached Morro Bay. We could barely make out the bow from the cockpit, the fog was so thick. Because of shallow water and long breakwaters, Morro Bay is a tricky entrance, even in good weather. In the fog, with a sea running, it can be impossible. We called the Morro Bay Harbor Patrol to ask their advice.

Was the entrance passable? "Yes," they replied. "The seas are not bad at the entrance." Well, that was something. But we could see nothing, good or bad, as we approached. The radar was on to help us "see," and the engine was on to give us more control. Stephen took the helm, and I watched the radar. On the radar screen the breakwaters appeared as two eerie greenish yellow lines with a narrow gap between them through which we had to pass. This would be an "instrument landing." We surfed down long rolling swells as we came to the gap. I began to wonder what the Harbor Patrol's definition of "not bad" was. We stared into the gray void as I gauged our distance from the gap on the radar.

"A quarter mile ... ah ... less than that."

"How much is *less*?" Stephen complained.

"I don't know," I replied. "We should be there right ... *now*."

"There, there, there!" Stephen yelled. And I could just then make out the gray rocks of the breakwater rising from the gray water, appearing through the gray air. At the last moment, a green marker gave us the key to the channel entrance. I heard a pounding. Was it my heart, or the waves on the rocks?

Slowly we chugged our way up the channel. With the warmth of solid land and buildings close by, the fog was less dense, and we could make out the channel markers, one at a time, leading us to a calm berth. With *Another Horizon* safely tied at the dock, we both sank into the cockpit. We looked at each other, and, I will have to admit, small begrudging smiles appeared.

We solved most of the problems that had developed on the passage. The engine overheating was traced to a disintegrating pump belt, easily replaced. The autopilot remote control had been switched on somehow, without our knowing it, and had caused us to believe the mechanism was broken, since the boat appeared not to hold its course. We vowed we would learn more about *avoiding* bad weather as the weeks progressed. And we agreed we would reef the sails earlier when the wind came up.

Stephen's seasickness, however, we would never solve in the nearly eight years we were at sea. It was his cross to bear. And me? At the moment I couldn't believe I was submitting to this way of life. Did I really want to go through more nights like that? I knew it would not be the last, that even with more weather diligence, we would have *many* nights like that—and worse. Was I crazy?

We were only two days into our eight-year odyssey, and I wondered what on earth I had gotten myself into. How on earth did I let this happen to me?

*   *   *   *   *

We harbor-hopped down the California coast. It was a good time for testing our systems, getting our sea legs, getting used to dark and stormy nights, and flying into harbors with only inches of visibility. And it was a good time for getting used to being on the go: sailing, motoring, anchoring, arriving, departing, tying up, refueling—all the things we were supposed to be good at. There were enough fire drills to remind us we weren't perfect, and that the risks of full-time sailing were present full-time. The anxieties of encountering bad weather, dragging anchor, things breaking, things going wrong, things being just a little bit scary were there all the time—not just on weekends, or even for a week's vacation. It seemed as if I was worrying all the time, and like Stephen's seasickness this anxiety would be with us for the whole voyage.

We met a few other sailors, but mostly we were by ourselves. It was September and October and everyone else was working! I missed the daily contact with office colleagues, weekend encounters with yacht club cronies, nightly talks with our daughter. I was lonely.

On the longer passages, when things were calm, I had time to think about the "lines" we had cast off, severed, stored away, and put on a plane—and I had more questions about whether I had done the right thing. On the Trial Run three years earlier, whenever things got dicey I could say to myself, "Only a few more months … only a few more weeks … do I have to endure." On that voyage, the end was always in sight. Now I was looking not at months, but years.

*   *   *   *   *

Our first anchoring drill (we had berthed in marinas up to that point) was in Prisoner's Harbor on Santa Cruz Island, in the Channel Islands off Santa Barbara. It must have been hysterical to watch us. First, motoring up and down the anchorage for half an hour, we couldn't decide *where* to anchor, and then we couldn't decide *how* to anchor. We held long discussions on the issue while we went in circles. We settled on anchoring bow and stern (with two anchors) parallel to the shore, with the bow into the wind. Not half an hour later the wind shifted 180 degrees. The other boats in the harbor (on one anchor) swung around to put their bows into the wind, and there we sat pointing in the opposite direction. "We have been known for our individuality," we quipped. But we felt stupid—world sailors, indeed! Not yet.

I did not doubt our ability to get the sailing (and anchoring) under control, even if I hated the storms, the black nights, the anxieties, and the risks. But I still didn't know about me. I was lonely *and* depressed.

*   *   *   *   *

In San Diego we settled down for several weeks to get ourselves ready to leave the United States. We would be heading south to Mexico and eventually to the South Pacific. We would not be in a big city again for at least a year, so we wanted to be sure we had everything we would need for traveling in remote places: enough food for months, enough supplies to last, enough spares to fix anything that might break. And enough courage to continue.

Our boat insurance company suggested that it would not be prudent to head south of the U.S./Mexican border before November 1st, the supposed end of the hurricane season. We were anxious to get going, but we had to bide our time, waiting.

On the evening of October 31st I wrote in my journal about "living on the edge." We had to be constantly on watch, I wrote, literally and figuratively. We had to keep thinking ahead so that we would not make mistakes. We knew if we ever got complacent, we were heading for trouble. We hadn't even left the United States and I was thinking these things!

On November 1st we powered out the San Diego channel, heading south. We were both nervous and elated, a mixture of feelings that would return time and again over the next eight years. The excitement of moving on to something new was always tempered by the tension of moving on to the unknown.

We stopped intermittently along the outside of the Baja Peninsula. The landscape was wild, dry, barren, beautiful. The fish and lobster were bountiful. Three-quarters of the way down the peninsula, we stopped at Bahía de Santa Maria, a large open bay with clear blue-green water, mountains at both ends, and pristine sandy beaches backed by undulating sand dunes. We tucked ourselves as far up into the bay as we could.

We had not been anchored long when some fishermen from a nearby fishing camp came by in their pangas (long, open boats with outboard motors) to trade lobster. We brought out a small bottle of cooking oil and two cans of "fancy" peas. Three lobsters were tossed on our deck. It didn't seem like a fair trade to me—canned peas for lobster!—but the fishermen seemed as delighted with our items as we were with their lobster.

On that lovely warm evening we watched shadows twist through the dunes as the sun set, and we savored our lobster, washed down with a bottle of champagne left over from our departure festivities. This was heaven.

The weather continued to be benign, and we met more and more boats also heading south. We had good passages, and we stopped in near-idyllic anchorages. Why, oh why couldn't I rid myself of doubts and longings? I missed our daughter. I was full of … well, I shouldn't forget that I had just turned fifty.

At the bottom of the Baja Peninsula we stopped at Cabo San Lucas and contemplated crossing the Sea of Cortez to Mazatlán. It's a two-day passage, notoriously rough, so we wanted to be sure we had the right weather.

In a couple of days the forecast sounded good—clear, average winds from the north—and we made preparations for leaving. Just at that moment we met Ryan, a veteran of many Sea of Cortez crossings. "The weather's not the best for a crossing at the moment," he said.

"And how's that?" we asked.

"There's a high about to pass over Idaho, and in 24 hours strong northerlies will blow down the sea and make the crossing uncomfortable. It doesn't seem bad in here, but it'll be awful out there."

Stephen had a weatherfax chart in his hand and could see exactly what Ryan was talking about.

"Wait until the high is over Texas," Ryan advised, "and you'll have an easy ride." It seemed incredible that weather in Idaho could be important to us in Mexico.

Two days later the charts showed the high approaching Texas. We left Cabo and had a beautiful crossing. Thank heaven for Ryan, and our weatherfax.

The weatherfax (a stand-alone instrument that operates on radio frequencies, transmitting weather charts not unlike the TV weatherperson's pictures) was a new piece of equipment, one that we did not have on the Trial Run. On that voyage, before weatherfaxes were readily available and affordable for small yachts like ours, we listened to the forecasts on the radio. But it was sometimes difficult to equate the forecasts with the weather we were experiencing. Often enough we'd say, "Looks good, let's go," and end up getting bashed a day or so later. In just four years the availability of weatherfaxes and their transmissions had changed the whole process of weather forecasting for small yachts.

In addition to that instrument, this time we had Stephen's vow to become a student of the weather. For each part of the world, as we approached it, he would study all the literature available to learn about the weather patterns and local idiosyncrasies. And we made a second promise to ourselves: we would be patient and wait for good weather before setting out. Once or twice when we forgot this vow, we regretted it.

*   *   *   *   *

In Mazatlán some friends from Berkeley came to join us for a few days, to sail down the coast to Puerto Vallarta. They arrived late on a Friday afternoon and we did not have time to go to the offices necessary to get them listed on our official boat papers. Mexico is full of bureaucratic business with which we were always careful to comply, but in this case we didn't see the point. They had their arrival cards (acquired on the airplane), they had their passports, and they had their return plane tickets. We were only going a few dozen miles down the coast, from one tourist town to another. There couldn't be any way for anyone to even know that they were on the boat ...

Until we were boarded by the Mexican navy.

They appeared in an old, gray, destroyer-looking thing that probably was part of the U.S. fleet in World War II, it looked that old. The ship came alongside and lowered an inflatable boat with four men on board. The English was halting, but there was no mistaking what they wanted: "We come on boat."

That was fine, we said, but I immediately had some misgivings. With the exception of the guy in charge, these chaps were so young—and so young with submachine guns slung from their shoulders, stumbling as they came on deck. I prayed that the safety locks of those guns were firmly in place.

We quickly determined that this was a routine boarding (such as our own Coast Guard frequently carries out), which was some small relief. But when the captain asked for our papers, we began to worry. Stephen tried a tactic he had used before in similar circumstances: he gave the captain everything he could possibly think of that might look like official papers. He hauled out passports, boat documentation, his U.S. Coast Guard captain's license, our radio licenses, our marriage license—and copies of them all. Absent was the paper (the "crew list") that should have had our friends' names on it, and the official stamp of the port captain where they came aboard.

The ruse was successful. The captain noted all four of our passports, and was happy with that. But then there was the issue of our fishing license. In Mexico at that time, every boat was required to have a fishing license if it had fishing equipment on board, whether or not that equipment was ever used. And every *person* on board had to have a fishing license, whether or not he or she ever used, or even intended to use, or did *not* intend to use that equipment. We had the fishing license for the boat and licenses for Stephen and me, but not for our friends.

The captain asked, "Fishing?" Just that, just the one word. It was a question that could be interpreted a number of ways, Stephen thought. We weren't fishing, actively fishing, just then, so he said, "No," trying not to look at the fishing pole situated on our stern, big as life. Again the captain seemed satisfied. Stephen was sweating, and not from the heat.

In the meantime, one of the "children" went below, with his gun and me in tow, to search our vessel. He peeked in the cabinets, examined the bilge, stared at the head (toilet), and lifted the top of the chart table, but didn't look inside. I didn't dare ask what he might be looking for, let alone how he expected to find it by his cursory search. Never mind, as long as he kept that gun pointed down.

A few minutes later I poked my head up the companionway to see how Stephen was faring with his papers, only to see the other three Navies in their inflatable casting off from our side. "Wait! *Señores, señores, su amigo, su amigo!*" I called. I fairly pushed the kid up the stairway and out into the cockpit. *Please, take this child with you,* I silently pleaded. *We have enough folks on board without papers; we don't need any more!*

*   *   *   *   *

One evening as we lay anchored in the small harbor of Melaque, our friend Ryan came alongside and asked if we'd like to take a food tour of the town. He had frequented the cobblestone streets of this village often, he said, and would be our guide.

We went first to the "cheap" taco stand where tacos were fifteen cents each, and then to the "expensive" stand where the price was twice that. The tacos looked and tasted pretty much the same to me—juicy good and spicy hot. With the tacos we were served rice water, which sounds awful, but it is a slightly sweet drink that is quite refreshing with the spicy food. We next tried some "churros," a doughnut-like confection that is cooked right on the street in huge vats of boiling oil. Strings of dough were sizzled in the oil and then rolled in cinnamon sugar. Fresher doughnuts you will never find. The evening was topped off with fruit bars—popsicle-like items of cream and chunks of papaya, mango, or banana. We were stuffed. And the total cost of this feast? Less than $4—for both of us.

I confess that I would never have eaten on the street like this without the advice of someone who knew the scene, someone who had no qualms (as I did) about what we were eating and how it was prepared. U.S. restaurant sanitation experts would have closed this lot down in a flash. The meat was chopped on an ancient wooden block. Had it been washed recently? The tacos were prepared with bare hands, and served on plates covered with plastic bags. Our dinner remains were stripped off the plates with the plastic, a new bag installed, and the next portion plopped on a plate that probably hadn't touched water, let alone hot water, in days. I did not think about these issues until later, and then it was too late. *We'll either be sick,* I thought, *or we won't.* We weren't.

Speaking of getting sick: fresh water would be a major health issue everywhere in the world, and we started grappling with it in Mexico. Anyone who has traveled in Mexico (and many other parts of the world) knows that you dare not even brush your teeth in the local water, even in the five-star hotels. We had three sources of fresh water: marinas, our watermaker, or purchased bottled water. The last was ideal as far as water quality was concerned, but to fill our 130-gallon tank we had to schlep those big 5-gallon jugs who knows how many miles, into our dinghy and out to the boat, then throw them up onto the deck, down the companionway, and into the cabin. It was an arduous and expensive task.

Our watermaker (a reverse osmosis desalinator that made fresh water from seawater) did just fine in clean harbors, or when we were under way, but it produced only 3.3 gallons an hour at considerable expense of energy. It was only practical for topping off the tanks as we went along. Getting water in the marinas was the easiest, but the quality of the water was always questionable. The Cabo San Lucas marina had its own desalination plant, and they claimed that the water was potable. We still treated it with a solution of iodine, which is supposed to be the best answer to killing the little amoeba things that can make you so ill. In Mazatlán, where we heard stories of cholera, we bought the bottled water and schlepped it. Finally, in Puerto Vallarta, we learned about filtering the water and outfitted ourselves with a complex three-filter system that purified the water completely—or so they said. We still treated it with the iodine solution, just in case. For the nearly eight years of the voyage we were never ill from the water we put into our tanks.

* * * * *

In virtually every country we visited, we were required to check in with the authorities on arrival and to check out on departure. The Immigration Office was usually the first stop, where passports were examined, visas purchased if necessary, and stamps acquired, all of it similar to processes at airports the world over. But because we were also bringing a boat into the country, we were required to check in with customs, and often the agriculture and health departments, and sometimes with the local port captain as well. There were usually forms to fill out and documentation to produce. Sometimes this exercise was done at a special arrival dock, and sometimes officials came out to the anchored boat. At other times we went ashore and walked to the required offices.

In Mexico they seemed to protract the process in every way possible. We had to check into the country *and* every port we visited. Visits to the offices of immigration or police, customs, and port captain were required nearly everywhere; in some ports there were intermediate stops to pay a port tax (usually about a dollar), or to have the papers reviewed and stamped by some other official. The process entailed many forms typed by the Mexican officials and many documents generated by us. The forms were typed on typewriters that were probably made in the 1920s. They were typed in many copies, using carbon paper.

We had made multiple copies of our documents, and eventually we learned to take them *all* with us every time we checked in, because just when we thought we'd figured out that they needed four copies of the boat documentation, they'd ask for six. (A cousin, of course, ran the copy shop around the corner, if we needed more.)

I'd love to know what they did with all those copies. Undoubtedly some were hand-filed, and others were sent to other offices for more filing. It all made sense when we remembered that Mexico had much more labor than it had capital. Labor-saving devices (such as computers and copy machines) were irrelevant. Just our little checking-in process kept a heap of people employed. It also gave us some contact with local people.

English in these offices was often sketchy, so the checking-in process gave us plenty of opportunities to practice our Spanish—which needed a lot of practice.

* * * * *

It was mid-December when we found our way to Puerto Vallarta. This was a comfortable place to be, and we found many more sailors like ourselves. There was a real sense of community among these folks, and we began to make fast friends. It began to relieve the loneliness of the previous weeks.

One evening after dinner we wandered into Old Town and found crowds in the streets. "What is this?" we asked a man standing near us.

"Fiesta de Guadaloupe," he responded.

We were standing in front of El Templo de Guadaloupe (the town's principal church), where most of the activity seemed to be concentrated.

"Just wait," our street friend said. "It all begins soon." "It" was a procession—a colorful parade of families, work groups, church groups, school classes, and unions that were coming to the cathedral to make an offering to the Virgin of Guadaloupe. Each group had a presentation: a dance (with fancy costumes), music (guitars, bands, mariachis), flowers, or banners. Some of the groups had a representative dressed up as the Virgin. Some presented the Virgin in her martyred state, complete with bloody wounds, carried by a handsome young man. One group of children executed this spectacle with a husky ten-year-old boy carrying a tiny five-year-old girl up the long flight of steps into the church.

We followed them inside, where the various groups sang songs. Periodically the church bells rang, and firecrackers were lit outside in the town square. Across the street, dozens of concessions sold food, balloons, cotton candy, and other festive wares. It was a fair, a festival, a parade, a pageant, a religious happening, and a community gathering, all in one. Everyone in town took part in some way, and although we were only observers, we could smile and clap with the locals as their family and friends in the procession passed by. We could exclaim with our neighbors when the fireworks banged; we could eat the food and buy a balloon. In our small way, we too could be a part of this occasion.

And then I remembered why we were making this voyage. This was what I loved about our new life: the color, the language, the dress, the food, the customs, the people of our new world. The depression of the last two months began to lift. My apprehensions and worries began to slip into the background. Stephen says he bore his seasickness because he did not want to miss what we experienced at each port of call. And like his seasickness, I learned to absorb my anxieties into what was, after all, a very exciting life. This was the new beginning to our new life. And the world, with so many more new horizons, lay ahead.

The Long Passage

Crossing the Pacific Ocean

We left Puerto Vallarta, bound for the Marquesas Islands of French Polynesia, on March 3rd at 10:20 AM. It was four years to the minute from when we departed on our Trial Run voyage to the South Pacific. It was a silly thing, that departure time, but superstitions are often built around silly things. The first voyage was successful; whatever we could do to replicate it might be desirable. We had 2,800 miles of ocean to sail across. It would take us about three weeks, a long time to be sure the planets were in proper alignment, the gods were smiling, and the moon was in the right quarter. We are not superstitious people, but there are enough legends about ocean passages that it behooved us to take no chances.

Although *Another Horizon* was the same model of boat as *New Horizon,* our boat on that first voyage, *Another Horizon* was newer, stronger, and better outfitted. And we felt we were now "old hands" at this ocean-crossing business. There were many reasons why this crossing should be just as successful as the last, but there was still a sense that we should pay attention to the gods that oversee such events. The old hands were wakeful throughout that night before leave-taking, and up and cranking at dawn on the third.

It was a glorious day, with gentle breezes and clear skies—another fine sign. This was far better weather than four years ago, when a late winter front came through San Francisco (our port of departure that time) leaving residual seas and winds.

I look back on that first blue-water passage and marvel at our naïveté. Before that departure day we had never been more than fifteen miles offshore and never more than a few hundred miles from our home port, and there we were launching an ocean passage of 3,000 miles! The first day, four years ago, seemed good: strong breezes, but manageable, and we fairly flew along. Then a second frontal system swooped down on us. For ten days we careened south in near-gale conditions with huge seas. Stephen was immobilized with seasickness, dehydration, and lack of nourishment. Holly and I calculated our chances of surviving the day, the next watch, the next meal, the next wave. Holly was a good sport, but at fifteen, there were moments when her bravery, patience, and goodwill ran out.

"This isn't fun. I want to go home." We were into the seventh day—1,000 miles from San Francisco, 900 miles from the tip of Baja, 1,500 miles from Hawaii, and 2,000 miles from the Marquesas, our destination. Just about as far from everything as we could be. "Can't we cut it short and go to Hawaii?" she wailed. We checked the chart. It would take us as long to get to Hawaii as it would to the Marquesas, given the winds and currents. We resigned ourselves to keep going south.

On the twelfth day, the winds finally abated and the seas lay down. Stephen began to recover. The temperature was in the eighties and we had enough stability on the boat to take our first shower. I can't begin to think about what we must have smelled like, but since we were all in the same boat, so to speak, we all smelled alike and were not conscious of our stink.

*   *   *   *   *

I thought of that beginning to our ocean voyaging as we pulled out of Puerto Vallarta, and wondered whether this starting-at-the-same-time business was a good idea after all. But this day off the mid-Mexico coast was too good to think anything but hopeful thoughts. After clearing the marina breakwaters we put up all our sails and turned on the stereo as loud as we could, for a little extra fortitude. Beethoven's Sixth Symphony (the Pastorale) came out of the cockpit speakers, which was a beautiful complement to the day and the event. A pair of dolphins came leaping by, as if to say good-bye. A giant manta ray came up out of the water like some fantastic airplane. His wingspan must have been about twelve feet, as wide as our boat. It was an exhilarating sight.

It was exciting to be sailing again toward another horizon.

*   *   *   *   *

Day 2 (from my journal): "It's the color of the water that is puzzling me. I am trying to think of all the blue words, to see if I can get it right: cobalt, no; electric, parrot, turquoise, no, no, no; aquamarine, good heavens no. I am looking *down* into the water; the light is different than looking *over* the water. Looking down, it's a *deep sea blue*. How original."

And then: "I had a taffeta party dress when I was ten or eleven that changed color from bright blue to navy as I moved in it; the water is like that."

*   *   *   *   *

Day 3: "We are beginning to get into the passage routine. Keep the watch, sleep, eat, read, sleep, keep the watch ..."

I remembered one occasion after we returned home from our Trial Run when I was talking to a number of colleagues about our ocean experiences. One woman asked how it was that my husband and I could manage a relationship in such a small space, out in the middle of the ocean. "It's not like you can slam the front door and go for a walk around the block to cool off," she said.

Even before our voyaging days, I had often made the point that Stephen and I got along better on the boat than on land. On the boat we were usually pulling in the same direction. Sailing almost always gave us a common goal, and we shared the tasks of reaching that goal. We gladly celebrated any accomplishment toward achieving that goal together. So yes, Stephen and I, fortunately, did well together on our little craft out in the middle of nowhere.

As this conversation with colleagues went on, another woman, announcing her ignorance, asked what we did at night. "The anchor rope, or whatever it is, can't be long enough for the middle of the ocean, can it?"

I smiled, and took this opportunity to explain our system of "watches." When under way, even for short passages, one or the other of us stands watch, on deck, all the time, morning, noon, and night. This means that we can continue to sail through the night, over many days at a time, without stopping.

Although there are various ways to work these watches, we chose to stand four hours on watch, and then four hours off. I began the day with the 8 AM to noon watch, Stephen relieved me to stand noon to 4 PM; I'm back for 4 to 8 PM, Stephen stood watch 8 PM to midnight, and there I am back at midnight, and so on.

The woman who had earlier asked about our relationship piped up. "Okay, I get it now. You get along because you never see each other!"

To some extent, she was right. The routine that develops on long passages has the off-watch person sleeping, resting, or reading much of the off-watch time. Sleep deprivation is always a worry on long passages, so we took every opportunity to be sure we were rested. We never knew when the weather or some other "condition" might develop that would interrupt our off-watch and wipe out the sleep time.

Our "together" times were usually meal times. They gave us a few minutes to share our thoughts about how we were doing, if we had any worries, and if we were pleased or not about our progress. Crossing an ocean is an all-consuming activity. It is hard to think about much else.

*   *   *   *   *

Day 4: "We have had near perfect conditions since we left Puerto Vallarta. The wind is just right, the skies are clear; we haven't touched a line or sail in forty-eight hours. The solar panels are keeping the batteries well charged, and the batteries are keeping the refrigerator going, and that is keeping the yellow-tail tuna we caught earlier today nicely iced. We will have at least six meals out of that fish."

It was fortunate on our little ship that although the captain was nearly always seasick, the cook was nearly always not. I could produce meals—albeit not necessarily beautiful, tasty, or balanced meals—under any conditions.

Edible food isn't too difficult, but palatable food can be hard to produce when the stove is heaving unpredictably up and down, up and down. Working on palatable *without the stove* usually involves a knife (pieces of vegetable, for instance, or a sandwich). When the boat is crashing about in heavy seas, the old adage "one hand for the boat, one hand for yourself" applies. But how do you hold the food item to be cut, and cut it with a knife in the other hand, when the boat lurches? The knife-holding hand jerks over the food-holding hand—not a good scenario.

Just keeping food under control on a heaving boat is a challenge. We had nonskid plates, but the food you put on them isn't always nonskid. And non-skid plates are not immune to the boat's lurching, which sends the plates leaping across the cockpit, spilling their contents on the way. Silverware is the worst. It cannot be left unattended for a moment. A spoon will fall out of a bowl in a nanosecond, taking a sticky spoonful of oatmeal with it and spreading the oatmeal in little bits across the width of the cockpit cushion, freshly cleaned of last evening's spaghetti sauce.

And now about that "captain" designation. Stephen and I always felt that the voyage was a shared venture, and that we contributed to it equally—so equally that we were both supposed to be able to do everything necessary to keep our voyaging life going. In the months leading up to our departure I took diesel mechanics courses and navigation classes, got my ham radio license, and acquired a scuba diving certificate and a first aid certificate. Stephen did all those things too.

However, when we entered a new country and the paperwork required the name of the captain, we always used Stephen's name. It seemed the appropriate one to use. In reality, as we plied the oceans, it was our habit to declare whoever was on watch the captain. It was this person who had to make decisions to reef the sails, make a course correction, radio an approaching vessel, change course to avoid some danger, or call the off-watch for help.

It was not always easy for me to assume this role—or for Stephen either, on occasion. We tended to look to one another for help, advice, or some indication of what we should do—together. This was, at times, a source of irritation.

"You're on watch," Stephen would yell from below. "You decide. I don't care." My tendency was to ask for help too often. Stephen's tendency was not to ask until things were already out of hand. I usually woke up when the boat started bucking, or yawing, or rolling, or displaying some other gross change in its movement.

"What's going on?" I would snarl (irritated that my sleep had been disturbed).

"I don't know. I'm trying to tack to get around this squall," Stephen might answer.

"So why didn't you ask for my help?" Mumble, mumble. It didn't matter by then; my captain would humbly take my assistance—since I was awake anyway. And the reverse scenario was always true.

*   *   *   *   *

Day 5: "It is surprisingly cool, especially at night. Stephen says I'll wish for this coolness soon enough. I know he is right. We are heading for 'sauna' country. The sailing weather continues to be picture-perfect. What a contrast to our first crossing four years ago."

The watch/eating/sleeping/reading routine was set now. We were comfortable with making the passage. I enjoyed sitting in the cockpit on my watch, alone, looking out over the water—nothing, absolutely nothing out there but our little boat and the two of us. I felt both very, very small and very, very tall. The smallness was all too evident. There are not many places in the world where you can get this sense of being a mere speck in the greater scheme of things. The tallness came from the confident feeling that we could harness Nature, make her work for us, keep her happy, and move across her sphere safely, making progress toward our destination.

"As long as the weather is good," I wrote, "I could do this forever. I really do love crossing oceans—as long as the weather is good. I'm not a fan of bad-weather ocean crossings (who would be?), but the challenge of crossing oceans includes managing the weather, getting the navigation right, and maintaining life while we sail ever-so-slowly all those miles."

*   *   *   *   *

Day 6: Just before sunset a red-footed booby came to rest on the bow pulpit. A second booby tried to land beside him, but it was apparently a tricky landing.

He made several attempts, flying the same approach pattern each time, heading up into the wind as he attempted to touch down, his wide webbed feet reaching out to grab the rail. He finally made it, only to fall off before he could get an adequate grip and balance himself. He was the best entertainment in days.

The two boobies finally settled together, squatting on the rail, facing aft, leaning into each other to help keep their balance against the wind and the bucking movement of the boat. By 9 PM the wind had increased sufficiently that we decided to reduce the genoa (large sail at the front of the boat), furling it in by about half—but the furling line jammed. Stephen went forward to check the jam and tried to shoo the birds away while he was there. They squawked as if to say, "How dare you?" He was close enough to swat them with his bare hands, but they did not budge, even with the sail flapping in their faces. They remained on their perch, swaying and leaning, past midnight, when apparently they felt rested and off they went.

I saw the Southern Cross in the sky this night. We hadn't yet crossed into the Southern Hemisphere, but there were signs that we were close, and I was happy with that.

*   *   *   *   *

Day 7: "The first sign of 'weather'—heavy clouds. If they get their act together, they will probably produce some rain. The wind is back down to 10–15 knots and we are galloping along. We are not going south as much as we should be, but when the wind shifts (as it should) more to the east, we will be able to correct our course.

"Up on deck I can see that our wake is full of foam. I watch the water for a sense of passage. Looking out onto the horizon, we might as well be standing still."

*   *   *   *   *

Day 8: Radio contact with other yachts that were also crossing the Pacific was a daily event. Each day, at 7 AM, we turned on the ham radio to an agreed-upon frequency. We gave our position to the other boats, in latitude and longitude degrees, and recorded their positions as well. If anything disastrous ever happened, we knew that there was a time in the day when we could contact other vessels for help. If we did not make contact at the scheduled time, we knew that the other boats would launch a search (contacting the appropriate authorities) to hunt for our boat, our life raft, or our remains. The radio contact was thus an important safety matter, but it was a social occasion as well. Out on that vast plain of water with nothing but a mate to look at, talk to, and eat with, a few words with some other humans was a special moment in the day. We looked forward to it.

*   *   *   *   *

Day 9: "We have had two days of higher winds and heavy seas, with lots of banging and crashing. The winds have moderated now but the seas continue to be sloppy. It's slowing us down."

As simple as it may sound, one of the day's greatest pleasures was to compute how many miles we had gone in the previous 24 hours. It gave us a sense of accomplishment. When we were moving over water without any change in the scenery—save possibly the color of the water (blue, gray, green, turquoise, gray-green, blue-gray, navy taffeta)—we needed something to show us that we had actually made progress. Our best day's distance on this passage was 170 nautical miles; our worst, 100. A nautical mile is about one-seventh longer than a statute mile, so to land-bound readers that's about 195 miles for the best day and 115 for the worst. That may not seem like much of an accomplishment for 24 hours, but our average speed was 5 knots (just 6 statute miles per hour), so 170 nautical miles in 24 hours was really quite good!

*   *   *   *   *

Day 11: Just before crossing the equator we entered the Intertropical Convergence Zone (ITCZ), an area where the weather patterns of the North Pacific collide with the weather of the southern ocean. The results of this collision are sudden changes of wind direction and velocity, serious calms, frequent squalls with torrential rains, and—worst of all—lightning.

We usually tried to dodge squalls, knowing they could pack winds of 30 knots or more, with blinding rain and lightning. We would track the squalls on the radar, watching their movement on the screen and planning our strategy—for example, storm is moving to the left, we move to the right. On the second ITCZ night, however, we were overwhelmed by squalls all around us; there was no way to dodge them all. And there was the lightning, flashing everywhere.

Lightning is a considerable danger to a sailboat at sea. We all know that lightning will often seek the highest object around for a strike. Out on the ocean, with nothing for hundreds of miles except our 56-foot mast, there was no question in our minds about where the lightning would be looking.

Usually when lightning was in our vicinity we would unplug all our electronic gear. If we were struck by lightning, that gear was vulnerable and would most likely be blown to bits. All of the equipment was grounded to the engine and the sea, but we also streamed wires from our mast rigging into the water, to further conduct a lightning strike away from the boat.

On this particular night in the ITCZ we were in awe of the lightning show. Huge bolts were flashing in every direction and more ranged overhead—horizontal bolts zinging across the sky directly over our mast. Since we had unplugged everything, including the radar, we could no longer track the squalls and had no idea which way to go to get away from them.

There was little wind, and the seas were relatively benign, so we were just bobbing around in the water. Stephen and I sat in the cockpit. Whoever was off-watch could not consider sleep. We looked at one another, silent. It was not necessary to say anything. We knew all the dangers the other was imagining. We held hands.

I can't say I was frightened; I wasn't. I knew we would survive this lightning storm. Even if we took a direct strike, we most likely wouldn't sink. At worst we'd lose the electronic gear, and although the electronic gear was important, we could do without it. We even had an old-fashioned sextant on board to find our way across any ocean, and we knew how to use it. So I wasn't frightened—no, not really. Just very, very anxious. It was another of those awful nights I had imagined, but did not know about, in Morro Bay.

South of the equator, where you are supposed to pick up the "predictable" south trade winds, we found light, fickle winds instead. Slogging around in lumpy seas with no wind to drive the boat was uncomfortable. We ended up motoring for long periods to move away from the calms and to keep our speed high enough to get through the ocean swells more smoothly. It was always a relief to feel the wind pick up, watch the sails fill, and get rid of the noise of the engine.

Using the engine on these long passages was a dilemma. We carried only 105 gallons of diesel fuel that could take us, if we so chose, about 600 miles nonstop, or about 5 days. Obviously, on a passage of 2,800 miles it was important to ration the fuel so it would last until the next fuel stop. And it was very important to leave enough fuel in the tanks to get us into port. We entered most harbors under power. We figured we didn't have to test our sailing skills that far, and we knew that sailing into many harbors in our sluggish-moving vessel was a design for disaster. So no matter what, we kept at least 5 gallons in one jerry can on deck until the very end of the passage. We did not allow ourselves to use those last 5 gallons until we were within a few miles of a refueling station.

*   *   *   *   *

Day 12: "We have put the ITCZ behind us and the skies are utterly clear. We can see clouds 'falling' off the edge of the sea. Watching this, it is easy to see why the ancients thought the world was flat."

*   *   *   *   *

Day 13: "For more than 24 hours we have had 10–18 knots of wind on the beam. The sky remains clear. We are clocking speeds of 6 to 7 knots. We are sailing in the 'trades.' This is the best."

*   *   *   *   *

Day 14: "Four years ago every day brought new challenges, accomplishments; there was the wonder of it all, the changes in way of life, the enduring, the jubilations, all for the first time. Nothing is new in this experience. Instead there is a sense of renewal, of finding things familiar and comfortable (in a manner of speaking)."

We poured a little rum into the sea—for Neptune—as we crossed the equator. It was dinnertime, so we opened a half-bottle of champagne, the only lapse in our "no-alcohol-at-sea" rule. We were already shellbacks (persons who have crossed the equator before), and so our ceremony was just sufficient to keep everyone happy. On our first crossing, when we went to great lengths to get things right, Stephen poured some of the champagne into the sea. I felt this was a great waste, and so I ensured no such repetition by having a cheap bottle of Mexican rum at the ready for Neptune, keeping all the champagne for us.

*   *   *   *   *

Day 15: "All of our fresh food has been consumed. I am getting into the can locker. It has been a long time since I've had a canned peach—about four years long." Keeping a balanced diet on long passages was a challenge. The leafy green parts were the most difficult. I draw the line at canned spinach, so when the fresh cabbage was gone, we ate more fruit and forgot the veggies for a while. South Pacific islanders have survived for centuries without green leafy things. We could manage for a few weeks.

*   *   *   *   *

Day 18: "How hot is it? The butter melts on your knife before you can get it to the biscuit."

*   *   *   *   *

Day 21: At 7 PM. I saw the tip of Hiva Oa's Cape Mataferuua off the starboard bow. "Land ho!" I shouted. Stephen rushed out to the cockpit to join me. The "land ho" moment was both exhilarating and tense. Here was where things could go very wrong: close to land where off-lying dangers—rocks, reefs, sand bars, to name a few—could turn a good day into a disaster. We were already in a bad way with our timing. It was dusk, and we would be approaching the island in the dark.

We had a policy of never entering a strange harbor at night, and although Baie Taaoa of Hiva Oa had been our landfall on the Trial Run, and so wasn't exactly strange, it was an unlighted and small harbor. And it had been four years since our last visit. We decided we would wander around outside the harbor until daylight. It was still 30 miles to the harbor entrance, which would take us most of the night anyway.

It was difficult to sleep on my off-watch that night. I was too keyed up. Approaching land, approaching land in the dark, approaching the end of the passage, approaching the end of the passage in the dark, I was too excited and nervous to sleep. The end had a certain similarity to the beginning—excitement and anxiety.

At 4 AM we were outside the harbor and started our "pacing," sailing back and forth—two miles east, turn around, two miles west. And then a squall swept in. We turned south to duck underneath it; the squall came south. We turned north to tuck behind it; the squall came north. The wind was from the east at 20 knots, so we couldn't go east, and we were too close to the island to go any farther west. We went southeast, and the squall came with us—or so it seemed. In fact the squall was simply expanding. We could see it on the radar, moving in all directions, like a huge amoeba-like mass. The rain was torrential, obscuring our surroundings, which were already black enough.

We were both on deck now, working the sails, hand-steering, yelling at each other above the wind, sloshing around in the rain. "Let there be light, and get rid of this squall," I intoned to myself. At 6 AM, I got my wish.

We made a final approach to Baie Taaoa, and before 8 AM we had our anchor down. I couldn't help but remember this moment four years earlier when, with Holly, we pulled into the same harbor. We were jumping for joy. We hugged and laughed and popped a bottle of champagne. We had crossed an ocean, we had found our landfall, and we had managed these things without major mishap. This time, like old hands, Stephen and I looked at each other, smiled, hugged, laughed, and popped a bottle of champagne. Our silly timing thing at the beginning of the passage could now be considered a good omen.

The final journal entry for this day says, "I really do love this, all of it, especially now that we are in harbor."

Black Pearls and Electricity

French Polynesia

Coming to the Marquesas, we were back in the territory we had sailed through on the Trial Run. We looked forward to returning to old haunts as well as investigating new islands and anchorages. And we wondered if we would find any of it changed. It had been only four years; what could possibly have happened in those laid-back, languid, tropical-paradise islands, where the biggest upheaval—a volcanic eruption—last happened centuries ago?

Hiva Oa looked the same. The harbor was the same small niche in the southern coastline of the island, with mountains surrounding the bay, jutting out of the water to 3,600 feet. The air was flower-fragrant and humid, the water tropical-warm, the beaches sandy and full of no-see-um bugs that soon had me looking like a bad case of chicken pox, driving me crazy with their itch.

No, nothing had changed. The spectacular visions of mountains, valleys, waterfalls, volcanic remains, and archeological mysteries—we'd seen it all before, so we could move on. Farther down the Marquesas chain was one of our favorite stops of four years ago: Ua Pou. Coincidentally, for the second time we arrived just before Easter Sunday.

The Easter Sunday service at the Catholic Church in town was exactly as we remembered it: crowded, crawling with children, hot, and with wonderful singing accompanied by drums, guitars, and ukuleles.

The priest spotted us after the service. Speaking French, he greeted us and asked if we were Catholic.

Stephen didn't quite hear the question and answered, "No, we came on our boat," as if that were another religion.

"Ah," said our priest, "Americans from California," as if that explained everything.

We stood near the back of the church as it emptied after the service, watching the people decked out in their very best church attire. A tall, darkly handsome man approached us and put out his hand in greeting. He was being friendly to strangers, a common-enough event in these islands. But he looked familiar to me. "Lazarus?" I asked hesitantly.

"Yes," he said, looking puzzled and surprised, and then *he* recognized *us.* "*New Horizon!*"

"Yes, yes."

"You came back!"

"Yes, we came back to see you." Lazarus laughed; he was clearly pleased.

On that earlier Easter Sunday we had met Lazarus in the afternoon when all of the townspeople came down to the beach to enjoy the sun and swim in the warm water. Lazarus paddled out to our boat on a tiny inflatable beach toy. He asked if we spoke English, which seemed like a silly question with our American flag flapping off the stern. But we were charmed by this young man's direct manner. "I want to practice my English," he said. "Can you come to my house for dinner tomorrow?"

We were treated to a feast cooked on several outdoor fires, but the highlight of that evening was the moment Lazarus pulled out his ukulele and began to play, and his four-year-old daughter danced. Vahea was a beguiling dancer even at four, her dark hair swaying, her arms rippling, her feet moving softly. Lazarus said she had learned from her mother, who had danced for her living at one time.

Lazarus told us that he was a composer too, that he had just made a tape, and that we might find it in the music store in Papeete, Tahiti. Later, when we arrived in Papeete, we went looking and found his tape *stacked* in the window of the store. Now, four years later, Lazarus told us he had been chosen "Man of the Year for French Polynesia," an honor recognizing him in particular for the Marquesan folk music he composed and performed under his Polynesian name, Ratoro—music that is now well-known throughout French Polynesia.

Although Lazarus was basically a humble man, he was quick to tell us of his accomplishments, and he reveled in our exclamations of surprise and admiration. He was captain of the island's pirogue (outrigger canoe) team; he was "chief" of the musician's union; he continued to compose, sing, and perform his own music; and, just to be sure his family ate and had a roof over their heads, he worked as a nurse at the island's ten-bed hospital. A busy man. His hero? Elvis Presley. His English? As good as any we heard in these islands. A busy, talented, smart young man. The four-year-old daughter from Trial Run days was now a gorgeous eight-year-old. A three-and-a-half-year-old brother, Joseph, tagged along, peeking out from behind her skirts.

After a quick stop at Nuka Hiva, the last of the hot, sticky, bug-ridden, resplendent Marquesas, we set sail for the Tuamotus (the second of five groups of islands that compose the whole of French Polynesia), a three-day passage of 350 miles.

In contrast to the mountainous and geologically young islands of the Marquesas, the Tuamotus are low—in most cases only a few feet above sea level—and very old. Most of them are simply coral reefs that once surrounded volcanic islands, the cores of which have slipped away into the ocean depths, leaving a body of water—a lagoon—in the center of a ring of coral.

Over the years, the coral has been ground down by wave action, and material deposited by the water has accumulated on top of the coral, creating occasional islets, or *motus*. Some of the islets eventually become substantial enough to support people, and these are the motus on which the villages of these isolated atolls are found.

Many, but not all of the encircling reefs have deep-water passes through them to enable ships to enter the lagoon. Getting through these passes can be a treacherous exercise, but once inside, vessels often find idyllic anchorages in the lagoons.

Our landfall in the Tuamotus was Raroia, the island on which Thor Heyerdahl's raft, *Kon-Tiki,* was wrecked in 1947. We had a special reason for visiting.

*   *   *   *   *

After 101 days of sailing and drifting 4,300 nautical miles from Peru, the end of *Kon-Tiki*'s historic voyage was relatively swift. The wind and current were carrying the raft and crew down on the reef, and they had no way to change their course. The raft's crew had known for several hours that they would not sail clear of the reef and had prepared themselves carefully for the terrifying landing. Mountainous waves washed over them, the roar so loud they could not think. Retreating waves sucked them back, repositioning them for another ton of water to rip through the logs, the rig, the cabin, and the men. Despite some retreat after each wave, the next wave launched them farther onto the reef until finally the remains of the raft wallowed in just a few feet of water. Incredibly, the crew—all six of them—survived the ordeal to jump off the raft and walk to the safety of a tiny motu nearby.

After spending several days on this motu, wondering how they would be able to reach civilization again, the stranded men were visited by some natives who sailed from a village 30 miles across the lagoon. The *Kon-Tiki* crew were transferred to the village to await the arrival of a supply ship that could take them to Tahiti.

The *Kon-Tiki* adventure over, the crew dispersed from Tahiti to pursue other ventures. One, a Swedish sociologist named Bengt Danielsson, returned to Sweden and his sociological studies. But he dreamed of returning to Raroia, to live there and study its people. Within two years Danielsson got his wish—a research grant—and returned to the island.

Upon returning to Sweden once again, Danielsson did what any good sociologist would do: he wrote a book about his experience. *Raroia, Happy Island of the South Seas,* published in 1953, was not a bestseller. But for anyone who has traveled in the Tuamotan islands of French Polynesia, it is a fascinating treatise. A friend had found the book in a used bookstore in Berkeley and gave it to us; we read it and decided we must visit the island.

* * * * *

Raroia is a typical atoll, with the lagoon in the center of a rough circle of coral. Danielsson's village was still there on an islet near the pass through the reef. It appeared to have changed little in the intervening years.

The minute we landed our dinghy on the beach, we were greeted by a mob of smiling children, chattering away in their local Tuamotan dialect. They quickly switched to French, which we could manage adequately and they could speak fluently, since French is the language of their schooling.

Would the children take us to the village chief? "*Oui, oui,*" came the chorus of eager voices. Running and skipping ahead of us, the children guided us to the heart of the village and the home of the chief. We gave him our greetings and asked permission to stay, anchored as we were, to visit the island over the next few days. He was happy to have us, he said.

We told the chief that we came to Raroia because this was the place where the *Kon-Tiki* had landed.

"*Oui,*" the chief answered, and pointed across the lagoon in the direction of the motu where the beaching took place.

Still in our halting French, we asked if he knew about Bengt Danielsson.

"Yes, yes. He came back and stayed on Raroia."

And did he know about the book that Danielsson wrote?

"Yes."

Had he ever seen a copy of the book?

"No."

Surprised by his answer, we told him that we had a copy on board *Another Horizon,* and that we would bring it ashore the next time we came to the village.

The next morning we saw the chief again, the Danielsson book in hand. Our edition was an English translation, so the text meant little to him, but the photographs caught his attention. In a matter of moments a dozen or so adults, along with our constant entourage of children, surrounded us to look at the pictures. The villagers began identifying the people in the photos: my uncle, my grandfather, my wife's father, the old chief.

"Are any of them still here on the island?" I asked.

"No, all gone. They have died, or they have gone to Tahiti."

I continued to turn the pages. "The church ... my older brother," said one of the village elders. As I turned to the last page of photographs, a woman looking over my shoulder exclaimed and pointed excitedly: "*C'est moi! C'est moi!*" She pointed to a young girl walking down a path. "It's me! It's me!" A girl of eighteen when Danielsson took the picture, Martine was now a robust woman of sixty-three, her hair graying, her face crinkled. From one corner of her mouth hung a cigarette that she could barely keep in place as she smiled. She could hardly contain herself, she was so surprised and pleased. The other villagers surrounding us broke into smiles and torrents of Tuamotan that we could not follow.

Although we cherished the book, especially after this encounter, it was suddenly very important to leave it behind. We quickly inscribed it to the village and presented it to the chief. The villagers smiled and laughed and continued their animated discussion. The pages of the book, now in the chief's hands, were turned over and over again.

Days later, we pulled up our anchor and headed for the pass to take us out of the lagoon. The children called from the beach, jumping up and down, trying to outshout one another. The older villagers came down the path to the water's edge and waved. And yes, there was Martine, her aging face still full of the pride and satisfaction of discovering her image in the Danielsson book.

* * * * *

Another favorite island on the Trial Run was Kauehi, also in the Tuamotus. We had enjoyed unparalleled hospitality on this island of sixty people, and the lagoon was as close to a Pacific paradise as it could be. There were white beaches and turquoise water full of brightly colored fish. Fluffy white clouds moved quietly overhead every day; the copper sun kissed the horizon every evening. During our earlier visit, we became particular friends with the recently deposed chief, Xavier, and his schoolteacher wife, Tanya. We had exchanged meals, gifts, hugs, and tears on our departure four years earlier. We wanted to visit them again.

As we made our way cautiously into the coral-studded lagoon, we noticed change immediately. The tiny motu in the middle of the lagoon, where we had enjoyed hours of glorious snorkeling on the previous trip, was now covered with small buildings, some of them standing out over the water on stilts. What was this?

After anchoring, we made our way ashore to look up the chief of the island, as is customary on a yacht's arrival. We found Pie (pronounced "pie-ee") to be the same, if a little more portly. And the chief of police, Pomare, was also more—how shall we say—"mature," but happy to see us again. On shore, in the village, we *felt*, more than saw the change. Over the next few days we pieced together the socioeconomic revolution of Kauehi.

The population had more than doubled, from 60 to 130. What had been a trading economy (copra cut from the plentiful coconut trees and traded for goods arriving by the copra boat) was now a cash economy. There were non-Kauehians living on the island, many of them single, without family. Instead of a one-room schoolhouse, it was two rooms with two teachers. The handmade, open wooden fishing boats had been replaced by sleek fiberglass runabouts with new outboard motors. The single village generator was just about an anachronism, because most people had one of their own, along with clothes washers (even though there was no running water) and dryers, and TVs.

And the cause of all this change? The black pearl. The demand for coconut oil, the end product of copra, had declined dramatically in the last decade, and Pacific Islanders, whose economy was dependent on copra harvests, were looking for alternatives. Black pearl farming was becoming a popular venture.

A Chinese-owned, Polynesian-managed company had invaded Kauehi and talked the locals into growing oysters and selling them to the company when they were ready for seeding with the tiny fragments that produced pearls. Highly skilled Japanese seeders visited the island periodically to seed the oysters, which were then hung in the waters around our idyllic motu of past times. These seeded oysters were tended to and eventually harvested by the off-island workers.

In the old Polynesian society, the chief controlled everything—that is, he told you where you built your house, which acreage you harvested for copra, who you married—and everyone shared the island together. It was an egalitarian society.

But now there were haves and have-nots. Some villagers' oysters were more successful than others. A few even paid the Japanese to seed some of their "private" oysters and reaped a few pearls on their own, making even more money than their neighbors. But some of the seeded oysters did not develop pearls, and their "farmers" were in debt because the Japanese seeders were very expensive. And some Kauehians (but not very many) continued to cut copra.

As a result of their newfound affluence, the wealthy villagers were buying more "luxury" goods, not just the subsistence materials—clothes, food, and building materials—as before. And there was clearly a little "keeping up with the Joneses" going on. If so-and-so had a bicycle, maybe I should have a bicycle—or a bigger outboard, or a fancier runabout. The conspicuous consumption award went to the police chief, who had purchased a car for his wife to visit her father who lived at the other end of the village, all of a five-minute *walk*. It was the only car on the island.

Another new feature was a restaurant of sorts where a cook produced meals for the off-island single workers who had no family to take care of their gastronomic needs. Josephine was a recent widow who, with her late husband, had built a pleasant homestead at one end of the village. Aside from her home, she had a large, open (but roofed) kitchen and dining area for her catering business. *Business.* There it was again, a new and strange (for us) way of looking at Kauehian life. One day a half dozen of us from boats anchored in the lagoon asked Josephine if she would cook us a meal—at noontime, when she did not have to provide for her charges. She was delighted.

The table was set when we arrived: a plate and a drinking coconut in a small bowl for each of us. Her menu was smoked fish, fried fish, poisson cru (raw fish marinated in lime juice and coconut milk), poi (mashed coconut, sugar, and tapioca), and coconut bread (wrapped and baked in coconut fronds). The meal utilized what was most available on the island: fish and coconut.

She would take no payment from us, as she did from her worker-patrons. But we brought her gifts from our boats: real coffee, a small bottle of rum (her favorite), and some pieces of vanilla bean (which she put into the coffee beans—it would make some exquisite coffee in a few days). The gift that caused some consternation, as well as hilarity, was a small tin of Crisco®. On opening this gift, she thought it was a skin cream and applied some to her face, saying it was "good for the baby—smooth skin."

"No, no," we exclaimed, "like lard, for cooking."

Josephine blushed at her mistake, and we tried to hide our embarrassment at her embarrassment, and we all ended up laughing.

We mulled over the changes in Kauehi for days. We watched the copra boat come in, selling huge numbers of "things" to Kauehians in exchange for *money.* We watched our Kauehi friends, and we wondered about the future of this island, and we had to conclude that change was inevitable. Was this no longer a tropical paradise? Nonsense. The way of life had changed, there was no doubt, but the puffy clouds were still there, and the white beaches, the swaying palms, and yes, some of the world's friendliest people.

The hospitality we had experienced before was renewed. On several evenings the village musicians came to our boat to play and sing. There were five of them; Andre was the leader. He played guitar and weighed well over 300 pounds. Paul and Francis played guitar and ukulele and sang quite well. But the star by far was 14-year-old Cyril, who played the ukulele like a pro and couldn't have weighed more than 80 pounds. Edward, a friend from the previous voyage, was just Edward and liked to be along for the fun. Edward weighed more than Andre. The stern of our boat was measurably submerged when we had all the musicians together in our cockpit.

We dined in a number of their homes, always entertained by the musicians. The day before we left Kauehi, Andre and his family invited the crews of the half dozen yachts anchored in the lagoon to a banquet. As usual there was music, and before long there was dancing. Edward took me to the floor. This was a spectacle to produce laughter on both sides—sailors and Kauehians. Imagine a semi-petite, fair-haired woman dancing with a huge Polynesian!

We had been at Kauehi almost a month, an exceptionally long time for us to stay in one place. Our inherent restlessness usually had us on the go more frequently. Finally we said to ourselves, "If we're going to sail around the world, we'd best get a move on."

In fact, the next step wasn't far, just 53 miles to Fakarava, a neighboring island. Fakarava is a comparatively large atoll, about 30 miles long and 10 miles wide. Most of the middle part of that acreage is, of course, water in the interior lagoon. After checking in, as usual, with the mayor and police chief in the village at the north end of the atoll, we sailed down the inside of the lagoon to the opposite end. One Manihi Salmon lived there, the great, great, great (maybe one more great) grandson of the last queen of Tahiti. (Note: Salmon is Stephen's last name—and my married name.)

We had come across the legend of the Salmon family in Tahiti on the previous voyage, when we checked into Papeete. The customs agent had flipped open Stephen's passport and beamed with pleasure. "We are related," he exclaimed, and launched into the story of their shared heritage.

Some generations ago, an Englishman by the name of Alexander Salmon married a Tahitian. One of their offspring married the fellow who became King Pomare V, and was herself the last Queen of Tahiti. When we learned later that a descendant of this pair, Manihi, lived in the Tuamotus, we resolved to visit him.

As we were anchoring at the southern end of Fakarava's lagoon, we saw a couple on shore in the distance. We knew that Manihi was the only person to live in this area, so we waved vigorously. I was a little busy with lines and anchors, but later I said to Stephen that I believed our host was sporting his

"Adam's suit," and the young woman … well, could I say her "Eve's suit"? Stephen mumbled that he hadn't noticed. My foot.

A few minutes later when we met Manihi Salmon, descendant of royalty, he had a piece of bright cloth wrapped modestly around his waist. We also met Cecilia, a young Italian woman who was "a friend," according to Manihi. *A very good friend,* Stephen and I confided to one another later. She had also donned a skirt, and might be described as having on her demi-Eve suit.

Manihi gave us a tour of his property. The land actually belonged to the government, he said, but as long as he maintained it and lived on it, he was afforded the privilege of keeping it. The property was like an estate, by comparison to other French Polynesian property. He and his wife had built a large A-frame house for their family, with walls that opened to let in the cooling sea breezes. The grounds were landscaped with Australian pines and many nonnative plants. His wife and daughter had left for the brighter lights of Tahiti, Manihi told us, while he and his son (about eighteen) worked a fish farm and "other enterprises."

Manihi decided we were "cousins," and invited us to dinner. Although we shared a last name, and were probably not in any way related, the designation "cousin" is not uncommon among Polynesians, meaning friends, distant relatives, maybe relatives, who cares, let's-have-a-party acquaintances.

Cecilia, Manihi, and another "cousin" (a Polynesian) from New Caledonia prepared salted fish with onions, lots of garlic, and soy sauce over rice, and a barbecued globe-eye fish. I brought a rice salad and chocolate cake, the latter eaten very quickly, and entirely. We also provided some wine. We had tentatively suggested it, as we were unsure if alcohol consumption was appropriate. (At Kauehi, for instance, only a drink like Kool-Aid was served with meals.) But Manihi had applauded our offer. Wine was a "taste" he had acquired, he said, during the eight years he spent in New Zealand.

Manihi's son appeared just in time for dinner. This young man, whose real name we never did learn, was referred to as "Baby." We loved the nickname, for "Baby" was like his father: tall and slim, extraordinarily fit, and muscular. They lifted weights, Manihi explained. Unlike his father, who shaved his head bald, Baby's hair was shoulder length, and he sported a large tattoo "necklace." He was a beautiful young man.

We had a memorable evening together, drinking wine, eating largely, toasting our familial connection, drinking wine, and eating largely.

The next morning Manihi came by *Another Horizon* to return the wine-glasses we had provided with the wine and to say his farewells. He and Baby were taking Cecilia to the north end of the island for her departure to Italy. And then he and Baby would be diving for turban shell (the "mother of pearl" interior was sold to the Japanese for making buttons). "A good way to make an extra buck," explained Manihi. One of his "other enterprises," we surmised. We wished them well.

* * * * *

From the Tuamotus we sailed on to Tahiti, the legendary isle of beauty and enchantment—an "earthly paradise." But we'd seen this before, and as beautiful as it was, we had our complaints. It was expensive ($1.50 for one carrot) and crowded (Papeete is a big city with 90,000 people) and noisy (cars and motorcycles raced by our very bow where we were tied up). We bought fresh food in the market, ate out once (all we could afford), enjoyed the company of some friends for a few days, and then moved on.

We zinged through most of the Society Islands, thinking ahead to new territory to the west. On Tahaa, however, we hesitated. There was something different here. As in Kauehi, we *sensed* it first … the change.

We went ashore for a walk along the main road of a village we had visited on the earlier voyage. We were pleased with the familiarity of the place; it had not changed one bit in four years, we said—or had it? The road was still unpaved and muddy; the houses were still plywood, open to the cooling sea breezes; the dogs and children still played along the shore. Finally we saw it. There were poles spaced along the edge of the road with wire strung between them, occasionally branching off to a residence. *Electricity* had come to Tahaa.

I had just finished reading some letters from friends at home describing the latest electronic controversies of publishing online, and exchanging e-mail on the Internet, and here Tahaa was just getting electricity!

What could this mean to them, the residents of Tahaa? A light at night? Perhaps a refrigerator, a radio, maybe a TV (we did see one)—a plethora of electrical delights that changed their lives inexorably? It was hard to relate our lives, even on the boat (which included lights at night, a refrigerator, *two* radios, and a TV), to a life where these things were such luxuries—and new luxuries, at that.

Island-hopping north, we arrived at Bora Bora, the extremity of inhabited French Polynesia in that direction, and the jumping-off point for the next step in the voyage. For some of our fellow sailors, the next step meant Hawaii and home to the West Coast; for the rest of us, it meant deciding on a route westward. While we were contemplating the various possibilities to the west, we settled in a well-protected bay on the south side of Bora Bora—Bahie Faanui.

One morning I awoke and stuck my head up the companionway to have a look around, as was my habit. I liked to know that we were still anchored in the same spot and that nothing untoward had happened anywhere in the harbor during the night. This morning I was immediately disconcerted by activities on shore. There were a few homes along the beach, and there was a flurry of activity at each. At one, there were two men on the roof laying long two-by-fours along the pitch of the roof and down to the ground. At the next house, three men were *removing* the porch at the front of the house. At the last, a couple was collecting pieces of yard furniture and leaning pieces of plywood against the front openings of the house.

"Stephen," I called, with more than a little tension in my voice, "what on earth is going on with the weather?"

Stephen, still waking up, grumped, "Some system or other heading this way."

"Wind?" I queried.

"Nothing extraordinary."

"I think the locals have a different weather report," I announced.

As I described to him what was happening on shore, he leapt from our bunk and went to the weatherfax machine to see if the overnight charts had come through. The charts suggested wind, but not the kind of wind for which you remove your front porch.

On our regular radio "sched" an hour later, we asked if anyone had other local information that might corroborate our observations. A friend in Papeete said they had watched the TV news the night before, and he gave us the bad news. The Papeete weather service was predicting winds to 60 knots that afternoon! "Well, I'd put two-by-fours on my roof too," I mumbled, "if I had a roof."

There were a half-dozen boats in our little anchorage, and after the long-distance radio net, we all began to remove anything on deck that would provide windage and thus increase strain on our anchors. I set about stowing the jerry cans in the cockpit and the leecloths below, and removing the sails from the rig, while Stephen freed up access to the "bitter end" of our anchor chain, so that we could dump the anchor and chain if necessary. This last precaution was taken in case conditions became so intolerable in the anchorage that we needed to escape—and we could not get the anchor up. That would be an extreme situation, but we knew from our reading that boats had been lost in harbors, in bad storms, because they could not get themselves *out* of the harbor.

We spent the whole morning preparing, and the whole afternoon waiting. In the end the wind peaked at 45 knots—a gale, but not a storm. I grumbled a bit while I put everything back in order the next day. The porch guys were probably grumbling too. But I think we were all really more relieved that the predicted winds did not develop.

Other than the beauty of Tahiti, Paul Gauguin's paintings, and Melville's *Typee* and *Omoo* (in the Sunday crossword puzzle), French Polynesia was probably not on everyone's map until 1985, when terrorists blew up the Greenpeace ship *Rainbow Warrior* in New Zealand. The ship was on its way to the southernmost reaches of the Tuamotus, where the French conducted nuclear tests.

Nuclear testing is only one of many issues between the French and the Polynesians, who would dearly love to be independent. The violence of this struggle erupted in Tahiti too. In 1983 a huge riot caused millions of dollars in damage, and just months after our visit, the Tahiti airport was burned to the ground, causing significant concern in the tourist industry.

But our pass through this tropical paradise was mostly full of peace, pearls, and friendly people—with perhaps a new radio, TV, bicycle, generator, refrigerator, or car. What our sail through French Polynesia taught us was that change is indeed inevitable. As the world continues to shrink, change is not only inevitable, it is expected, and we should not complain. If the electric power poles in Tahaa seemed out of place and intrusive to our sensibilities in this tropical paradise, the Tahaa natives don't notice them. But they do notice, I have no doubt, the electricity they now have in their own homes. A better life?

A better life.

What Do You Do All Day?

A Day in the Life of Another Horizon

Many people, musing about our life, seem to find it hard to imagine. They think of it as an extended vacation: so you sightsee, eat, drink, go from one place to the next—and then what?

There was no typical day in our lives—not one, in nearly eight years. One day, however, I decided to record everything that happened, as it happened, just to see how it turned out. We were anchored at the south end of Fakarava, off Manihi Salmon's piece of paradise.

* * * * *

6 AM: I'm awake. The sun has just risen. I'm listening to the wind, which came up during the night, and I'm wondering what the weatherfax is going to tell us. Will it be something to worry about? While lying here, still, I've been thinking about our evening with Manihi and his friends. The conversation was wide-ranging and contained some gems I want to remember. I'm scribbling away in my journal as quietly as possible so that I do not disturb Stephen.

* * * * *

6:30 AM: We are both up now, folding the bedding, putting on water for coffee, trying to decide what to have for breakfast. Probably French toast, with the three-day-old bread. How different is this from anyone's life? Not so different, so far, except perhaps for the three-day-old bread. Since I make it, it has no preservatives in it, and in our not-so-very-cold refrigerator, it does not stay fresh long. At three days, it is *really* old, hours from becoming moldy, I gauge. I'm lucky to have some eggs, off the supply ship in Kauehi. I'd tried powdered eggs in Mexico, with little success, and decided that since we

42

shouldn't be eating all that many eggs anyway, we'd eat eggless unless there was a lucky opportunity, as in Kauehi.

* * * * *

7 AM: Breakfast in the cockpit. Stephen is mulling over the weatherfax charts received during the night. There is a front close by, which could affect our weather today. We talk about that for awhile. It's not like "better take an umbrella to work," but more like "should we do anything to save our house should a storm blow up?" That sounds like a heavy conversation, but we approach it in a matter-of-fact way. We'll monitor the current conditions, check the weather reports as they become available during the day, and decide what our options are as the day progresses.

* * * * *

7:30 AM: Every day at this time we get on the ham radio and check into an informal "net." A group of us that arrived in French Polynesia at about the same time decided to keep in touch via the ham radio. Cory is net control today and calls for check-ins. We identify ourselves by radio call signs. About ten boats check in this morning.

Cory calls us each in turn and directs the conversation. "Any questions or traffic for *Another Horizon?*" he asks.

"WEH" (that's Vicki).

Cory: "Go, WEH."

Vicky asks our location and when we think we will be coming to Papeete.

"In a few days, depending on the weather," we reply.

Cory calls for Ira, who arrived in Papeete yesterday with a serious staph infection. We hear Ira's report about a consultation with a doctor and visit to a clinic. Manny (still in Kauehi, 250 miles away), who had a similar infection last month, compares notes with Ira. Don, a physician, comes up and offers some advice. Medical help, even in these remote islands, is almost always available over the radio. There are several people out here who are physicians and who are willing to help with our medical problems. It's not easy, however, since the doctor usually has to diagnose from afar, relying on our descriptions of the problem. And then there is the issue of medicines. Do we have what is needed on board? We have an excellent medicine chest, we think, and are able to provide stopgap help on occasion. Fortunately, Ira is in "the city" and will be able to get the antibiotic he needs.

Other boats report their locations and share bits of news or information that would be of interest to the group. Because we have the weatherfax, and because Stephen has become an excellent student of weather, he has become the net's weatherman. He gives his daily weather report. The front is immediately on everyone's mind. Some ask Stephen questions about the speed the front is traveling, how much wind we might expect, and from which direction. Once again Stephen says he is not a wizard, but gives his best guesses. He also adds that he is an amateur at this weather business, and every skipper should use the information with that in mind.

One of our friends reports that their freezer is now empty, and they are turning to canned meats. Could anyone recommend an appropriate wine to drink with Spam? The net closes with that bit of humor, as most of us wonder what the luxury of having a freezer must be like.

*   *   *   *   *

8:10 AM: With the net closed, Stephen switches the radio to a weather report from Raratonga in the Cook Islands while I finish washing up the breakfast dishes. No dishwasher here, and in order for things not to get out of hand, we do the dishes after every meal.

*   *   *   *   *

8:30 AM: We hop into our dinghy to go to the next motu. We are interested in what the tides and currents are doing in the pass between the inside of the atoll and the open ocean. At the end of the next motu we can see the pass and we observe that the tide is flooding (coming in). From the turbulent water on the inside, however, we are sure that despite what the tide tables say, the flood started some time ago. All of this is important because we must time our departure through the pass at slack water, during the change between water coming into the lagoon and water going out. At other times the currents through the pass could be dangerous. We will come again tomorrow to try and confirm the timing of the incoming and outgoing tides.

*   *   *   *   *

9 AM: We are back on board *Another Horizon,* and Manihi, "Baby," and Cecilia come by to say good-bye. They are leaving to go to the village at the other end of the lagoon, 25 miles away, where they will be diving for giant turban shells. We wish Cecilia bon voyage, and good fortune to Manihi and Baby. We regret that this "family connection" is coming to an end.

*   *   *   *   *

9:30 AM: The wind has shifted to the north and is a steady 15 knots. We are lying parallel to the beach and are no longer protected by the motus. A two-foot wind chop has developed in the lagoon, and we are bobbing up and down; it is decidedly uncomfortable.

Having eaten the last of our bread for breakfast, I realize it's time to make some fresh bread. It would be welcome for sandwiches at lunchtime.

For the rest of the morning we take turns on the computer, working on our correspondence. While the bread dough is rising and I'm not on the computer, I fix the end of the boom vang line that is fraying. Then I do a little laundry (by hand, mind you) and hang it out on deck to dry. I also make some more notes in my journal about Manihi and his life.

* * * * *

11 AM: A huge squall sweeps down on us. I hurry to take in the laundry, while Stephen closes the hatches and ports. It gets very uncomfortable below with everything closed up, a bit sauna-like. The squall passes and after twenty minutes of sweating below, we can open the hatches and ports again. I rehang the laundry, hoping it will dry before the next squall. In retrospect this was probably a lousy day to do laundry. It may never dry, and a heap of damp laundry below is not pleasant.

Noon: We have tunafish sandwiches made with the fresh bread, a new recipe that turns out well. The winds continue to build behind the squall, and the boat is really pitching now in the choppy water. Stephen is beginning to feel a little queasy and takes a pill so he won't be seasick. This is the worst for him, being seasick at anchor. It's bad enough during the passages, but at anchor it seems unfair.

I have to move the laundry farther aft because the hull pitching in the wind chop is throwing saltwater spray along the side of the boat and onto the laundry. If salt water gets into clothing it acts as a moisture wick, attracting dew, rain, and spray of any kind, leaving our clothing forever damp, dank, and musty-smelling. Why on earth did I do laundry today?

* * * * *

1 PM: The wind has backed to the northwest and our stern is facing the beach. I can see a huge coral head just below the surface only a boatlength away from the stern. This is not a good situation. If anything happens to our anchor tackle, we will go up on the beach, or smash into the coral head, almost immediately. In other circumstances we would change our anchorage or, if necessary, leave and head out to sea. But there is no other anchorage nearby that

would be more protected. And there is no way we could get out the pass to open water now, the tides and currents being at their worst at the moment. By the time the next slack begins it will be dark, and we would not be able to see well enough to negotiate the unlighted pass. We are stuck here, like it or not.

We think the weather front must be passing through, but we can't be sure. The wind continues at 15–17 knots, and we are bucking up and down in the short, steep waves coming down the long stretch of lagoon. Stephen is concerned about our nylon snubber line on the anchor chain. He can't tell if what he's feeling when he holds the line is the line chafing on coral, or the chain chafing on the snubber line. We begin to fret. We alternate watching our position, feeling the snubber and anchor chain, and pacing from bow to stern.

*   *   *   *   *

1:30 PM: I get around to washing the lunch dishes. I check our food stores for something to do, while nervously looking out the ports to check our position. We are just about out of fresh food; only potatoes and onions are left. Most meals are made from cans these days. I will be glad to get to Papeete and some fresh food. Thinking up palatable meals from canned goods requires some creativity. Staring at the can locker, I mentally rearrange the cans into three meals—hopefully enough to last to Tahiti. Perhaps we'll catch a fish on the way, but we can never count on that.

*   *   *   *   *

2:30 PM: I'm very tense about the weather and our anchor now. With Manihi gone, we are quite alone. If anything were to happen, we'd have no outside help. Despite the turbulent water, I decide to dive overboard and look at the anchor chain. This should tell us if there really is anything to worry about. Wearing a snorkel mask, I can easily see that all is well. The anchor is well dug in. In addition, I can report to Stephen that the anchor chain is wrapped tightly around a small piece of coral. Although it will be the devil to unwrap when it's time to leave, it will keep us off the beach and the coral heads behind us, and there is no danger of the anchor dragging. There is an unusual strain on the foreshortened chain, however, but the chain is fairly new, and a hefty size. There is no reason to think it would snap in anything less than a gale.

As long as I'm in the water, I decide to swim for 15 or 20 minutes to get some exercise. Being pinned on the boat in bad weather always makes me itchy. When the weather is questionable, we do not like to be far from the boat. Even now that we know that the anchor is unlikely to drag, going ashore doesn't *feel* like a good idea.

While swimming, I watch a school of unicorn fish (a "horn" protrudes from their forehead) and swim after a huge fish, four or five feet long, that I have never seen before. (I discover later in my fish book that it is a *mara,* or Napoleon fish, a relatively rare sight in these waters.) I feel much better after this swim, both from the exercise and the knowledge that the boat is secure.

＊　＊　＊　＊　＊

3 PM: After showering I check the water tank gauges and see that both tanks are getting a little low. With all the wind, the wind generator has been keeping the batteries well charged, so we decide to run the watermaker for a couple of hours. This will put about eight gallons of fresh water back in the tanks. Not much, but we can usually do with about that amount on an average day. So, by running the watermaker for two hours we should replace the water we are using today.

＊　＊　＊　＊　＊

3:30 PM: I decide to read for a little while. I'm in the middle of two books: Collins and LaPierre's *Freedom at Midnight,* and E. M. Forster's *A Passage to India*—an interesting combination. One of the things we like about this lifestyle is the time we have to read. We complete, on average, four to five books a week. India seems far away at the moment, but we'll get there eventually. Although fiction continues to be our mainstay, we have picked up a number of historical studies recently. I say "picked up" because we often trade books with other boats in anchorages. We started out from San Francisco with over 400 books on board, half of them reference books and half of them leisure reading. Although it is difficult at times to find someone with similar tastes in literature, when we do it is fun to swap.

Stephen, in the meantime, is trying to figure out how we can rig a better whisker pole topping lift (part of our rig for flying the spinnaker sail). Our current topping lift is not satisfactory.

The wind is abating somewhat. We are no longer heaving, bucking, or pitching—just bobbing.

＊　＊　＊　＊　＊

4:30 PM: I study some charts for awhile, to familiarize myself with our next passage (to Tahiti, a 250-mile run, two and a half to three days). I want to check on possible obstacles in the way, and possible harbors of refuge if the weather goes bad. Three days isn't a long passage, and weather forecasts are usually good enough to get us safely through that period. But it doesn't hurt to know what's out there. By looking at the charts, I discover that we have not yet plotted our course for this passage, so I turn on the GPS to put in the waypoints. This is always a satisfying task for me, seeing what our course will be, how many miles we will transit, what the navigational hazards or aids will be—pinning down the details of a passage. I get excited to be on the way. We have the route, we're ready to go—but the weather has other ideas at the moment.

* * * * *

5 PM: The cocktail hour. Some awful French box wine and vodka with Tang is all we have left. We really *must* get on to Papeete. I open a bag of spicy Mexican peanut mix. It's not too stale. We sit in the cockpit and talk some more about Manihi and what we learned from him. We talk about the next passage and agree that we'll not leave tomorrow; the unsettled weather could make the seas uncomfortable. We should give them a day to settle down. Unless something else suggests another delay, we'll definitely leave in two days.

* * * * *

6 PM: We listen on the ham radio, alternately to the Pacific Maritime Net (a formal net for boats all over the Pacific) and the evening weather report from Rarotonga.

* * * * *

6:30 PM: Supper in the cockpit. I've made the remnants of our barbequed mackerel into a fish stew with the last potatoes and onions. Making a meal on *Another Horizon* is both more efficient *and* more time-consuming than in a regular kitchen. I gather the ingredients, reach for a pot and pan, wash the veg in the sink, chop what needs to be chopped, add spices, open and close the frig, stir the stew at the stove—all without moving an inch. The galley standing space is just two feet square, with the fridge, stove, and sink each located on one side of the area. However, the refrigerator is *under* the right counter, and in order to get into it, I must move everything off the counter to lift the cover. The counter space is limited and the stove has just three burners. I rarely use more than two at one time. To extricate the right-sized pan, I have to move three others in front of it.

* * * * *

7 PM: We have a radio "sched" with Bob in Berkeley. He and Dave have been our loyal home-base contacts. We talk once or twice a week, passing messages to family, friends, and our business manager. Bob and Dave are our link to the mainland, and could be an emergency network if needed. We learn from Bob that Holly has returned to the Bay Area, following the end of her first year in college. We are relieved that she is "home," staying with friends and working at her summer job. We arrange with Bob to do a "phone patch" in a few days. This patch enables us to talk to someone via a phone and radio link. Although not quite the same as talking on the phone (we have to speak in succession, using the verbal "over" to signal the other person it is their turn), it is better (and cheaper) than anything else. Of course, radio conditions are not always good, and the call can be a frustrating series of yelling, static, and noise—ending with an inadequate, "We'll try again another day."

Two other hometown friends with ham radio rigs come up on frequency. It is good to hear the voices of old friends, so many, many miles away. These radio contacts with the world we left behind are wonderful. I'm not homesick now, I'm not yearning, but oh, it's so good to hear familiar voices, no matter how distorted, over the radio. This "can-string-can" link keeps us connected— "centered," they'd probably say in California.

* * * * *

7:30 PM: The wind is almost calm and from the west. With the wind from that direction we surmise the front hasn't quite made it through. I'm making notes in my journal about our radio contact.

* * * * *

8 PM: We play a couple of hands of Piquet (a card game). Stephen wins both.

* * * * *

8:30 PM: Another squall hits us. The wind is 20 knots and gusting from the southwest. We are more in the protection of the motus again, so there is less chop in the water. In the course of the day, the wind and *Another Horizon* have clocked through almost 360 degrees. The anchor chain must be *really* wrapped around that piece of coral now!

Because it is pitch-black—no moon or stars—we can't see the motus, and with Manihi gone there are no lights on shore. There is no reference point with which to gauge our position and any movement of it. Instead, we read the instruments. The depth under the keel is 33 feet, a good sign. The wind is gusting now to 25 knots, not so great. By looking at our cabin compass, we can see the boat swinging with the wind more to the south, also a good sign. Perhaps by morning this crap will have passed through here. It has begun to rain.

* * * * *

9 PM: We go back to reading our books, listening for the rain to stop so we can open the hatches again and get some air. The cabin is stifling. The wind has risen to 30 knots.

We turn on the radar to see how extensive the squall is. It is big, and likely to be around us for another hour, we judge, a long time to listen to the howling wind. I try reading again, but it's too difficult to concentrate on anything. I am restless.

* * * * *

10 PM: This is not a squall—it's a near-gale. The winds are a constant 35 knots. We continue to monitor the instruments. The radar has one huge green blot on the screen, the storm is so big. Our main concern now is the sun awning that covers the boat from the mast to the stern. In this wind it's like a sail. To try to take it down would be disastrous, but to leave it up could also be disastrous. We watch it nervously. Why didn't we think to take it down earlier? The wind is from the southeast now.

Despite the knowledge that the anchor is secure, I can't help but be nervous. We said the foreshortened chain should hold in anything short of a gale, but now we *have* a gale. My mind roams over the options—changing anchorage, putting to sea.... It's a futile exercise; we've already noted that these are *not* options this time. But I do it anyway just to remind myself that we have to get through this storm *as we are.*

* * * * *

10:30 PM: We struggle with the awning. It has to come down; it is in danger of being blown to pieces. Each corner that we untie becomes a thrashing "wing," beating wildly. I drag the yards of cloth into the cockpit, bunching them up as best I can out of the way. Our usual careful folding process is out of the question. We both make mental notes to deal with the awning earlier in the future, if we expect higher winds.

There is no point in trying to read, let alone sleep. We will pace the boat, checking the instruments, the radar, the compass, until this thing passes. It is nerve-wracking.

* * * * *

11 PM: I'm getting tired, but the sound of the wind in the rigging is *so* loud. Despite the fact that I really can't see anything outside, I make regular trips up the companionway to peer into the black. It's been a long time since I can remember feeling so isolated. Other times I have taken comfort in having another boat in the anchorage to talk to—but there is no one else anchored within 250 miles. And now that it is night, there is no more radio activity, short-wave or ham. Of course I would never admit on the radio that I was worried about our situation—never. But just asking someone else how *they* are doing helps put our situation into perspective.

They are likely to respond, "And how are you doing?"

To which I would answer, "Oh, just fine. Wind is up, noisy, but we checked the anchor this afternoon, and it looked fine. So we're fine, just fine."

* * * * *

Midnight: I'm lying down on a cushion in the salon for a moment. I'm really tired.

* * * * *

12:05 AM: I think I fell asleep.

* * * * *

6 AM: The next morning. The sun has just risen, the wind is *calm*, the boat is still. I sigh. The bread is only a day old.

Kava and Pigs

Samoa and Wallis

At one end of the open-air market in Apia, the capital of Western Samoa (now known as just Samoa), there was an enormous hand-carved wooden kava bowl more than two, maybe three feet across. It stood on its characteristic sturdy legs; it looked well used. A group of men were standing around the bowl, passing a coconut shell filled with the murky liquid. *Manuia lava* (Samoan for something like "cheers") they mumbled, dribbled a little of the kava on the dirt floor, and sipped the rest. We stood on the sidelines, watching.

One of the men approached Stephen with the coconut cup. I smiled. The stuff tastes truly terrible, and Stephen was going to have to drink it. Ha! For once I wasn't sorry to be left out of the game. Kava drinking is usually for men only in Samoa and other South Pacific islands. I was allowed to take pictures of the men enjoying their morning drink, but only Stephen was invited to sip.

Kava is made from a root plant that is steeped and chewed and twisted and squeezed to produce a dishwatery liquid of foul taste that many Polynesians love. Kava drinking has different rituals and is associated with different behavior in the different countries. In Samoa it is consumed with a certain amount of decorum, including the dribbling and mumbling before sipping, and the kava bowl provides an opportunity for socializing among the men. The kava bowl in the Apia market is more informal than usual, but there is still some protocol observed, and the sense of sharing is achieved by passing the same coconut shell around the circle of men that surround the bowl.

And what were the women doing? They were selling their fruits and vegetables in the market alongside. They sat on mats on the ground, behind low wooden tables on which their wares were displayed in very orderly fashion. I asked a couple of them sitting close together if I could take a photo of them. They smiled. By the time I had my camera in place, four of them had moved together, leaning into a center, to be sure they were included. I snapped. "Thank you!" they chorused, as if they were pleased to be the subject of my photograph, instead of it being my pleasure to capture their radiant smiles.

One of the women, with useful English, asked me my name.

"Tina," I said.

There were expressions of doubt and confusion on the women's faces. My conversant asked, "That is your name? Tina?"

"Yes, it's short for Christina—a nickname for Christina, which is my Christian name," hoping that would explain away whatever the doubt and confusion was.

"Tina! Tina is a good name. It means 'mother' in Samoan." She quickly translated this, or something like it, for her friends. Huge smiles with my name repeated a number of times. A little laughter. I was delighted. *"Mother" fits me well,* I thought.

The population of Apia is less than 40,000. As the capital of a country, therefore, it is rather small. We found the place to be a charming combination of the old ways (like the kava bowl) and a struggle to get into the twentieth century. There were businesses here with computers, and some people who knew how to use them. But the government offices were a graphic example of the rough road of progress, and the difficulty of putting aside the old to get on with the new.

The government offices were spread out in a number of ramshackle, old colonial buildings—wooden, two-story structures with outside staircases. But in a dominating harborside location, the New Zealand government (which had had close ties with Western Samoa since World War I) had built a brand-new government building, eight stories high, that would enable Samoa's government offices to consolidate. The new building had stood nearly empty for over a year.

We spent an evening with an Australian couple who had come to Apia on a contract job in telecommunications. They explained to us the *matai* system—that is, a hierarchy of village chiefs who look after their people by, among other things, getting them hired for jobs they are not qualified for. Our friends explained that there was this sort of manipulation in the government, as well. It's not exactly corruption, but part of their cultural heritage. The Samoans are trying to reconcile their old way of doing things (hiring your brother-in-law) with more contemporary ideals (get the job done on time, and on budget).

Perhaps the most charming event of Apia is the daily police parade. At eight o'clock every morning but Sunday, the police force, in their smoke blue uniforms—tunics and *lava lavas* (long straight skirts), with white pith helmets and sandals—and accompanied by their own twenty-piece band, parade from their barracks down the main road, a half mile to the new (nearly empty) government building. Grouped in front of the building, an honor guard raises the national flag, the band plays the national anthem, and all of Apia comes to a standstill. The ceremony completed, the band and police contingent march back to the barracks. The whole bit takes maybe twenty minutes. All traffic stops on the main road between the barracks and the new government building. "You'd be foolish to drive this route at 8 AM," a local told me. "Everybody knows, but there's still a traffic jam every morning," he said. But no one seemed to care. Twenty minute traffic jam? Why worry?

Every time we returned to the San Francisco Bay Area and were caught in a freeway mess, we thought of this tiny city and its daily traffic jam—just twenty minutes—while the band played on.

While we were in Apia we petitioned the appropriate authorities to visit the second largest island of Western Samoa, Savai'i. Visits to this island were carefully regulated, and required special permits. We prowled among the various old government buildings to find the appropriate offices (several) to get the papers we needed to make the visit. It wasn't altogether clear to us why a special permit was needed. There was perhaps a historical reason, long forgotten, and as is so often the case, no one thought to do anything about it.

The passage between the islands was an awkward one—too long for a day, too short for an overnight. We opted for the night passage, since it would be easier to slow down for daylight than speed up to make an entrance before dark. We decided to leave Apia Harbor with the last of the day's light, but at the last minute we were delayed by a radio contact.

We eventually pulled up the anchor just after dusk. By the time we had motored to the harbor channel, it was really quite dark. The channel was straight and not difficult to negotiate, but it was narrow, with unlighted reefs on either side. We didn't want to wander left or right, but straight and narrow was really no problem. What we didn't anticipate was a fresh wind that blew right down the channel and a short, steep chop that developed as the wind pushed the water through the narrow opening in the reefs. The bow bucked; the mainsail, raised inside the harbor, swung and banged. We couldn't quite see the coral edges of the channel. I was pissed with the situation and started muttering to myself about leaving too late, a bad beginning to a passage, and how I hate nighttime passages.

Suddenly off the port side came an unexpected and loud, "Talofa!" (the traditional Samoan greeting). Shee-it, what was that? It turned out to be a local fishing boat, an 18-foot open dory, surfing in on the wind wave we were bucking. The half-dozen fishermen in it could see us easily with our navigation lights, but we had not seen them at all, as they had no lights. In the glow from our midmast steaming light we saw their faces as they roared by, grinning, hands raised in greeting, all very congenial. We were terrified. We could have run them down. We never saw them. They scared us half to death.

Stephen was instantly seasick in the steep, sharp waves. My anxiety about the night passage increased. The fishermen had set our teeth on edge. I was already petitioning the gods to get this over with quickly. And thankfully, the gods delivered. The wind blew well through the night, and at dawn we were at the entrance to the bay of Asau, the town we were to visit on Savai'i.

Savai'i is one of the larger islands in the Pacific—a volcanic island with some 470 old craters. Although there hasn't been an eruption since 1911, the history was evident everywhere we looked. The island appeared to us as one huge, gray lava bed. Lava pools had been carved out of the seabed around the village; the anchorage itself was formed by lava streams that had rolled down to the shore and solidified in the cold water. There was an overlay of vegetation everywhere, but the predominant geography was jagged lava rock.

We put ashore in our dinghy, tying up to an old wooden wharf, and walked along what looked like the main road that ran along the edge of the lagoon. Every head turned to look at us. We smiled and said, "Talofa." Giggles from the children, wide smiles from the mothers. The men were all working in the fields.

Some of the children asked, "What is your name?" in carefully practiced English.

"Tina."

Gales of laughter.

"No, no, it really is Tina."

More giggles. The older women all wanted to know where we were going, as if walking through the village was a strange thing to do. A few with a little more English asked where we were from.

"United States."

"Long way from Samoa." Yes.

To one of the few young lads we said, "Samoa is a beautiful country."

He said, "No."

"No? Why not?"

"Only a few cars and trucks. In America many cars and trucks."

Yeah, we would have said, *and you have clean air, safe streets, quiet villages, and no traffic jams, either.* But I don't think he would have understood.

Matti and Temo, two boys about ten or eleven, walked along with us for a while. They seemed to like walking with us, looking into our faces—looking for something, I don't know what. They liked being seen with us too; that was clear. They lavishly greeted friends along the roadside while keeping pace with us.

We had been wary of leaving the dinghy at the wharf, and groaned when we returned to find a half-dozen children sitting on the rocks close around it. We had had these experiences before: the kids crowd into the dinghy and want to be taken to the big boat; or they get in the dinghy while we're trying to launch it and bounce on the inflated sides, refusing to get out; or they swim out and hang on to the side so you can't row. A nuisance. As we approached, the children stood. *Here we go,* I thought.

We tried a little, "What's your name?"

"Tulu." "Paulus." "Serina." They were shy.

We asked, "See you tomorrow?"

"Yes, yes!" Excited.

We launched the dinghy into the water and rowed away to their "Good-bye, good-bye" as they raced down the wharf waving. We smiled. We would look forward to seeing them tomorrow.

That evening we watched a lone fisherman rowing quietly around the anchorage in his *paopao,* a narrow dugout canoe. We waved but he turned away from our gesture. We watched for a while, but were distracted by dinner. The next morning we came on deck, preparing to go ashore again.

"Where are my sandals?" asked Stephen.

"I thought you left them on deck, next to mine."

"Not here," he said. "I *know* they were there." "Not here now," he said, "but yours are."

We knew of this. A Norwegian boat that we had spoken to had had the same experience here. They had left sandals on deck. The man's were gone the next day.

"They only take what they can use, and only if you leave it lying about, seeming to be careless," our friends had warned us. We had forgotten.

When we pulled the dinghy ashore the next day, we were greeted by a young man with a small child in tow. He spoke surprisingly good English. Would we come to his home? he asked. We'd be delighted, we said. Lamenko lived only a short distance from the wharf. His home was in a large clearing and part of a group of *fales* (thatched houses). Samoans often live in family compounds, and Lamenko had all his family around him—parents, brother and sister, and children … a gaggle of children.

Lamenko asked us to sit in the only two chairs available. A low table was placed before us, and his wife, Lotte, appeared with hard coconut bread and drinking coconuts. I'm not a fan of coconut milk, and the bread was dry and tasteless. It is very difficult to be enthusiastic about food you do not like, and eat enough so as not to give offense. This would be our trial for the next few days as Lotte and Lamenko repeatedly invited us into their home and fed us.

As we sat and ate, the family gathered around us, sat on the bare floor, and watched. The youngest girl sat in front of us and fanned us with a large palm frond. We had experienced this disconcerting aspect of Polynesian hospitality everywhere. Polynesians do not eat with their guests. They eat what is left over after the guests leave. We found it difficult to gauge how much we should eat—to be polite and appear as though we were grateful for the food, but to be sure there was enough left for our hosts later.

In the case of Lotte and Lamenko, we soon surmised that they were subsistence farmers, like most of the villagers, and lived pretty much hand to mouth. Although we sipped and nibbled, I could tell Lotte was watching carefully to be sure the food was acceptable. I crunched and gulped. And we had just eaten lunch too.

We tried to distract them from watching the eating business by taking some Polaroid pictures. This was a big hit, and indeed, it distracted them well. But since our visit now exceeded some time element, and we had given them something they needed, apparently, to give something back. And what they had to give was food.

Lamenko brought out a bowl of *ufi* for us to eat. Glory, I thought I was going to gag. I'm not sure what *ufi* is exactly, but it looked and tasted like a bland potato (and when is a potato not bland, you ask?). So it was a root vegetable clearly, cooked and mashed, and we ate it, washed down with more coconut milk. Blaach! I needed a swig of pure orange juice, or carrot juice, or whiskey.

The next evening was Thursday and we had heard that the Congregational Church in town was having choir practice. We went ashore and wandered into the village to have a look. Choir practice turned out to be *everyone* in the congregation learning the hymns for the Sunday service. The church musician and choirmaster stood in front of the congregation and patiently taught them the harmonies by rote. It was fascinating. Some of the villagers knew some of the hymns, and some were learning for the first time. There were no hymnals, or song sheets, or even printed words. Since most of the people cannot read words, let alone music, everything was taught by rote. And the result? We agreed to return Sunday and find out.

The singing on Sunday was as we expected—loud, amazingly in tune, and inspired. The pastor of the church approached us after the service and asked if we would join him and his family for Sunday dinner. We had to decline, regretfully, and we could tell that this was a minor offense. But we were already in trouble with Lotte and Lamenko because we had agreed to come to the Congregational Church service instead of their church—the Latter-day Saints.

This mistake was an embarrassing lesson: once "taken home" by a Polynesian family, you must remain loyal to that family, or they may lose face. The fact that we had accepted Lotte and Lamenko's hospitality meant that we were sort of adopted by them, and were expected to do everything with them. Their status in the town was lifted considerably because we had eaten in their home and shared time with them. We committed an enormous *faux pas* by deciding to go to the Congregational Church for the Sunday service, and I fear that Lotte and Lamenko were embarrassed that we were not with them at their church.

We tried to make up for it by having Sunday dinner with them. That is to say, we sat and ate dinner while the family sat around and watched us. Oh, how hard this was. Lotte had gone overboard in her preparations. To them it was a feast, but to us it was all bland, gray, and mostly starch. There were several root vegetables, a couple of coconut concoctions, *bisua* (coconut cream with tapioca) and *supo* (noodles with fatty beef ribs), and the favorite Samoan beverage, watery cocoa.

This day the young girl who had fanned us on previous visits was missing. Attending Sunday school, Lamenko explained. That seemed odd, as the rest of the children were all at home. In her place at the fanning job was Malua, one of the many boys in the family. I had noticed on previous visits that Malua watched me closely, and one time he came close to feel the fabric of my shirt. Watching him that Sunday, I suddenly realized that Malua was a *fa'afafin*, a boy brought up as a girl. Although that's not a practice seen much today, on the more traditional island of Savai'i it was not surprising to encounter this phenomenon. With only one girl child, Lamenko's family needed more girls to do the female jobs (e.g., serving food and fanning the guests); so a boy was chosen to fill in. Whether by instruction or choice, Malua had developed effeminate body language, his voice was high-pitched and had a singsong quality to it, and he was clearly *interested* in being a female.

The *fa'afafin* do not dress as females, nor do they dress in pants and shirts as many Polynesian men do today. The few times we encountered *fa'afafin*, they were dressed in muu-muu-like costumes, or *lava lavas*, or with a cloth tied around the waist and a T-shirt (Malua's preferred garb).

As we left Lotte and Lamenko that day we told them we would be leaving Savai'i the next day. They expressed regret and asked if they could see us in the morning to offer a safe voyage. We agreed to meet them at the wharf.

In the morning we rowed ashore with a bag of clothing for the children, some canned goods from the food locker (green peas and yellow peaches—anything with color), and some pens for the children's school.

The whole family had come to the wharf. Lotte presented us with a wide woven pandanus mat, and her father intoned a blessing for a safe passage. Lamenko shook our hands but said nothing. The children stood by quietly. Malua never took his eyes off me. Our thanks were effusive for all of their gifts, but most of all for their gift of friendship. We pushed off in our dinghy and rowed out to *Another Horizon*. The family stood on shore, watching, but strangely did not wave.

* * * * *

In all of the South Pacific, entering into lagoons or harbors through the passes in the surrounding reefs was a source of anxiety. Despite the number of reef entrances that we made successfully, we never got used to it. No two were alike, and none of them was easy. There was always a leap of faith that the chart was good enough. At Suvarov in the Cook Islands, we searched for an hour before we found the cut through the reef. The GPS coordinates we had calculated on the chart were two miles off. The chart (which was the best available at the time) had hardly been updated since Captain Cook's time.

And if finding the opening to the pass was not enough, there was then the issue of *when* to enter the pass—a subject that could occupy Pacific sailors for hours. Tides and currents were the major factors. Was the tide rising or falling, the current going in or out? And at what time were these events happening? (Of course you never had a timetable for the exact place you were, so you had to extrapolate from an island miles away.) The location of the opening of the pass in relation to the wind also needed attention. (Would the wind be pushing the sea swell into the channel, or might there be an eddy just outside—or inside—as a result of the confluence of currents?) And you couldn't forget to consider the phase of the moon!

The old salts advised observing the time of slack tide, and planning to go in or out an hour (or so) later the next day. At Makemo in the Tuamotus we spent three days inside the lagoon, watching the currents in the channel—in, out, slack, out—no, no, it should be "in" now. Well, it looks like "out" again. Some experts will tell you that there is always *some* "out." We made a chart of our observations, and just to be sure, we asked a local fisherman when he thought the slack would be. He shrugged his shoulders.

As we left our anchorage at Makemo, I noticed a number of people on shore watching us. Well, that wasn't so unusual. What was unusual was that they weren't smiling and waving. If I had had the time and the binoculars in hand, I might have seen their eyes bulging out, and an expression on their faces that said, "You've got to be kidding."

We proceeded to the inner end of the pass and looked out. The water appeared calm. No swells, breakers, or eddies—that we could see. With Stephen ever-faithful in the rigging, and me manning (absolutely) the helm, we carried on. Just as we approached the end of the channel, the water began to swirl in enormous whirlpools. I swerved to avoid one. But ahead there was another—larger—with standing waves and a pull so strong that we could not escape. We were sucked into the vortex. Here was Charybdis? Was this the end? "I don't believe this," I screamed at Stephen, and looked up. Stephen was swaying in the rigging, holding on for dear life, too preoccupied to even yell at me to stop yelling.

I put the engine throttle to the maximum rpm. The roar dimmed my screaming, and the surge of power pushed us out into calmer water.

The issue now was: if this could be the experience after days of watching, what were our chances when we arrived to go *in* through the next pass? We wouldn't have the luxury of watching for days ashore. We would arrive outside the pass, take a look, and if the water appeared calm …

The channel into the lagoon at Wallis (a French protectorate, west of Samoa) was located on the windward side of the island, which meant the sea swell crashed ashore around the opening. This swell meeting an outgoing current could produce ten-foot standing waves, we had been warned. Going through in those conditions would be unthinkable.

We had hoped to arrive in the late afternoon, before the sun set, to go through on a slack tide and with enough light to see any coral dangers. But as hard as we sailed, we just couldn't quite make it. We were frustratingly close, but finally concluded it would be too dangerous to try so late, and in the dark. Now what to do?

We could sail away from the island for hours and then come back, but we didn't want to take the chance of missing our window again. So we hove to. Heaving to, managed by an arrangement of reefed sails, put the boat at a near standstill. We simply drifted, with the wind pushing us gently away from the island. When the sun rose the next morning, we had drifted less than five miles.

We approached the pass with our usual trepidation, Stephen in the rigging and me at the wheel. The pass was very narrow, and there were no navigation marks until we were over halfway through the reef. Huge seas were rolling directly into the pass, rolling us from side to side, gunnel to gunnel. Stephen yelled that he couldn't make out the markings—there were too many, and all close together. Hell's bells. I was fighting the wheel to keep the boat on course—but what course? I screamed mild profanities. Stephen yelled at me to stop screaming, but I couldn't. Screaming was my way of venting my anxiety.

I yelled at Stephen, "Which way, which way?"

He yelled back, "I don't know!"

When we got close to the marks, it became clear at last. New marks had been set up, but the old ones had not been removed. The new ones were not exactly next to the old ones, so the patterns of "lefts" and "rights" were confusing until we were right on top of them. We swept through the maze at an appalling speed, made a right turn into the inland water, and suddenly all was well. The water was flat, the marks were clear, I stopped screaming, Stephen stopped yelling, the island sparkled, and the sun beat down into water of crystal clarity.

We ventured into a tiny anchorage at the main island. There were three other sailboats already anchored there, and we invited them to join us for "sundowners" that evening. One of the boats was Norwegian; the crew spoke excellent English, and good German. One was Russian; they spoke little English but passable French. One was French; they spoke no other language. We manage passable English, high school French, vague German, "tak" in Swedish, and "Kahk deelah" (That's life) in Russian. The conversation was lively, and the more sundowners we consumed, the funnier the exchanges became.

The next morning we hitched a ride into the main town, Mata Utu, with a Frenchman and his Wallisian wife and discovered that it was a fete day.

"What fete is that?" we asked.

The two looked at one another. "Mata Utu day, we think." I had read that Wallisian towns often had a holiday just for their town, and it was often in conjunction with special church activities.

In town, we asked others about the fete.

"Fete de Marie," said the woman who gave us directions to the church.

"Fete du Kava," the French navy personnel said.

The proprietress at the restaurant where we had lunch said, "Fete de l'Assomption," and with that we remembered the day's date, August 15. Of course ... Assumption Day.

What we found in town was a curious mix of activities aimed at raising money for the church. A church fair! But not like any church fair I can remember.

There were thirty to forty dancers in front of the church, the women sitting, the men standing behind. They wore all-white clothing with colorful crepe paper streamers around their necks and waists. The dancing was typically Polynesian: graceful, slow-moving, not what you'd call exciting. As we stood at the side watching, we saw townspeople walking among the dancers and stuffing something down the fronts of the women's blouses. It looked, well, not very polite. I asked the woman standing next to me what was happening.

"If you like the dancing, you give money." I was sure I had translated that (from the French) correctly, but Stephen said I must have it wrong.

"If you like the *dancer,* you give money," he said. Whatever. He pulled some bills out of his pocket. Oh, yikes.

"You're not going to do it, are you?" I pleaded. "What if you pick the wrong one, or give some offense without realizing it? That happens," I whined. He frowned and mumbled, but stayed put.

When we had seen enough of the dancing, we walked around behind them and saw one of the most outlandish sights of the whole voyage. The field behind the church was filled with rows of roasted pigs lying on mats of woven coconut frond, with their snouts and legs sticking up to the sky. They were laid out according to size, from little piglets to gigantic sows. Some were on platforms of other foodstuffs, including fruits, kava, and other root vegetables—even a case of Coca Cola, in one instance.

"And what is this?" I asked another onlooker, hoping the French would be simple.

"Everyone gives on this day. If you don't have money, you bring one of your pigs as a gift. If you have money, you buy one of the pigs." Throngs of folk from all over the island were wandering up and down the rows, deciding on their choice and placing bids on the one that suited.

About midafternoon it began to rain, one of those lovely tropical downpours. We ducked under a roof overhang at the side of the church. Although some others joined our temporary shelter, most people just kept on doing what they had been doing. The dancers danced, the pig selling continued. The pigs held up all right: what was a little water to wash off some of the cooking fire ash? But the dancers soon became a more colorful sight. The strips of crepe paper they had lavishly hung about their necks and tied around their waists began to bleed bright red, yellow, and blue splotches down their white shirts, skirts, and pants. They danced on undaunted, smiling. The paper money, now billowing inside the shirts, was turning a bit soggy too, I imagined.

The rain did not dampen spirits or any of the other activities. Speeches were given, canoe races were started, and everyone got wet as the rain continued on and off through the afternoon. At the end of the day a traffic jam of pickup trucks converged on the church lawn to haul away the pigs. Onlookers praised the buyers' choices; the winning bidders were nearly licking their chops. We retreated to *Another Horizon* for some pasta with canned spaghetti sauce, leaving the pigs with their feet in the air to our memories.

* * * * *

The cultural traditions we discovered in the Pacific stand out, vivid and exotic. But on reflection there are interesting parallels in our culture. Our social drink is tea or coffee (and not kava, thank heaven), and we sometimes use it in a way similar to the Samoans' use of kava—as an opportunity to have a chat with some friends. We bring or buy "white elephants" at our church fairs instead of pigs. But the idea is the same. Like Josephine and Lotte, who cooked what they had on hand, the people of Samoa and Wallis gave what they had on hand. A cup of friendship would have to be kava; a gift to the church, if not money, would have to be a pig. It was what they had to offer.

But what struck us most about these experiences, beyond the colorful traditions and beautiful setting, was the generosity of the islanders—not just to their friends and neighbors, but to two boat people who just happened to sail to their shores.

The King and I

Tonga

We had heard that they would kill 1,800 pigs for the agricultural festival in the northern islands of Tonga—because the king was coming for the festival. I had to imagine that such a slaughter would obliterate the entire pig population of the island group. It was hard to imagine that there were even that many pigs on these islands. But that's what they told us: 1,800. They had apparently killed most of the chickens too, not so long before, for some other festival, which is why we would pay forty-three cents each for eggs imported from New Zealand.

The 170 islands of Tonga are spread in a north-south line over 500 miles long. The thirty-four islands of the northern group, called Vava'u, are hilly and thick with vegetation. They reminded our Seattle friends of the San Juan Islands. The Vava'u group is bordered on two sides by a reef that protects the islands from any sea swell. The anchorages are sheltered and plentiful.

With fine white beaches, clear water, coral gardens, abundant fish, and friendly locals, Tonga—and especially the Vava'u group—was as close as one could get to a voyager's paradise. Although I have never acknowledged that I had a best-liked country out of the sixty-one we visited, Stephen is quick to say that Tonga was his all-time favorite.

Tonga is Polynesia's oldest and only remaining monarchy, and the king of Tonga was the first king we had met. Royalty are as intriguing to Tongans as they are to the British, and we were swept right along. Anytime the king was to appear, we were there.

For days before the agricultural fair, we heard of the king's coming. The locals were abuzz with this news. The women talked about what they would wear, just as if the society page reporter would be there.

I listened seriously to the women's advice about dressing conservatively if we were to attend the fair. I scoured our clothes lockers for the best of our wardrobes. For Stephen we managed navy slacks, a white dress shirt (long-sleeved), and a tie. Although there was a blue blazer in the hanging locker, I finally convinced him that he would get heat prostration if he wore it. In a dress (a dress!) I looked decent, if not gorgeous.

When we arrived at the fairgrounds we wandered among the exhibits of taro, yams, sweet potatoes, watermelon, and pineapples, all lined up for judging. But judging what? The biggest? The most perfectly shaped? We couldn't tell, but from the looks of the growers and the scowls of the judges, this was serious stuff. There were food stalls too, where some of the exhibits were being eaten. (Unlike in Wallis, we never saw the results of the pig slaughter, for which I was grateful.)

At one end of the field we came to the parade-viewing area, where we found the king's special viewing tent being swept clean of every fleck of dust—not an easy task in the hot, dry field. We cast about, looking for the best vantage point for our viewing.

One of the king's attendants began herding us to the dignitaries' tent, an open-sided pavilion that provided the only shelter from the sun. With regret I had to say, "Ah, no, I don't think this is our place."

"Please," the uniform responded.

"But we don't have the invitation," Stephen protested (we had noticed that the people entering this tent were proffering white envelopes).

"Sit!" the guard commanded, pointing to two chairs in the middle of the tent.

"Well, okay, okay," we mumbled, and with some embarrassment stepped over the feet and legs of our fellow guests to find our seats. There were a few who turned and stared.

"The guard made us," I wanted to say. We certainly didn't want to offend anyone, the guard or the dignitaries.

Just then a large black car pulled up in front of the king's tent.

"Why would you have a black car in a tropical country?" I murmured to Stephen.

"If you're king, you get to have whatever you want, even if it doesn't make sense to us." Oh! I suddenly realized that the broad backside maneuvering out of the car was the king. Once a large and very heavy man in the Polynesian tradition, the king had recently lost many pounds on a diet. He was somewhat stooped from his former six-and-a-half feet, and hardly the "ample" king we had read about. Although we all applauded his arrival, King Taufa'ahau Tupou IV turned without acknowledgment and quickly entered his tent. Well, let the games begin.

From our spot among "the dignitaries" (and didn't I wonder who they all were), we watched dancing, drill teams, blaring bands, and parading horses. In the middle of the show there were speeches, of course. They were in the Tongan language, so I spent this time gazing at the people, the pigs, the ... wait ... what was that about "private sector" and "quarantine?" The speaking became more intense. A political diatribe? "San Francisco" … could we have heard him right? I tried to pay more attention, but the sprinkling of English words (for which there was no Tongan equivalent, apparently) gave us no clue about the subject of this talk. No one around us had enough English to explain.

Awards for the best, biggest, or brightest taro, goat, pig, and sweet potato were announced. Festival organizers were acknowledged and applauded; they had done a splendid job. We smiled and applauded at appropriate places—that is, when our dignitary neighbors did—while we were seated in our cool tent. Our fellow voyagers, most in shorts and T-shirts, were in the back of the crowds standing along the railing at the edge of the field, with the sun beating down relentlessly. In our going-to-see-the-king duds, we were comfortably seated; we were offered refreshments, and our view was front-row.

"Never, ever laugh at me in a dress," I later told my shorts-and-sneakered friend.

"Believe me," she answered.

* * * * *

We were anchored behind a small island on the reef that defines the end of the bay between Utungake and Kapa. We could see across the reef to the next island, Pangaimotu, which was joined by a causeway to the main island where the town of Neiafu was located. The islands were a beautiful puzzle of interlaced fingers of reef and motus, spotted with little islets, any one of which could be the dream of a South Pacific isle.

In this anchorage at Mala we met William—a thirtyish fellow, slight by Polynesian standards and industrious, although I wasn't always sure what he was industrious about. His wife made respectable tapa (bark cloth), and we purchased several pieces from her. We stayed a number of days in this anchorage, and William became a daily visitor with one or another of his numerous children. One day he asked if we could help him deliver a small boat with an outboard across the bay. Could we follow him in our dinghy, pick him up after he delivered the boat, and bring him back across the bay? Of course. I elected to help him, as Stephen was busy with some boat chores.

On the way across the bay, alone in the dinghy, I could go fast enough to get our normally sluggish craft to rise up on the water and plane. In this way I could speed across the bay, keeping pace with William's larger boat and engine. He gave me a thumbs-up; he liked that.

I picked him up on the far beach, and we started back across the bay. William grabbed the bowline of the dinghy and hung on, imitating me when I had been planing earlier. Sadly, I had to make it clear that I couldn't plane with him in the dinghy because he was too heavy. He laughed, and then became quiet and thoughtful. Suddenly he turned to me and said, "You the boss?"

"Sometimes," I said, "but not usually."

"He good man, your husband." A statement, not a question.

"Yes, he is."

"You fly home; your husband sail from here?"

"No, we sail together."

"Oh, you cook good for him, make things okay," William said.

"No, I sail too."

"You do!" Incredulous. Broad smile. He liked that too. This was clearly a new concept for William: a woman who could and would do what men do.

William was a good husband too, I think. He worked hard selling the things his wife, Anna, made, and he kept close contact with his children. I was sorry to leave his company when we left for Kenutu.

* * * * *

The food we ate in Vava'u was one of the islands' outstanding features. We were several times invited to a traditional Tongan feast. We sat on mats on the ground; dozens of seafood and vegetable dishes were served on banana leaves. Shells were used for bowls, fish were wrapped in seaweed, and we used our fingers to eat it all—messy, but delicious.

At these feasts there were often local dancers to entertain us. The lithe young women oiled their bodies, which gleamed in the fires around the clearing where we sat. To show appreciation of their skill, it was the custom to "paste" paper money on their oiled skin. I kept a strong hand on Stephen's arm. I could tell that this pasting operation was delicate, and as in Wallis, I was nervous about the possibility of doing it "wrong" and causing embarrassment.

The Tongans teach their young how to dance at an early age. By seven, they are experts whose charming, fresh, and somewhat naïve dancing is a delight to watch. I eased my iron clutch on Stephen, and he was the first to approach the youngest, shyest, and in my opinion most beautiful of the little girls. She was six, if a day. Stephen leaned down to pat a large bill on her back. There was a low noise of appreciation from the adults sitting on the sidelines. They were clearly pleased with Stephen's tribute, and so was I.

* * * * *

Along the line of Tonga islands, between the Vava'u group in the north and the Tonga tapu group in the south, there are the Ha'apai, a spread of low-lying islands thickly interspersed with reefs—a dangerous path to negotiate in a sail-boat. The reefs were more often than not unmarked, and the charts, we eventually calculated, were about a half-mile off. We could not, therefore, apply GPS positions to the charts. Instead, we navigated the old-fashioned way, using our eyes. With Stephen high in the rigging, calling out instructions to me at the wheel, we picked our way through the maze of reefs.

We made our way to an anchorage at Lifuka, where on shore we met Sara, a noticeably thin woman with an iron handshake. It was the first time I have heard the bones of my hand crunch when taken in the hand of another. Trying not to wince, I looked into her face. She had no idea she was causing me pain. She smiled a genuine smile of welcome and friendship. Sara was, she told us, in charge of repairing the ceremonial mat-skirts of the queen.

Tongans wear tapa mats like overskirts around their lower bodies. Although many of the mats are small and unobtrusive, others, especially those for special occasions, are large and seemingly cumbersome. Sara ushered us into a spare cabin where mats were laid over long tables up and down a twenty-foot-long room. The tapa was remarkable for its color: a deep, dark mahogany shade—the color for royalty, Sara explained. With immense pride, she showed us the repairs she was making, and how she tended to the fragile beauty of these garments. She explained that mats are often handed down for generations, and for most people the tattier—and therefore the older—they look, the more valued they are. The queen didn't care to look tatty, however, so Sara was tidying the mats for her.

*   *   *   *   *

The next morning we heard on the radio news of a strong earthquake near Japan. A tsunami was forecast to sweep across the whole of the Pacific.

Tidal waves, or tsunamis, are only dangerous when they hit land or shallow water. In the middle of the ocean, they appear to be an ordinary ocean swell. But when land gets in the way, the wave plows into it, revealing its immense size. And it is not just the size of the wave and the amount of water that comes on shore that does damage. When the wave retreats from the shore, it sucks the surrounding water out with it. Entire harbors have been emptied to mud flats as a result.

None of this sounded especially appealing to us. We were, in fact, a trifle worried.

Although there was apparently no way to predict the size of the wave—and therefore its effect on shore—it was apparently not difficult to predict the time the wave would move through our area. We were told it was traveling at 500 miles an hour, and we could therefore expect it to pass through our area about midday.

Our strategy was to leave the anchorage and head away from land until we knew the wave had passed. We were glued to the radio all day, listening to reports from the islands across the Pacific and following the progress of the wave. The reports from the islands at the appropriate times became disturbing. Nothing was happening. Was the speed of movement wrong? Was the time of the original earthquake wrong?

When the wave hit Hawaii, the experts there reported its height to be just under two feet! I believe this is called a nonevent. Sighs of relief came crackling across the radio waves. We headed for Nomuka, to anchor for the night before heading for Tongatapu, the capital of Tonga.

*　*　*　*　*

There are two things about Tonga that are unique in the South Pacific: the king, and the king's music. The king we were getting to know; his music, we were startled to discover, we already knew.

While attending Oxford for his education, the king heard the marvelous English church music, including that of Handel, Mozart, and Brahms. He acquired copies of the music, brought it back to Tonga, and gave it to his royal choir person. "Teach this music to my people," he said.

His royal musician was a clever man, and he constructed a special notation that could be easily interpreted by the choir. No long years of piano lessons to learn the traditional notation were needed—besides, there were no pianos. Nor did anything require them to "read," since so many adults were only marginally literate.

The teaching of this music was far-reaching. In the northern islands, 300 miles from the capital, we attended a service at a Wesleyan Methodist church, the primary Protestant sect of these islands. There were perhaps eighty people in attendance. At mid-service it was time for a choir anthem, and the pastor asked the "choir" to assemble. About sixty of the eighty people rearranged themselves into the center of the church and began to sing. They had no hymnals or sheet music. They sang it all by heart, and it sounded familiar: it was Handel. An erstwhile musician myself, I was confident of that identification. I couldn't be sure, but it had many of the musical elements of the Hallelujah chorus from the *Messiah*. (Baroque composers often wrote multiple pieces using the same themes.)

Although the Tongans had learned the classical composers' music—the notes—they had not been taught much about the dynamics of this music.

They sang it all in true Polynesian style, at one sound level: *loud*. I was amused to hear in the quiet moments of our service (during prayers or silences for whatever reason) the singing from the Anglican Church a few hundred feet down the path, also very loud. In any case, this rendition of some Handel choral piece was magnificent, though definitely incongruous in this simple wooden church, open on all sides to the tropical breezes, with the choir dressed in their decorative pandanus mats.

Sunday is sacred in Tonga. Absolutely nothing happens on that day. You are not allowed to do any work, to swim, or even to cook. What is there to do? Go to church.

The strong religious faith of the Tongans is not unusual in the Pacific. Although it often took a few attempts before the conversions took hold, the missionaries were very successful. Whether or not their faith remains strong we could not tell, but for whatever reason, the islanders and especially the Tongans attend church religiously.

Stephen and I, on the other hand, are not normally churchgoers. We attend midnight masses on Christmas Eve and look into cathedrals for their architecture, art, or music, but we generally shy away from formal church services. But in Tonga, we attended church at every opportunity.

The king's chapel in Nuku'alofa, the Centenary Chapel, is not what we'd call a chapel. It seats 2,000 people, and in our experience there was never an empty seat. There was a choir of some fifty voices accompanied by a brass band, not an organ (I do not believe there was one). They played and sang the hymns of Wesleyanism and the anthems of Bach, Handel, and Mozart. We attended a service there twice.

On the first Sunday, we came early to the churchyard to watch the congregation arrive. I knew we would see some of the finest *ta'ovala*, the mat skirts worn by men and women alike. Many men wore formal Western dress—white shirt, tie, and suit jacket—on their upper body, but with a handsome Sunday-best *ta'ovala* coming to their knees. Bare legs and sandals completed the outfit. The women wore long skirts, with the *ta'ovala* worn as an overskirt.

The first arrivals came in a long, white stream two hundred strong: young, beautiful Polynesian women walking to church, all in white dresses, their gleaming black hair long, but carefully and neatly braided down their backs. They were students from the nearby Queen Salote College, who came early each Sunday to lead the gathering congregation in preservice hymns. We watched them flow through the church doors and were quickly drawn inside by their singing.

Upon entering the church, we learned that as foreigners we were to be seated in a special section at the right front of the church, with an excellent view of everything happening throughout the chapel. The minister that Sunday was a visitor himself, not the regular pastor. He was a younger man, with a passel of small children, as it turned out.

The service was in Tongan, but periodically the minister would give us a précis of "what's going on" in English. This was both cordial and astonishing. He could not have known we would be there that Sunday, so his translations had to have been extemporaneous. To have made them at all was very generous. He was obviously well-educated, well-traveled, and his English was above average for a Tongan.

I hardly cared that I couldn't understand most of what he was saying, since the people-watching was excellent from our slightly elevated visitors' section. It was unfortunate that the king was not in attendance that particular Sunday—and I'll bet the young minister was sorely disappointed too. (We had heard that the king had flown to New Zealand for a special meeting of some sort.) The opposite, or mirror platform to ours was the king's seating in the chapel. Two ample chairs of throne-like quality were positioned for the king and queen, so they too would have a fine view of their subjects.

Although I loved watching the families (the children, if not attentive, were exceptionally well-behaved), it was the choir and the band that held my attention. The sound of this combination was so unusual, but so grand. A brass band playing hymns is quite a noble sound; it made the music soar to the rafters of this lofty church.

The hymns sung by the congregation were as we had heard them in other Tongan churches, with full harmonies and sung without written music in hand. As the people of Savai'i had, the members of these congregations *all* went to choir practice during the week until the harmonies were well ingrained. This was an extraordinary concept to me. In effect, everyone belongs to the choir. I wondered what happened if you were tone-deaf.

Having heard the almost-Hallelujah chorus for the anthem in Vava'u, I was eagerly awaiting a similar treat in the king's chapel. But this church experience would continue to surprise us.

As the collection offertory was announced, the minister's four children, ages about four to twelve, came forward and gathered around a microphone. The eldest played a guitar in accompaniment to the four of them singing "Jesus Loves Me" (in English!), to the tune of "Doe, a deer, a female ..." from the *Sound of Music!* (It works.) The children were dear. Every face in the chapel had a smile on it.

*   *   *   *   *

It was rumored that the king was not a well man. We heard that he flew to New Zealand regularly for medical checkups. When we saw him at the agricultural fair, he was stooped and moved ponderously. It was with great concern, then, when one day on the waterfront of Nuku'alofa we heard a gun salute begin. The volleys continued. After several went off, we began to count them.

We knew that when the king's mother, Queen Salote, died in 1965 they fired a 65-gun salute—one for each of her years. We were fearful that we were hearing the beginning of a similar salute to the king. He was seventy-six years old that year. But after a few dozen shots, the sound of guns ceased, and we breathed a sigh of relief. We could not imagine the distress—emotional, political, economic—that would result from the king's death. In 1965 the country was virtually shut down for six months of mourning. But if this volley was not, thankfully, for the king, the question remained: what was it for?

We left the restaurant and began wandering the streets of Nuku'alofa. We sensed that something was going on. It's an eerie feeling when you know something is afoot, but can't make out what it might be. We asked some storekeepers.

"A holiday," they said. "Stores are closed."

But why?

"Just this morning."

When will you open again?

"Later."

After several exchanges like this, we finally pieced together that the king wished to honor a couple of dozen soldiers who had served in a United Nations peacekeeping mission in Bougainville, Papua New Guinea. Sending his troops to this "long-distant" place was an unpopular move for the king. Why should they—Tongans—spare their soldiers to this neighboring country that couldn't keep its own peace? Very unpopular.

The king apparently hoped to make some amends by honoring these troops on his parade ground that afternoon. He ordered the shops to close, and the word was spread that the soldiers would make an appearance. The whole town turned out.

We stood on the fringes, restive in the heat under some meager trees, watching the children nearby play with sticks in the dust. The king's band marched onto the field and played stirring music; the soldiers marched around the ground, standing tall; the king appeared and said some good words. The king's pastor offered a prayer. And then the band began to play—pianissimo—and all around us the people began to sing, uncharacteristically quietly, almost whispering.

The harmonies rose gently from the ground—the women seated under the trees, the men standing by the trunks, the young girls bunched in the back, the boys sprinkled around watching in envy the men they wanted to be. They sang, softly, the harmonies they knew from church. We couldn't understand the words, but the music was familiar. After a few moments the English words to the tune came to me: "What a friend we have in Jesus."

The music came from the blades of grass, from the leaves of the trees, from the dust of the road, from the still air hanging over the parade ground. We were moved to tears without even understanding the magnitude of the moment. The sound they created all around the parade ground gave me goose bumps— in 90-degree heat.

The following day, Sunday, we returned to the king's chapel and saw some more of the king's hoped-for appeasement. The service was dedicated to the Tongan armed services, all 400 of them—nearly all of them in attendance. We had never seen such proud men, and a sprinkling of women, in uniform. At the end of the service, the band played the introduction to the national anthem, and the rows of uniforms rippled as the troops stood, as tall as any people can (and Tongans are not an especially tall people). The pride was palpable. The anthem, played by the band and sung by all 2,000 people in the chapel, was magnificent.

The king was absent—in New Zealand for a medical appointment.

More Sheep Than People

New Zealand

The birds were the first clue. An albatross glided by, followed by shearwaters that gave way to some gannets. No more boobies and terns; we were too far south. The water's color went from tropical blue-greens, silky aquamarines, and ripe indigos to a deep khaki with a slate blue overlay of sky reflection. Cold, cold-looking water. And a distant cloud, a Polynesian navigational hint to the close proximity of land, stood us in good stead. We were nearly there, to Aotearoa, "Land of the Long White Cloud"—the Polynesian name for New Zealand.

The morning we pulled into the harbor at Auckland we were struck dumb by the sight. After nearly a year of traveling among tiny island nations, hot and dusty, with populations of a few hundred to a few thousand, here was a real city with suburban sprawl, skyscrapers, cantilevered bridges, and traffic.

Despite modern advances in transportation, New Zealand is an isolated place, and our check-in procedures included all the precautions of a country that wants to protect itself. Immigration officers were the first to arrive. After stamping our passports, they warned us that we could not leave the boat until Agriculture had come by. New Zealand has few agricultural diseases, non-native critters, or bugs, and they take extraordinary precautions to keep it that way. Any vehicle such as a boat or plane that enters the country must abide by stringent regulations, especially with regard to foodstuffs: no eggs, honey, meat products (fresh or canned), fresh vegetables, or fruit. Our sailing guides had alerted us about the regulations, and we carefully consumed nearly everything on the list before reaching shore. The guides also suggested that we should not arrive completely clean, as that could be suspect, so I purposely kept a couple of eggs, the dregs of a honey jar, and half of a browning cabbage ready for the official's black plastic garbage bag, to take away and destroy.

The agricultural official who came on board remarked that we seemed especially well prepared. We told him about the information we had received in advance.

"Not everyone is so smart," he said. "We had a large yacht in here recently that had a freezer *full* of meat."

"How awful," I said somewhat facetiously. "You had to destroy it all?"

"No," said our official, "I told them if they wanted to consume any of it on the spot, on the boat, they could. So they fired up their barbeque, cooked the whole lot, and had a party. Invited us and everyone on the street to join in. Quite an event, especially at nine in the morning."

* * * * *

It did not take us long to steep ourselves in civilization again, although our first trip to a shopping mall was a bit overwhelming: crowds, bustling, everything moving at a pace that left us standing befuddled. But our yearning for things we had been without for so long led us quickly back into the consumer mode. It had been a long time since we had been able to buy cheese, a pair of shoes, a mold-retardant cleaner, flour that wasn't full of bugs, a new bathing suit, or a decent bottle of wine—the odd things that you find you need, or really want, when you can't get them.

The grocery store was particularly welcome. We greedily tossed lettuce, spinach, broccoli (green, green, and green), kiwis (the fruit), oranges, delicate peaches, and plump chickens into our grocery cart. We had become temporary vegetarians in the islands, passing up the tough, frozen, imported meat, or the meat hung in open-air markets in 90-degree heat, with flies swarming it. Just not appetizing. Now, in a place with high standards of handling and packaging, we excitedly pored over the stacks of lamb, beef, pork, and sausage.

But not the kangaroo meat. New Zealand's neighbor, Australia, was trying its hand at exporting it. In typical Western supermarket style, they had a promotion table at the entrance to the store. The table was laden with leaflets about this tender alternative to chicken. Its nutritional value, calories, recipes, the whole gamut of food information was there. And a video. The tape loop—continuously running—showed the cute hippity-hoppities bounding across the Outback, nibbling bushes, nuzzling joeys in their pockets—for heaven's sake! Who would buy this meat? It was tantamount to showing Bambi in a promotion for deer meat, or Mary with her little lamb. We stuck with the chicken.

* * * * *

After checking into the country, we had tied up at the marina in the shadow of the Royal New Zealand Yacht Squadron in Auckland. The RNZYS was in the throes of challenging the United States for the America's Cup, that conspicuously extravagant, how-much-money-can-we-possibly-spend sailing race that grabs the sports news now and then. I wouldn't say we were branded the enemy, but we trod softly when we entered the Squadron building.

One day we were walking the premises with the Squadron's public relations person, and we just happened to mention The Cup.

"So, where are you going to put it *if* you win?" we asked.

"Oh, it will go right here," she said, as she showed us a prominent display point and indicated how it would look, as if there were no question that the trophy would soon occupy that spot. Kiwis, in their isolation, are a determined, proud, and *confident* lot.

And Kiwis *are* avid sailors. It was probably only a matter of time before they produced enough supersailors to win the premier yachting event of the world. Even so, with a population of only 3.5 million people, this possibility seems fairly astonishing. However, we were told that there was a sailboat for every ten people in Auckland, and we watched for weeks as that urban population took to the water *every day* in flocks of sailing craft, racing. We often wondered who was doing any work in Auckland; everyone seemed to be out on the water, racing, *every day*.

After a brief trip to the States for the Christmas holidays, we started a sailing jaunt north from Auckland, reveling in the Southern Hemisphere's warm weather during our American winter. Our first stop was Kawau (pronounced "cow-wow") Island. In the evenings we sat at anchor in Schoolhouse Bay, and as the wind died we heard a virtual symphony of bird song. One surely was the bellbird, his song sounding like his name.

Next stop moving north: Tutukaka (a Maori name). It was a tiny harbor and an "angler's paradise," we were advised. Indeed, there was hardly a sailboat in the place, and nothing much else other than a bar where the day's catches of marlin and swordfish were recorded. The weather forecast began to look iffy, so since Tutukaka didn't hold much interest for us, we decided to make a run for the Bay of Islands, at the north end of New Zealand, before the predicted gales swept the area.

The Bay of Islands is just that, a large bay filled with islands of all shapes and sizes, with many anchorages from which to explore this piece of the "Long White Cloud." We walked on Urupukapuka (we loved these Maori names), where the remains of early Maori settlements were still evident in the ground: pits where they stored their foodstuffs, terraces on the hillsides for cultivating the *kumara* (a kind of sweet potato), and sheered-off hilltops for a *pa* (a reinforced enclave from which to defend the settlement from attack). At another anchorage we went ashore to pluck large, juicy mussels from the beach rocks and scrape through the sand with our fingers to pull out *pipis*—tiny, tender clams. There was seafood stew for dinner. In yet another cove we visited the remains of a nineteenth-century whaling station, complete with blubber vats and a still-intact boiler.

* * * * *

No one can visit New Zealand and not be aware of the native people. The Maori number around a half million, or about 14 percent of all Kiwis. About one in twelve Kiwis is at least half Maori, and with land reclamation just beginning, there were at least another quarter million ready to assert Maori heritage. But demographics of today aside, there is history to be dealt with here.

Relations between the Maoris and other New Zealanders were tense at times. The conflict dated back to February 6, 1840, when the Waitangi Treaty was signed. In that treaty the Maoris turned over their lands and their government to the British in return for protection from other foreign intruders.

More recently, the Maoris have protested that the British, or Pakeha (white persons), have not upheld the spirit of that treaty—that is, they took more land than they should have and have treated the Maoris poorly. As if to underline these ills, Waitangi Day, February 6, continues to celebrate this unfortunate treaty and the beginning of modern-day New Zealand.

On this February 6th we were in Waitangi, along with several hundred Maori agitators. They disrupted the ceremonies and speeches; tore up a mock treaty, using the scraps for some unmentionable activities; ripped the New Zealand flag from its staff and stomped on it; spat at the Crown representative; and in general did as much as possible to disrupt the usual pomp surrounding this important—albeit controversial—historic day. This event was talked about in the papers for weeks afterward, and we could always start an interesting conversation with any (pakeha) Kiwi by telling them we had attended Waitangi Day. "Bloody hell, did you now?"

* * * * *

Following this spirited event we turned south again to return to Auckland, stopping in a few spots we missed on the way up. At Whangaruru, we took a bit of a hike. The trail went from plains of grazing sheep to marshes with reeds and cattails—where we flushed out a pheasant—and from hills covered with cactus and palms to forest jungles so damp and humid that huge toadstools grew at the side of the trail. Birds chirped and twittered in every bush, but the constant clicking of cicadas sometimes rose to a deafening pitch. And orchid plants five and six feet across roosted in the limbs of the trees. All of this in a three-hour walk seemed an outrageous wealth of botany and beauty.

From Whangaruru we returned to Tutukaka, in part because it was a convenient day's sail, and in part to visit some Canadian friends on a yacht now berthed there. We had planned an overnight stay, dinner with our friends, and we'd be on our way. But the wind strengthened during the night and was howling at 40 knots by morning. Worse than the wind was a mean swell, rolling directly into the entrance of the harbor. We'd stay an extra day, we decided, and have a longer visit with our friends.

The extra day turned into five. By the third day the swell at the entrance to the harbor was about ten or eleven feet high. The entrance to this tiny harbor is only 100 feet wide, with ugly rocks on either side. Trying to exit through this gap in those conditions would be foolhardy. For days we couldn't even see the entrance or the ugly rocks because of the huge breaking waves.

Fortunately, our friends had a car and could take us away from the "angler's paradise" to see some of the countryside. One such trip took us to limestone caves out in the middle of a cow field. Dodging the bulls, we made our way down into a valley in the field where, hidden beneath the trees, were three huge caves. I'm not terribly keen on caves, being just a little claustrophobic, but encouraged by our friend Gary and a strong flashlight we clambered into the first one, wading through streams and climbing over rocks. After making our way deep into the cave, we turned off the flashlights and looked around. All about us were thousands of tiny lights, like stars in a black heaven: the Milky Way in a cave. They were glowworms! It was magical.

By the sixth day we had had it with Tutukaka, our good friends notwithstanding. The swell was still nearly nine feet high, but the waves were not breaking over the entrance. We ploughed our way through them, wondering once or twice at the wisdom of this move, but finally broke free. Once out of the channel we turned south and flew back to Kawau, where we settled into our quiet little cove—a birdlover's paradise—and listened to the bellbirds.

*   *   *   *   *

There are fifteen sheep for every human in New Zealand—that's almost sixty million sheep! But so far we had seen far more sailboats than sheep. Where were they, the sheep?

"They are on the South Island," our Kiwi friends said. "Head south and you can't miss them." We packed a car and drove south to an adventure of spectacular scenery, geological wonders, natural encounters, lovely architecture, and honest, congenial people.

On the west coast of the South Island there are two large glaciers that descend from high alpine mountains toward the coast, petering out in subtropical forest—an unusual configuration. Although you can walk on your own through the forest and across the river to the edge of the glacier, we decided to take a guided walk onto the glacier itself.

We were provided with hobnailed boots for ice climbing, and our guide carried an ice pick to hew out steps when the glacier face became steep. Ropes and pitons were hammered into place as we went along.

Before beginning our climb, the guide was explaining some of the techniques of ice climbing that we would use. Suddenly, a half-dozen boulders rolled down the riverbed nearby.

"The glacier is advancing some ten feet every day," our guide explained. "That was about one-fifth of today's advance."

A few minutes later we were high up on the glacier when there was a noise akin to a sharp thunderclap, a rumble, and then a roar that echoed down the mountain.

"Part of the glacier face above us has probably sheered off," our guide explained—a little casually, I thought. "Don't worry, this part of the glacier is quite stable." In our present position, several hundred yards up the glacier bed, we could hardly do anything but believe him.

After we returned to the forest floor, gasping somewhat from our exertions and from the icy sights, we couldn't help but exclaim: "A far cry from sailing the tropical blue oceans!"

The South Island of New Zealand was as far south as we went on this voyage, and the bird life again reminded us of our position. At the tip of Otago Peninsula, a flock of Royal albatross (the largest bird in the world, with a ten-foot wingspan) was breeding on a clifftop. Yellow-eyed penguins, the rarest of the penguin species, were climbing slippery sand dunes to their nests outside Dunedin. Elsewhere we saw Stewart Island shags, the flightless takahe and weka, and that awkward-looking national emblem, the kiwi—all seen nowhere else in the world.

Driving back north, we stopped in Wellington, the capital of New Zealand, and looked in on the Parliament chambers. New Zealand has a unicameral parliament with just a House of Representatives. The "Debating Chamber" was in session that afternoon, and we had a rare look at a British-type parliament in action. We found the Members muttering, talking, and calling out insults in typical British fashion while their colleagues persevered with their speeches, debate, questions, and answers. "That's rubbish." "You said that last week, and nothing's happened." That sort of thing. At one point, when a particular corner of the chambers had been especially noisy, the Speaker cracked his gavel and admonished them like schoolchildren. He had heard enough from them, he said, and if they couldn't hold their tongues, they would be asked to leave.

As we were leaving the chambers, I spoke to the elderly attendant who had guided us to our seats.

"Quite hilarious," I said.

"Ah, yes," he responded, "a regular comedy show."

In the city of Napier, in addition to some of New Zealand's best wines, we found a city that had been almost entirely rebuilt in the 1930s after a devastating earthquake. It was reincarnated in the Art Deco style of the time and had been quite remarkably preserved and architecturally sustained in that style.

In a huge field on the outskirts of Napier, the Second International Kite Flying Contest was being held. And where had the First International Kite Flying Contest been held? Berkeley, California, right next to the marina where we had spent years of our previous lives. Did we come a quarter of the way around the world to see something we could have seen in our own backyard?

The very best part of our whole stay in New Zealand was the very best part of every country we visited: the people we met. On this motor trip we stayed in bed-and-breakfasts, most of which were "homestays"—a guest bedroom in a private home. We met a wide range of the country's people this way: a policeman in Picton, a wealthy Scot in Dunedin, the arts council executive of Napier, a deer farmer in Te Anau, an auto electrician, and even some sailors.

And sheep? Yes, quite a few. Herded by tractors now more than by dogs, they often stopped all traffic while they crossed the road to another pasture. The sheepdog was still around, sitting shotgun on the tractor and barking his instructions from there.

* * * * *

We sailed out of Auckland for the last time in the rain, but as we left the channel for the open bay a fresh breeze came up, on the beam for a change, and we steered north. Our first stop? Kawau, of course. Returning to an anchorage, especially one we liked, was like coming home—something familiar. We didn't often do this, as we were usually looking for new experiences. But this was an especially pleasant place to which we didn't mind returning. In the evening we listened to the birds. The tui was still about, raucous and loud; a silvereye and a gray warbler sang; a redpoll and a fantail were there; but the bellbird was not to be heard. Well, summer was over, and I suppose like us, he had decided it was time to move on. Low-pressure systems, with their winds and rain, were making their way farther south now, and nights had more frequently become the two-blanket kind—sure signs that we needed to find warmer waters soon.

For convenience's sake, we stopped at Tutukaka again. Our friends were gone, and the "paradise" was still not that interesting, so the next morning we powered back out that narrow entrance. Just as we hit the inevitable swell rolling onto the shore, we felt a horrid vibration through the whole boat. Something was amiss with the propeller, or its shaft. A peek into the engine room confirmed that the prop shaft was turning erratically. Damn.

We immediately shut the engine down and spent all day sailing the boat in very light winds. We were gloomy with thoughts of having to find a boatyard to haul the boat out of the water and find the problem, just when we thought everything was ready to head north to the islands again.

Then along came the dolphins. There is something about dolphins that turns a cursed day into a day of wonder. There were about two dozen of them, and they seemed happy to see us. They raced us, rolled under us, veered left and right just in front of us, and broke water right at our side. We talked to them and laughed at their antics. A proud mom and dad swam with a baby, not two feet long, between them. Every time they broke water—in unison—the little tyke threw himself to the surface a little too vigorously, his rudder (tail) came out of the water, and he flopped back in with a splash. The parents were patient.

After spending about a half hour with them, we had to pay attention to navigation and the sails, and we left our observation posts. The moment our attention was diverted, they left. But their good humor, playfulness, and joy of life remained with us.

The light wind held sufficiently to get us to anchor in the Bay of Islands with time—and a few rays of sunshine—to spare.

The next day we dove over the side in rather chilly waters to look at the propeller. Our problem, it turned out, was a "sacrificial" zinc anode—attached to the end of the propeller—that had come loose, and by this time had fallen off. (These "zincs" neutralize electrolysis in the water to keep metal objects, such as propellers, from disintegrating.) Our task now was to find a way to get the boat out of the water so we could replace the zinc.

There is a large tidal range in the Bay of Islands, averaging about ten feet. Taking advantage of this, pilings have been placed at the edge of the water here and there where you can bring your boat alongside, tie off, and wait for the tide to go out, leaving the boat high and dry, sitting on its keel. They call them "scrubbing posts," and they are in high demand for cleaning boat bottoms as well as making emergency repairs below the waterline. We had never tried these posts before, and it turned into a nerve-wracking experience. You feel very vulnerable balancing some 30,000 pounds of boat on a few inches of keel. But it worked. We got the new zinc on and floated off on the next high tide.

We were ready to cross oceans again.

The Storm

Latitude 28 South, Longitude 176 East

One year before our crossing from New Zealand to Fiji, a fleet of yachts made the same passage at about the same time of year (May, June). It's the ideal time of year to be going north—not too early, not too late. On the 2nd of June that year the weather forecast was perfect for a New Zealand departure. A low-pressure system was off to the east, its "backside" presenting steady trade winds between New Zealand and the islands north—the perfect passage conditions. But a second low developed in the north near Tonga, deepened rapidly, and dropped like a bomb toward the southeast, right in the path of the fleet heading for the islands. The second low bumped up against a high over New Zealand *and* the low off to the east, creating a "squash zone" with a steep pressure gradient that threatened high winds. Just looking at the weather maps for those few days in June gave me the heebie-jeebies.

This storm, having raged over the June birthday of the Queen of England, is called "The Queen's Birthday Storm." In some ways it was comparable to the "perfect storm" off Gloucester, Massachusetts, in 1991—a rare confluence of weather patterns that created conditions unimaginable even to experienced seamen.

While in New Zealand for the winter, we heard innumerable stories from survivors of the Queen's Birthday Storm. In light of their experiences, we (and every other ocean sailor in the area) were rethinking our storm strategies, reviewing our emergency equipment, and even purchasing more equipment.

We met a number of sailors who had experienced this storm.

"I looked back across our stern, and up to find the top of the wave," Margaret told me. "When I found the top, and realized I was looking up at the same angle as to my old fifth-story office, I turned forward and never looked back again. It was too frightening."

Joe and Rebecca had been taken off their catamaran on the second day. "A large commercial ship came by and asked if we wanted to abandon ship. We didn't know what to say. We were fine at the moment. But the ship's captain

82

told us that he was here now and that later, if we got into trouble, he didn't know if anyone could come back to us. We had only a few minutes to decide. We abandoned ship." I have run their scenario over in my mind a million times. What would I have done?

Gallant rescue efforts took the crews of six boats (including Joe and Rebecca) to safety. One boat was scuttled purposely, after the crew was taken off, so that it would not remain a hazard to navigation, and one boat went down with all hands. Ironically, however, the other five boats survived reasonably intact. If their crews had remained on board, they probably would have survived too.

What would we have done? I did not want ever to be in that position.

* * * * *

Up to this point in the voyage, our attention to weather patterns had kept our longer passages relatively benign. The idea for the passage from New Zealand to Fiji was to hop on the backside of a low-pressure area (with the wind spinning clockwise, blowing moderately from the southeast) and ride it north—which, on the 27th of April, we did. But about halfway across the South Fiji Basin, the ball of low pressure was blocked unexpectedly. It swung in a wide circle to the east and south, and came up behind us—in the middle of the night.

* * * * *

It was about 8 PM, and total darkness had just set in. We had seen squall-like clouds off to port earlier, and now in the dark we saw that they had lightning in them. We changed our course to starboard, but soon there were clouds with lightning in that direction too. We changed our course to steer between the squalls, but it wasn't long before we were surrounded by them. We could see them on the radar: small cells that expanded and contracted, formed and dissipated. They began to pass by us without incident—no wind or rain. They didn't seem to be anything to worry about.

At 11 PM Stephen turned the watch over to me, saying "All's the same." I spent a few minutes looking around to assure myself he was right. There were just a few squally areas here and there; otherwise we were sliding along quite nicely. I went below for a second to locate some crackers to munch on. As I came out of the companionway, looking aft, I could see blackness that was blacker than the black around it. Before I could even check the radar, a huge squall some 20 miles across (we determined later) was upon us. The wind went from 15 to 40 knots in seconds. The force of the higher gusts knocked us off course. Seeing that the boat was overpowered with so much sail area flying, I tried to lower the mainsail immediately. It wouldn't come down. I screamed for all hands to help get things under control.

Stephen and Alan (a friend from home who was along for the passage) came flying from below, wide-eyed, trying to absorb the situation quickly. I asked them to work on the sails while I took the helm off autopilot, to better steer through the mounting seas.

Our best course was to run with the wind to keep from broaching in a cross wave. I looked at the wind direction indicator at the top of the mast (lighted by our masthead navigation light) to keep my bearing. Then it began to rain—a hard, driving rain. Looking up, my eyes filled with water. Lightning and thunder followed one another in rapid succession; there were blinding bolts of lightning directly overhead. "Stay away from the mast," I screamed above all the noise. I felt very vulnerable. Lightning by itself is unnerving, but lightning with 40-knot winds seemed unfair.

In the meantime, the boys had somehow furled the genoa in a spaghetti of sheets and furling lines. The mainsail sheets were loose, spilling as much wind from the sail as possible. The top of the sail had parted from the mast, and in the lightning I could see where it was stuck. There would be no way to get it down without climbing the rigging, but with the lightning all around, that was out of the question for the moment.

Alan was now watching the storm on radar. We were in the middle of it, he reported, and traveling with it. It seemed to be keeping pace with us, or us with it. How could we extricate ourselves from this monster? If we changed direction to angle away from it, we ran the risk of being swamped by the waves, or losing the rig with the big mainsail crashing in the high winds. We inched our way to starboard, widening the angle between our course and the storm's as much as we dared. It took two hours before our tracks diverged and the squall, with its lightning and high wind gusts, went on its way. We now had *only* a steady 40-knot wind and huge seas with which to contend.

Through all of this, Stephen was violently seasick. He had not been feeling well since the beginning of the passage, and with the worsening weather his condition had deteriorated. By the time the squall went off he was incapacitated, leaving it to Alan and me to get us back on course. With the autopilot engaged again, our hands were free for the sails. Alan is big and strong, but since I knew the rigging, I suggested he stay on deck to pull things when they needed pulling, and I climbed the rigging in hopes of freeing the mainsail.

The boat was pitching wildly. I had my harness on with two tethers so that I could stay clipped onto some part of the boat with at least one of them. Climbing the shroud steps was a slow process, clinging to the shrouds, unclipping and reclipping the tethers, forcing myself up another step. A little voice in my brain kept repeating, "Concentrate on the task at hand and don't look down." The higher I climbed, the wider the gyrations of the boat, at times nearly flinging me off. Finally I reached the snag. The wind was pushing the sail so hard against the rigging that it took an enormous effort to pull it off and push it down. I felt like screaming. And quite possibly I did. No one would have heard, not even Alan just 40 feet below. But the sail finally came free and fell to the deck.

With the mainsail down and lashed to the boom, and the genoa furled in a mess, we were wallowing in the seas. The genoa mess was too much to untangle in the dark, so we pulled out the stays'l (a small sail between the main and the genoa), which was just enough to keep us rising to the tops of the waves, and not foundering dangerously in the deep troughs of the seas.

With this, Alan and I traded two-hour watches for the rest of the night—what there was left of it.

By morning the gale-force winds and commensurate seas had not abated. The weatherfax charts showed the low-pressure system right on top of us. The squall we had experienced had been part of a front connected to the low. In the daylight, we untangled the genoa and mended the mainsail. It felt good to straighten and fix all the ills of the previous night. We continued sailing with only the stays'l. It was just right for the immediate conditions. By evening we were feeling confident again, coping with the winds, riding the seas competently.

And then the wave hit.

Just 24 hours after the squall, a huge rogue wave rolled over us like a bulldozer. The force of the wave turned the hull 90 degrees and completely engulfed the boat. The cockpit filled with water. When we came up for air, the boat shuddered, shocked.

Any ocean sailor will tell you that it isn't so much the wind that causes trouble at sea, but the concomitant seas encountered. There are usually two wave actions on the open ocean—a long swell created by the weather pattern covering a large area (the "prevailing swell"), and a short-wind wave created by the wind velocity in the immediate area. A high swell and a big-wind wave create rough conditions.

It is not unusual, however, to have more than one sea running. Swell from a storm thousands of miles away can affect local conditions, especially if it is from a direction different from the prevailing swell in the area. Large swells from two—or more—directions and high-wind waves create *very* rough sea conditions. On top of this there is the periodicity and the varying height of the waves. Waves are never "regular." There are theories about one in (say) a hundred waves that is much higher than the weather conditions warrant.

You put all of this together in the "washing machine," and occasionally you get the rogue wave—the hundredth wave from one swell configuration, meeting the hundredth wave from another swell train, meeting the hundredth wave of your wind wave—and wham! One Very Big Wave—a wave that can easily overwhelm a small boat.

*   *   *   *   *

Our crew, above and below, were shocked by the impact of the rogue wave. It took a moment before anyone realized that the autopilot had failed and that the boat had brought herself up into the wind, her sails flogging furiously. The wave's water had rushed over the deck and filled the one hole available to it— the cockpit. Fortunately, the cockpit drained quickly, but we were unable to get the autopilot to work again. The force of the wave had apparently jarred something loose.

We were demoralized, and just didn't have the stamina to try and fix it, or to rig the wind vane (the backup, nonelectrical self-steering system), or to hand-steer in these huge seas, especially with Stephen's condition worsening. It was time to heave to.

The heaving to maneuver, which we had used outside the pass to Wallis, was not only a good way to bide time at night, but it was also a perfect strategy for this moment. With the sails backed and the wheel lashed over, the boat sat almost still in the water, riding over the waves like a cork. It was relatively quiet and comfortable, even with the 40-knot winds. The crashing diminished and the motion of the boat was less violent. We continued to keep our watches, but it was far, far easier for the off-watches to get some sleep, something we all needed at that time, and the on-watch was far less tense.

Although we continued to keep our watch schedule, there was nothing to do but keep a lookout for other ships. We saw none. In the morning we discovered by the weatherfax that another low-pressure system had formed just south of us and was heading our way. The isobars were close together, indicating that the wind in this system could rise to 65 knots (hurricane force). We needed to get moving again. We uncovered the problem with the autopilot— the arm attached to the steering post had parted from the post. Repairable, but not in the current sea conditions. We rigged the wind vane on the stern and it worked perfectly. We resumed our race north, hoping to outrun Mother Nature. Within hours, the huge low, with its winds, waves, and lightning, finally veered off fully to the east, leaving us with a good southerly breeze to finish the passage in just nine days. We arrived at Suva, Fiji, without further incident.

* * * * *

Days after our storm experience I realized that I had never once thought we might have met another Queen's Birthday. After all that dithering, chewing, and fretting about this passage while still in New Zealand, and all the worrying about the chances of our getting "bombed," it never occurred to me that something like that might be happening.

How could we put such horrendous thoughts out of our minds? The ability to put aside fear and focus on getting through the hideous situation, whatever it might be, is an important aspect of sailing the high seas. Stephen can do this far better than I can. His fear-tolerance level is much higher than mine. And his ability to focus—on anything, at any time—is extraordinary. As wimpy as I am at times, I too can suppress my fear, have done it, and knew I'd do it again (and again) before the voyage was over. It was one of the reasons we could do this crazy business of sailing around the world.

Of the three storms—ours, the Perfect Storm, and the Queen's Birthday— our experience was by far the least dangerous. In fact, by storm standards it was hardly a blip. Stephen's determination to become the best weatherman he could, held us in good stead nearly every day of our voyage. But no weatherman can predict the whimsies of Mother Nature all the time. The Queen's Birthday "bomb" was not seen even by professional weather forecasters until it was too late for most of the sailing fleet in the area. No one could have predicted that our low-pressure system would stall and, as a result, be blocked by the high to the east.

When Mother Nature changes her mind and does the unpredictable, we have to be ready to take it on the chin. That this happened so infrequently in our eight years was really quite remarkable. We are often asked, "What was the worst weather you encountered at sea?"

At latitude 28 south, longitude 176 east, this was it.

Just Kava

Fiji

In Fiji, it is the custom when visiting a village to call on the chief of the village first and ask permission to visit. There is a ritual called *sevu sevu* surrounding this request. The essence of the ritual is to present the chief with some *yanqona*, or kava root, as a gift.

In Suva, the capital of Fiji, there is a market where we went to buy the kava root for the *sevu sevu* we anticipated in the outer islands. At one end of the second floor of this open-air building we found several stalls with Fijians selling kava. I was not sure what to ask for, or how much, or how to know what was appropriate for a *sevu sevu*.

We were lucky at the booth, where we made our first inquiry. Va said she understood exactly what we needed. "How many *sevu sevu* will you need?" she asked. We hadn't any idea. She let that bit of ignorance go, and showed us how much kava we should give at each ceremony, and how to wrap it in the newspapers and tie it with twine. We finally shrugged and said ten *sevu sevu*, and Va pulled a huge bundle of root aside, wrapped it carefully, and deposited it in our tote bag. We had no idea if ten was the number, but given the amount of kava root this ten entailed, we wouldn't have room for any more, anyway.

At the reef-encircled island of Beqa (pronounced "Mbengga"), we anchored at Vaga Bay, where we knew there was a traditional village. We rowed ashore and were greeted by Mele, the village chief's spokesperson, who said he would guide us to the chief's home. Ben, the chief, was there waiting for us along with a contingent of village women, many with babes in arms, all sitting on mats on the floor of Ben's *bure*.

Like most native Pacific homes, the *bure* was a small, sparse dwelling with little furniture. Beds were mats spread on the floor when it was time to sleep, and food was eaten sitting on the floor from dishes held in the hands. A few religious images hung on the walls; a small table in the corner was bare of object.

We slipped off our sandals as we entered the *bure*, and sat on the mats in front of Ben. We gave our kava gift to Mele, who in turn gave it to Ben. (You do not give things, or talk, directly to a chief; you work through his spokesperson.) Ben picked up our kava, carefully wrapped in newspaper and twine, and patted it while he intoned a chant of some sort. At various intervals the women chanted something back. There was a little clapping of hands toward the end. Mele then invited us to greet the chief and shake his hand. We approached with as much respect as we could, keeping low, almost crawling, nodding and bowing as tradition commanded.

Then we brought out the Polaroid camera. Everyone was thrilled. We took a picture of Ben. We gave the picture to Mele, who gave it to Ben, who crowed with delight at the sight of his image beginning to appear on the paper.

The Polaroid camera was a cultural icebreaker for us. We pulled it out whenever we thought the locals would enjoy it, and inevitably we were quickly surrounded by groups of people wanting their photos taken. Pacific Islanders are no longer ignorant of the Polaroid camera, in the way *National Geographic* articles used to tell us decades ago. They know now what it does, but they still love watching their image appear on the square of blank paper, as if by magic. Since they rarely own a camera of any sort, having an image of themselves was still uncommon. To be able to give them an *instant* photo made us very popular.

And this time, true to form, we were asked to take pictures of Ben and his wife, Ben and the women, the women and their babies, Mele and Ben—until we ran out of film. We had learned to bring only one film pack of ten exposures at any given time. With an encounter like this we'd go through all the film we had, however much that was, trying to keep up with the requests. "Oh dear, just ran out of film," brought disappointed faces, but it kept the activity from costing us a fortune and kept villagers in the coming days happy too.

Following the *sevu sevu* ceremony, Mele and an entourage of villagers gave us a tour of their village. As we walked, Mele called out to various members of his family, and we became interested in the kinship relations.

There were just 117 people in the village, and everyone seemed to be related to the chief. On the surface this was no surprise, really. South Pacific islanders often talk about "cousins" or "fathers" when the relationship is not that at all, but a good friend or an uncle. Mele told us that both he and his wife were in-laws of the chief. We puzzled over that for a moment. Then another of our villagers explained that Ben and his brother married two sisters. *Two sisters from another village family?* Well, no, two brothers married two sisters—that is, two brothers married their sisters. We had read about this inbreeding, but had not realized it was still practiced—at least not within our "modern" generation. I still couldn't figure out how Mele and his wife were both in-laws of Ben, but decided I wouldn't push that one.

Fiji is one of the more unusual Pacific island nations for preserving so much of their traditional life. Even in colonial times, the Fijian government had a *laissez faire* attitude, and the power of the local chiefs prevailed. Even the introduction of a strong tourist trade had not entirely interrupted the traditional way of living in many parts of Fiji, particularly the more remote islands—and Beqa was certainly one of these.

Since the position of chief is inherited, there is a strong inclination to keep the "royal" line close to the chest, so to speak—hence the intermarriages, although not usually quite so intermingled as Ben et al.

* * * * *

The *sevu sevu* ceremony is a holdover from warring times, when lesser chiefs needed to stay in the good graces of the more powerful leaders, bringing them gifts to show their gratitude. Strangers made this offering too, just as we had, so that the chief was given the option of accepting them or not. If it was determined that you came in peace, you were received into the village "family"—the chanting Ben and the women performed was their declaration of acceptance. And even strangers then became like family and were given the run of the village, and all villagers were expected to be hospitable toward them. We were usually given a tour of the village by the spokesperson or someone else close to the chief. It was an opportunity for the village to see that we were in good graces with the chief, making it acceptable for us to move through the village on subsequent days.

Our walk with Mele brought us to the village church, which was being rebuilt. According to tradition, the building of a church is a communal activity. All the men, and many women, were putting in time toward the effort. And alongside this activity there was the inevitable kava bowl. The workers drank from it now and then—and that they were drinking from it now and then was pretty evident. The building effort was languid, with more resting (and drinking) than building.

Kava drinking in these remote villages, the more traditional villages, was more apparent than in the larger communities because of the social aspect of the drinking. Since in Fiji just about everything, such as building churches, has a social aspect to it, drinking kava can occur on a daily basis. When the villagers gathered to do something together (such as build churches) it was natural to see the kava bowl nearby. As in Samoa, the kava bowl was of more interest to the men than to the women.

* * * * *

Suva, the capital of Fiji and our initial landfall, provided a quick introduction to this country of two cultures. Most native Fijians are Melanesian, and physically are quite different from the Polynesians to the east of them and the Micronesians to the west of them. They are short, square, and darker than Polynesians, with frizzy hair (not found in the other two groups).

The more fascinating part of Fiji's demography, however, is the Indian population. Even more fascinating was the way these two cultures rubbed elbows. Stephen and I had visited Fiji, ever so briefly, some years before on the way back from a business trip to Australia. We remarked then how well the two populations seemed to coexist: separately, to be sure, but peaceably. Indeed, Fiji was then an extraordinary example of intercultural democracy. But in the intervening decade or so, things had changed. They were still living separately, but not exactly peaceably.

The Indians first arrived in Fiji in the late nineteenth century, when they were recruited to supply labor for new sugar plantations. The British colonials had been considerate of the native people, and laws had been passed that would keep Fijians from being exploited as field workers—that is to say, Fijians couldn't and wouldn't work in the sugar fields. Life in India was never easy, so it was not difficult for the British to convince thousands of people from their most crowded colony to come to Fiji as indentured workers. Between 1879 and 1916, some sixty thousand Indians were imported. Most of them would never return to India, and it took most of the rest of the twentieth century for them to acquire common civil rights in their new country.

The Indians of Fiji are now nearly half the entire population of the archipelago. And this is, in part, the reason for Fiji's unrest. The question is how to have a government and economy that is fair to both sides; how to preserve the life and culture of the indigenous people, and also credit the Indians' history and contribution to the country? One of the difficulties arises from a total lack of intermingling between the two. It appears that they do not work together, and that there is virtually no intermarrying, which seems astonishing in this day and age. And since most of the land is held by Fijians, it is nearly impossible for Indians to own anything. So they rent—and sell. The Indians are the entrepreneurs of Fiji; they have established and run most of the businesses. Thus they live mostly in the urban areas of Nadi, Lautoka, and Suva.

While exploring the outer islands of Fiji, we were hardly aware of the Indian presence, but in Suva, where so many of the Fijian Indians live, you might almost believe they were in the majority. The smell of curry was the first sign. In the open market in the center of town, we found Indian merchants with *mountains* of curry powders spread out before us. The aroma was so powerful, it made my eyes water. Outside of Suva and Nadi we never saw an Indian face, and in some ways that was regrettable. On the other hand, it painted the picture of Fiji for us: a strong, traditional, entitled native culture almost overwhelmed by strong, tenacious outlanders who felt they had a place here—a right here—too. But they were not native, and that is a fundamental difference.

*   *   *   *   *

After bidding the folks of Beqa good-bye, we motored a few miles to a small island south of Beqa, but still within its surrounding reef. This was Yanuca (prounced "Yanutha"), where we had heard firewalkers lived. We anchored in an idyllic cove with crystal-clear turquoise water lapping on a white sand beach, backed by a dense jumble of palms, pandanus, and reeds—a typical South Pacific scene.

We were greeted on the beach by Nimilote, who said he would take us to the village to make *sevu sevu*. The village was on the other side of the island, and Nimilote led us along a path through the thick vegetation. As we walked we asked him questions. Yes, he was a firewalker. He and others from Yanuca worked the tourist hotels around Nadi. He was then twenty-three years old, and had been firewalking since he was nineteen. He was taught to firewalk by his mother.

When we got to the village, Nimilote kept wandering off, chatting with other villagers. Finally, he came back to us saying that there was some difficulty.

"The chief is away, but I will find another chief."

There is more than one chief?

"There is a second chief."

Okay, we thought, a vice-chief. We continued to wander about the village. There was some calling back and forth between Nimilote and other villagers. We walked farther afield. Nimilote seemed agitated, then looked worried. Finally, with some relief in his voice he said, "Here, I think this man can help us."

A small group of men, young and old, were coming down the field. There was an extended conversation in Fijian. We waited patiently. It was hard to say what the problem was, but I was guessing that Nimilote was embarrassed because he couldn't find anyone to take care of the ritual that he knew we expected.

Finally he said to us, "This will be okay."

"This is the second chief?" I asked.

"No, another chief." Maybe, maybe not, but he certainly qualified; he was old.

We were invited to sit down immediately in the dust and weeds of the fallow field, and we "did" our *sevu sevu*. (I am still unsure whether one "does," "says," "has," or "makes" a *sevu sevu*.) It wasn't the careful ceremony conducted by Ben at Beqa. It was very brief, and there were moments when I thought that this "other" chief had already had more than enough kava. Nimilote guided us through the ceremony, as he knew he must, and then escorted us back through the village to our anchorage.

Nimilote was an unusual young man in Fiji. He was concerned with his native culture, his village, and now with us because we had completed the *sevu sevu*. But he also had high ambitions. He talked a little about going farther afield with his firewalking talent. Today the Hilton, tomorrow the Four Seasons—if not precisely what he said, that was the gist of his talk. For a young man to have ambition, to be enterprising, and to look beyond his village was very un-Fijian. To want to break away from the traditional communal life and be an individual with separate talents went against the grain of traditional Fijian village life.

Nimilote spoke excellent English, and was an exceedingly polite and courteous young man. At our beach, he helped us launch our dinghy from the shore and waded into the water to push us off. He winced as he stepped on the coral with his bare feet. So it's not that his feet were so callused that they couldn't feel those hot coals. The secrets of firewalking continued to elude us.

From Yanuca we made our way around the south coast of Viti Levu, Fiji's largest island, to Fiji's second-largest town, Nadi (pronounced "Nandi"). We anchored by the Sheraton Fiji just outside the town and splurged with a dinner at the hotel.

The young woman who waited on our table was named Sera, and we enjoyed engaging her in conversation. Where was she from?

"The Yasawas," she said with an expression that suggested we wouldn't know where that was, or care.

"But where in the Yasawas?" I asked.

"You know the Yasawas?"

"Yes."

"A village."

We couldn't overcome our assumed ignorance. "Which one?" I persisted.

"Soso."

"Oh, that's wonderful," I said. "On the island of Naviti."

Sera beamed. I had finally won her confidence. I explained that we were on a yacht, and that we expected to sail to the Yasawas in a week or two and would surely be stopping at Soso. Was there anyone in the village she would like us to see or take a message to? She frowned and asked for our dessert order. Perhaps she hadn't understood us, or perhaps she wasn't supposed to engage in idle chatter with the people she served, or perhaps we had stepped over some boundary we weren't aware of. I was sorry if we had offended or embarrassed her in any way.

But with our banana fritters, she produced a small pink slip of paper from a Sheraton Hotel phone message pad. On it was a note in Fijian.

"For my mother," Sera said shyly.

"For your mother!" I blurted. "When did you come here from Soso?"

"A year ago."

"You haven't been home since?"

"No, it is many islands away."

"You haven't seen your mother in over a year?"

"Yes, this is so." Nor had her mother seen Sera in over a year. This was clearly a precious message. We would find our way to Soso come hell or high water.

We were met on the beach by Tema, the Soso chief's granddaughter, who explained that the chief was not in the village that day, but that she would take us to the chief's brother for the *sevu sevu*. So, another second or "other" chief.

We were invited to enter Siti's *bure* and sit on the floor mats. We placed our kava on the floor in front of us, as we now knew to do—we were old pros. Meli, the appointed spokesperson, picked it up and handed it to Siti, who patted it and said the words of welcome. We engaged in the requisite chitchat, and finally we got around to our message for Sera's mother. Could someone take us to Ana? Tema would be happy to, she said.

We made our inspection of the village first as Tema led us, pointing out the chief's home, the church, the village hall, the school, her sister's home. Eventually, on the far side of the village, we came to a small compound where Tema said Sera's family was gathered.

There was a rapid exchange between Tema and family members in the area, then much calling, and finally Ana appeared. I asked Tema to explain our mission to Ana. We held out the small slip of pink paper. Ana was slow to reach for it; I don't think she quite believed it was for her.

We watched Ana look at the paper intently, finger it, squint at it, pass it from hand to hand—and then we realized that she could not read it. She did not know what Sera had said. But it was clear from Ana's face she did not need to know the exact words. As a mother separated from my daughter by "many islands" myself, I could easily imagine what this message must mean.

Ana was a short, squat woman with few teeth, rheumy eyes, and graying kinky hair. She was not pretty nor handsome, but when she smiled with the happiness of hearing from her daughter so far away, she was quite beautiful in her own way. A basket of shells appeared and was handed to Ana, who picked out four white cowries—good luck charms—to give us. She collected shells to sell to tourist stores, Tema told us, and these were her most prized shells. Ana so wanted to return the gift she had just received. There wasn't a way to tell her we were just glad to have had the opportunity to bring her Sera's message; it was too large a sentiment to transmit. We gathered the shells from her out-stretched hands. It's enough to say that we were *all* happy at that moment.

* * * * *

The island of Yadua, north of Viti Levu, was surprisingly hilly; to make *sevu sevu* we had to hike from our anchorage over a small mountain to reach the island's only village. It was a long, hot, sweaty hike just to dump a few twigs of yangona. Was I getting tired of this ritual? Cynical? We had made enough *sevu sevu* in situations that obviously didn't mean anything, that I wondered why we bothered. The ceremony in the dirt of Yanuca with an "extra" chief, who had already had too much kava, was an example of a time when I'm not sure it was necessary. But there was no way to know when it would be important and when not. We had to continue to make the effort, just in case. We did not want to offend any village. Visiting the villages was an important part of our cultural immersion in Fiji.

We started out from the anchorage in our usual shorts and T-shirts, plod-ding up the switchback trail, gaining altitude quickly. We met Eta on the way up the hill. She was coming over to our anchorage to fish, she said. She had a wonderful smile. We trudged on. Then we met Luciana, Eta's younger sister. She was on her way to join Eta. She had a wonderful smile, like Eta. The fishing was best on our side of the island, Luciana said. How much farther did we have to walk to the village? A shrug, several fingers displayed—was this minutes, hours, or miles? English was a variable language here. Sometimes it worked, sometimes it didn't. We trudged on.

We had brought the conservative clothes ashore in bags—long pants for Stephen, skirt and blouse for me—and we changed at the top of the hill when we were in sight of the village. There was no sense soaking them in sweat too early in the game.

Two hours later we panted into the village and met Eleslie, who took us to her father-in-law, Andre, the chief. *Sevu sevu* was performed with all the words, the chanting, and the clapping. This was an important *sevu sevu,* and we were glad we had taken the time—and lord knows, the effort—of climbing over that hill.

Shortly a handsome young man by the name of Pita appeared. He said he was the chief's son. He would give us the village tour. As we walked toward the church (always an important site to visit in a village), we saw a woman inside a tiny structure beating a wood drum. What was this?

"It is noon," explained Pita, and the drum was to let everyone know that. The town clock.

School was dismissed and the children swarmed down the hill. They obviously already knew about the visitors and wanted to have a look. We were soon engulfed. It was difficult to tell the girls from the boys, for everyone's head had been recently shaved.

"The only way to get rid of the lice," Pita confessed. The Polaroid came out of the backpack, and the fun began. The kids literally danced around us in their excitement.

Pita told us that his village was very old. How old? Several generations. There were 200 or so people living there, almost all of them native to the village. The only outsiders were the schoolteachers (three), a nurse, and Pita's wife, Eleslie. Eleslie was from Lautoka, and from the pride in Pita's voice, she must have been a prize for him.

We found the church unfinished, but with a roof over it. "Enough to be usable," Pita said.

"But there is no building being done now?" we asked.

"We don't have the money for materials," Pita replied. "We are trying to raise the funds to buy these things." The villagers sold fish to get cash for things they had to buy—oil, flour, clothing—but otherwise their life was as near the subsistence level as it could be. As he explained this to us, I still couldn't see how they would find the funds for church-building materials, but I sensed that pressing this point might reveal too clearly how poor this village was, and that that might be embarrassing.

Back on our side of Yadua we enjoyed the seclusion for swimming, cleaning accumulated slime off the bottom of the boat, walking on the beach, and hunting for shells. Across a narrow isthmus of land that formed one arm of our little bay, we came to a beach partially open to the sea and partially sheltered by a rocky reef. On the beach there were hundreds of chambered nautilus shells. With their internal spiraled partitions and round white backs striped in burnt red, these shells are treasures, even to those who don't care about shells. They are so beautiful, seemingly fragile yet ingenious in their gaseous buoyancy in the water.

The shell books will tell you that these cephalopods are found the world over in warm seas. They are free-swimming, and hence you might run into one just anywhere, bobbing about. Why, then, did so many of them die for whatever reason, and their shells land on this particular beach—not in our anchorage cove, or on Vanua Levu nearby, or Rabi further north, but right here on the south side of Yadua, on the north side of Talai Bay? It is difficult to

find a *perfect* nautilus with no chips, dings, scratches, or washed-out stripes—
the shell collector's dream—but find one we did.

＊　＊　＊　＊　＊

At Yadua I had wrapped our last twig of *yangona*. It was time to say *mothay*,
good-bye, to Fiji.

Fire and Brimstone

Tanna, Vanuatu

It was a vision of Hell. Standing on the very edge of the caldera, we looked down onto three vents swirling, steaming, glowing, smoking, moaning, whistling, growling, swishing. One vent emitted plumes of thick black smoke whose rising was accompanied by a roaring that sounded like a jet plane taking off. The opposite vent looked like a pulsating fountain of lava, with small showers jumping. Every few minutes it erupted like a cannon shot with a display to rival any Fourth of July fireworks. The middle vent was a seething mass of hot lava, glowing brighter, rumbling like a tornado bearing down on us ... and then it exploded, sending masses of lava into the air, reaching a height far over our heads before the hot rocks turned downward to fall back into the caldera, inches from our toes. This was Mt. Yasur, "volcano" in the local indigenous language. Mt. Yasur is on the southern end of the island of Tanna, at the southern end of the island nation of Vanuatu.

* * * * *

Vanuatu, formerly the New Hebrides and independent from the British and French only since 1980, is a 730-mile-long chain of 74 islands populated by about 200,000 people, mostly Melanesians. The indigenous peoples are known as ni-Vanuatu, or people from Vanuatu. We had not planned to go to Vanuatu because of the high incidence of malaria there, but friends had convinced us that we should not miss this fascinating country. Taking our malaria prophylactics religiously, we sailed first to the island of Efate and the capital city of Port Vila. After checking into the country, we sailed south to the island of Tanna. There is only one decent harbor on the island: Port Resolution, in the southeastern corner, where we made a cautious entrance through the reef.

Early on our first morning we dinghied ashore and happened upon Nelson, a young Tannese about nineteen, with English just good enough for us to understand each other. We learned from Nelson that there was a male initiation rite taking place in one of the several villages that surround the bay where we had anchored. Could we attend?

"I would like to take you there," Nelson replied. And we began a hike along a narrow dirt path.

We passed through Nelson's village first, crossing a wide, open space surrounded by *fales,* which are dwellings loosely constructed of cane, with thatched roofs. After greeting Nelson's mother in front of their *fale,* we carried on along the dusty path to the next village. Here we found four boys who had been circumcised two weeks previously. For two weeks they had been sequestered with members of the village male population to learn about men-things.

They had only this day emerged from the ritual seclusion to participate in the festivities being prepared by their families. These chaps were about eight or nine years old, dressed in obviously new *lava lavas*—bright colored squares of fabric wrapped around their waists. A single feather was stuck in each boy's kinky hair. Their expressions were appropriately serious for the occasion ... until we pulled out the Polaroid camera.

Mothers straightened the feathers, Nelson grouped the boys in some unexplained order, and we snapped the picture. And a picture of the mothers. And a picture of Nelson and his "cousins." And a picture of the mothers with other children. Until we ran out of film.

Our picture-taking had only mildly interrupted the intense food preparations going on around us. Nelson escorted us to each activity, explaining the cuisine. A pig that had been roasting in a stone oven was uncovered before us. Banana leaves were removed from the top of the oven, and then the top stones, still too hot to touch, were rolled away with sticks. The smell that began to escape was heavenly. More leaves were removed to reveal the pig, so thoroughly cooked that the meat separated from the bones at a touch.

In another corner of the village center we watched *lap lap* being prepared. A group of women sat on mats on the ground, each woman intent on her task in the preparation. Wide banana leaves were laid on top of a loose weaving of palm frond "string." Root vegetables—tapioca or taro—were grated into a fine pulp and patted into an inch-thick layer on the banana leaves. The blood of a calf was next applied, and then small chunks of meat—goat, beef, and pig— were evenly planted into the pulp. Some liquid from the pulp was wrung from cheesecloth onto this spread. The banana leaves were folded over to produce a closed packet about two feet square that was then tied with the string. The packets were thrown one by one into another stone oven.

Next to another rock oven we watched another pig being prepared for roasting. Large chunks of flesh were speared and thrown on the fire to sear the hair off the skin. A freshly slaughtered goat was being skinned nearby.

Nelson delighted in showing us the preparations, and the villagers were obviously proud of their abundance. We, on the other hand, were trying not to appear disgusted (I mean, calf's blood on grated taro?), squeamish (it was the skinning of that *freshly* slaughtered goat), or rude (I really couldn't watch them skinning the poor thing). At least we didn't have to eat any of it. Wrong.

We were invited to sit on some mats and sample some of the *lap lap* that had been cooked. I tried one made with tapioca and pig. It was a doughy, greasy mess that tasted like a doughy, greasy mess. The one made with taro was less greasy, but very bland—even with the calf's blood.

Nelson explained that the status of a family is measured by the amount of food they are willing to share with the rest of the village at a time like this. All told, eighty *lap laps* were prepared, and two pigs, a calf, and a goat were slaughtered. We did not know, nor did Nelson share with us, if eighty *lap laps,* two pigs, a goat, and a calf is big status or not, but it seemed likely that there would be more food than the hundred or so people invited to the feast could possibly consume. I said something to that effect, and Nelson replied that the extra food would be distributed to everyone in the village when the party was over.

After appropriate thank-yous to the villagers, we departed, promising to come back later for more of the festivities. We headed back to the boat to eat lunch. Canned tuna fish sandwiches never tasted so good.

As promised, we ventured back ashore later in the day, and Nelson was quickly at our side to guide us back to the celebrating village. I was pleased that he wanted to help us. For one thing, I wasn't sure we could find our way through the winding paths that led to so many different villages.

"You are in good time," said Nelson. "They will be dancing soon." Wonderful! We were excited at the prospect of seeing native dancing.

But some things have changed with time on Tanna. The food may be cooked as it has been cooked for centuries; the rite of circumcision may be observed as it has been for all known time; but for dancing there was now a ghetto-blaster with American rock music blaring incongruously across the village center. And they danced more like Michael Jackson than ni-Vanuatus. I asked Nelson how they had learned to dance like this.

"They see videos at the missionary center," he replied.

It is said that the United States' biggest export is its popular music. To hear this music and see this dancing at this "primitive" occasion on this remote South Pacific island was all the evidence we needed to believe that assertion. I am not a connoisseur of Michael Jackson-type dancing, but these young people appeared to me to be brilliant dancers.

During one of our excursions on shore with Nelson, we discovered that he belonged to the Jon Frum group, one of the last "cargo cults" in the Pacific. In the late nineteenth century, the Tannese people became intently interested in the possessions that the missionaries brought with them to this island. During World War II, the U.S. military intensified this interest when they came to Vanuatu with a wealth of goods and services, the likes of which the Tannese had never seen. No one is certain how the quasi-religion started. But somewhere around the time of the Pacific War, the Tannese began talking about a mysterious person, Jon Frum, who would return to Tanna someday and bring them an abundance of material goods, making the people of Tanna wealthy and prosperous. Over the years the movement has evolved, melding concepts of Christianity and other historical events into its beliefs.

We had many questions for Nelson: "Who was Jon Frum?"

"He came here during the big war."

"Do people talk to him?"

"The old grandfather talked to him during the war."

Just then, lo and behold, here came the old grandfather down the path. Unfortunately, he did not speak English, and Nelson seemed reluctant to translate our queries. The old man was wearing an army dog tag around his neck and I couldn't refrain from pointing to it.

"Yes," said Nelson, "when the old grandfather spoke to Jon Frum, he got that tag." I dearly wanted to reach out for the tag and read it, but I was sure that would not have been appropriate. Given Nelson's reverence for this person, I did not want to jeopardize his relationship with the old man.

As we continued on our way with Nelson, we asked more questions. We heard that Jon Frum is also John the Baptist.

"Yes, they are the same."

"But Jon Frum is from America?"

"Yes, from America." Oh … kay….

"Do Jon Frum people get together once a week like the Presbyterians and Seventh Day Adventists [the other predominant religions on Tanna]?" we continued.

"Yes, but we do not have the Bible. We sing and dance stories about Jon Frum."

"Do people talk to him now?"

"Sometimes at night, the spirit of Jon Frum comes to certain people and teaches them a song. Then they teach it to us. These are the songs we sing when we get together on Fridays."

"You are waiting for Jon Frum to come back?"

"Yes. On Fridays we are waiting for him."

"Will there be a sign so you know?"

"He will let the special people know. They are able to see into the future and know he is coming. They will tell us."

We did not know it at the time, but we were soon to meet one of these "special people."

*   *   *   *   *

Early one morning we left Port Resolution in a pickup truck (the modern mode of transportation on the island) that we had hired to take us around the island. We had with us for a guide one of the most engaging young persons we were to meet in the whole South Pacific. We were lucky with John. Although his family did not have the money to pay for his formal education past the fourth grade, he had traveled extensively in Vanuatu and spent two years in Australia, where he had perfected his English. Now in his twenties, he was quick, intelligent beyond his educational background, and a delight to have in our company.

In just a few minutes from Port Resolution we had our first glimpse of Mt. Yasur. We were at the back side, where the lava had been blown and ground to a fine sand, then molded by the wind into a huge sand dune, spilling down onto a flat plain. It looked like a gray desert, with bleached trunks and roots of trees partially buried in the sand, like so many bones of long-dead animals. We could not hear the volcano here, and could see only the occasional puff of smoke.

Tanna is mountainous in the interior, and the road across the island (only 17 miles) was tortuous. As we lurched up the first peak, jolted in the back of the pickup, we could look out over the valley where a dozen streams of smoke announced the presence of villages hidden in the trees below. In fact, there are some 22,000 people on Tanna, living in 92 villages and more than 700 tiny settlements, most of them in the central belt through which we were traveling. The populations are in clusters, each distinguished by a different language. The languages are so different that knowing one does not help in speaking the others, John informed us.

"Why is that?" we asked.

Historically, John explained, the island districts remained isolated and did not mingle except in warfare, so there was no exchange of languages.

"You wouldn't want your enemy to know what you were saying," he added. John said he had a goal to learn all seven of Tanna's surviving indigenous languages; he could speak five of them so far.

The matter of language for John, and for all ni-Vanuatu, is further complicated by the national language, called Bislama. In the mid-nineteenth century,
when literally hundreds of languages existed in the islands, a pidgin language
began to emerge to facilitate trading with English-speaking sailors. The language further developed with the arrival of missionaries, and further still during World War II. This common language, Bislama, has become the
all-important communication link throughout this far-flung island nation,
where even today more than 100 indigenous languages are still spoken. It was
not surprising, however, to hear John say that the indigenous languages are
dying out.

"Nelson doesn't know 'his' language; only Bislama," he said. This state of
language made John's feat of learning all of Tanna's languages not only astonishing, but also admirable.

Somewhat like Caribbean pidgin, Bislama is incomprehensible to the non-
native ear, but when it is read phonetically, you can usually figure out what is
going on, more or less. For example: "Hamas yia blong yu" means "How many
years belong you," or "How old are you?" Some words are hard to understand
even when you look at them or say them, but with some imagination they can
make sense. For example: "miyu" means "me/you," or "we," or "us."

One of my favorite Bislama expressions is "titti-titti hang down" which
means "old woman." "Titti-titti stand up" is, naturally, "young woman." I have,
ever since Tanna, watched closely my, um, tittis to determine my, ah, age group.

* * * * *

There are on Tanna these days three "religious" groups: your ordinary brand
of Christians (Presbyterian or Seventh Day Adventist), the Jon Frum people,
and the *kastam* villages. This last group is intent on living in the old way, the
"custom" way, dressing as they did before the European invasion of missionaries, in traditional grass skirts and *nambas* (penis sheaths). They live in tree
houses, dance the old dances, and follow the old superstitious religious beliefs.

On the way back across the island we visited one of these villages. The people welcomed us and invited us to wander about the village. Stephen observed
that the women all stood around with their arms crossed over their chests. "I
think it has something to do with the fact that they don't wear bras," I murmured discreetly. Even the "titti-titti stand ups" had pendulous breasts that
would certainly jiggle uncomfortably when they walked. When they started to
dance, it was clear why the women's arm-crossing stance had become habitual.

The dancing we were invited to watch was all of a jumping-skipping variety.
Although the villagers performed three "different" dances for us, they all

looked pretty much alike to us. The men stamped their feet for a while, then ran in circles. The women waited (arms crossed on chests) until the appropriate moment and joined in, skipping around the circle or jumping in place. Each dance appeared to use these elements in different sequences, but the significance was lost on us. There was some chanting involved as well, which perhaps told a story, as these dances often do. But even with some explanation from John, we were unable to follow anything other than the vigor and intensity of the movements.

With continued admiration I watched John explain to the villagers in their local language that we had other places on the island to visit that day, and regrettably we had to leave. Well, that's what he *told* us he said.

*   *   *   *   *

The next objective was the Jon Frum village. Our conversations with Nelson about the Jon Frumers made us eager to learn more.

At first glance, the Frum compound looked similar to other villages we had already visited, with *fales* built around a large open space. But in this village, a number of flags were flying at either end of the open field. Two were very old and tattered, and we had to get very close to see what they were. Stephen recognized them: a U.S. Navy flag and a U.S. Marine Corps flag. A village man standing nearby told us they were both from units stationed in Vanuatu during World War II.

We were especially interested in seeing the Jon Frum church, and John said he would look for one of the village elders to ask permission. He left us momentarily and returned with a small, spare, elderly woman whose name was Elizabeth. Skinny as a rail, wearing what we would call a housedress, Elizabeth had a bright, almost furtive look to her. With John as our interpreter we talked with Elizabeth, who claimed she was Jon Frum's number-one prophet.

At one end of the open *fale* church to which Elizabeth escorted us, there was a large red cross. During World War II, the ni-Vanuatus admired the American Red Cross for all the medical materials and healing abilities they brought to the islands, and they adopted the red cross as a symbol of their religion.

With little prompting, Elizabeth was pleased to tell us about her religion. She told us, for instance, that Jesus was a black person and that the people of Tanna crucified this Jesus. He was then reborn as a white man (which was her explanation for why there are black people and white people in the world today). And, yes, it was Jon Frum who baptized the *white* Jesus.

Elizabeth's father knew Jon Frum during the Pacific War. Her father gave her the Marine flag that flies over the village. Elizabeth explained that she fed

Jon Frum every day in the church. He came down from the volcano and had a meal with her each night. And he told her things, and gave her American money every once in a while to thank her for her services. To illustrate, she ran to her house and brought back a small jar in which she had stored some coins. There were two 1991 nickels, a 1965 quarter, and on a chain with other trinkets, what looked like a 1923 buffalo-head nickel. Elizabeth went on to explain that Jon Frum would come back to reveal to his people where Hell is, why people suffer, and who on Tanna had killed Christ. She also told us that Noah built his ark on Tanna, and that during the flood it went aground near Tanna, and all the animals swam ashore. There are remnants of the Ark in the hills of Port Resolution Bay, she said.

During all of this exposition, our friend and guide, John, looked at us carefully as he translated. "This is their belief," he said. I could tell he wanted to say "it's unbelievable," but he was careful about repeating the stories as Elizabeth was telling them, and adding, "This is what they believe." My respect for John continued to grow. He would not interject his own feelings about Elizabeth or her cult.

At one point in our conversation I thought I heard Elizabeth say something about Napoleon, and I asked John if I had heard right.

"Yes," said John, "Napoleon was another ..."

"Manifestation?"

"Yes, manifestation of Jon Frum." We remembered that Nelson had tried to tell us about something that happened during the 1700s; this must be it. Although many of the stories that Elizabeth told us were probably learned from missionaries, John said that Elizabeth was illiterate, and so he did not know where she could have acquired the historical information. It was just one of the many mysteries about this religion.

By this time the light of day was waning. We bade Elizabeth good-bye and our truck turned toward an object with many mysteries of its own: Mt. Yasur.

* * * * *

We returned to the back side of the mountain across the volcanic desert of our earlier drive. Then we skirted the edge of the mountain and found a road that led through a forest and up the only part of the mountain still covered with green vegetation. Shortly we came out onto another, higher, desert plain, where we abandoned the truck and started a short, steep climb to the edge of the volcano crater.

As we arrived, the day's light was not quite gone. This gave us an opportunity to experience the emergence of the volcano's visual extravaganza as nighttime approached. The viewing area at the rim was about 50 feet long and just a few feet wide. We approached via a wooden stairway built up to the rim.

We had heard a number of stories about visiting the volcano, including tales of people who had been killed by flying lava during an explosion. There were other reports of strong winds that attempted to suck everything from the rim into the caldera. To say we were cautious on our approach would be to ignore our trepidation. But did we even stop to think about whether or not we should do it? No. And if I had stopped to think … well, what would I have thought? Dumb, dumb, dumb? People killed, and sucked into the inferno. Dumb dumb dumb.

At the top of the stairway we *were* wary, inching our way toward the edge. I crouched down almost on my hands and knees, afraid of that wind (60 miles an hour, we were told). Somewhat timidly, we paused back from the edge until one of the vents erupted. We knew it would be startling, even frightening, the first time, and we wanted to let that first experience happen away from the edge.

Kaboom! There it went, without warning, startling us and throwing us back away from the rim with the force of sound and light. There was no wind. We had been told that explosions rarely come in immediate succession, so the space of (unknown) time between them was a good time to creep to the edge and look in. Crouched low, we crawled forward.

There it was: Hell. A constant and fitful motion was joined by noises that were both familiar and indescribable. The Devil was down there, we were certain.

The story of the visitor and guide who had been killed here only a few months before suddenly came to mind.

"Where were they when this happened?" I asked John. He looked around, and said, "Well, just about where you are standing."

Stephen and I looked at each other, silently. "How did it happen?" I asked.

"The lava doesn't often come over us," he said, "and when it does, it's falling slowly enough that we should be able to get out of the way." John explained that normally the explosions were as we were experiencing them: eruptions of lava rock that went straight up and fell back slowly, like a Fourth of July rocket. But very occasionally the explosion sent debris out at an angle, and the fast-moving pieces can come out across the viewing area. It was during one of these incidents that the two people were hit by the lava.

"Is there any way to know when this will happen?" Stephen asked John.

"No."

This volcano experience was something that, as a child, you would tell your mother about *after* you had done it, because she surely would have forbidden it otherwise. It is possible that we should have questioned our judgment for engaging in this activity. But looking down into that caldera that night was truly thrilling.

*   *   *   *   *

The next day the weather started to change, and we stayed close to the boat. With a front approaching, the wind backed to the north, coming into the anchorage and making the water rough and uncomfortable. We knew that as the front passed over us the wind would back farther to the southwest, putting us downwind of the volcano. The thought of volcanic ash all over us was not appetizing; the chemicals in the ash could also destroy the finishes on the boat. As it was, enough of the ash and volcanic sand had already found its way into the rigging and had been tracked on board by our shoes and clothes. Despite our wish to explore more of Tanna's mysteries, we decided it would be better to leave before the ash descended. The sulfuric smell of the volcano had already begun to invade the anchorage.

The next morning, as we made ready to go, Nelson and his little cousin Mapmap (pronounced "mopmop") came out in their dugout canoe to say good-bye. As a final exhibition of Tanna's extraordinary offerings, Nelson called the local dugong (sea cow) by clapping his hands in the water. The strange elephantine creature came to the surface at this beckoning and rolled over and over, as if in pleasure at seeing us, or perhaps to say good-bye too. We took one more Polaroid shot of our two friends as a parting gift. Their smiles and "tankyu tumas" were heartfelt, and were felt in our hearts. They watched solemnly from their canoe as we raised our anchor.

We knew from Elizabeth that the hills to the left side of Port Resolution sheltered a piece of Noah's Ark. As we pulled away from the shore we regretted not having had time to look for this phenomenon. And (we had so desperately wanted to ask Elizabeth) what about the elephants and lions? Where were they? It mattered not. Here, there was a dugong.

And did Noah have two of *them* on board?

Splendid Isolation

Pacific Reefs

When we purchased *New Horizon,* the boat on which we made our Trial Run to the South Pacific, there was a ham radio on board. Stephen was immediately enamored by the idea of radio communications. As a young lad, he had had some interest in this field, and was delighted with the opportunity to become reacquainted.

Our reading suggested that having ham radio capability on board a cruising yacht would be important, especially in the Pacific. "Capability" meant not just a radio, but an appropriate license, as well. As Stephen is never one to do things halfway, he had, by the time of our Trial Run, achieved the highest level of ham-radiodom: an Extra Class license. This enabled him to broadcast on any ham frequency at any time.

In addition, he learned the "sport" of ham radio, and became an avid listener and "DXer" on the ham radio bands. DXing is the radio pastime of collecting ham radio contacts in other countries in order to earn various awards.

As we made our way around the world, there were places we visited that were classified as rare or nearly so, in one or another DX competition. It thrilled Stephen to be the rare station that hundreds, even thousands, of other ham operators vied to contact. A tiny reef hundreds of miles from anywhere, accessible only by boat, was a rare contact indeed.

Minerva Reef, between Tonga and New Zealand, is a ring of coral that is completely submerged, even at low tide. A natural opening through the circle of coral allowed us to enter the lagoon and anchor inside. From a distance, it would appear that we were anchored in the open ocean. Without any land visible, we looked to be afloat in the vast water. The ever-so-slightly submerged reef blocked the ocean swells, however, and kept the water inside the circle *relatively* calm—in good weather. We had to plan this visit carefully.

Five years earlier, sailing for Minerva would have been risky—at least beyond our tolerance for risk. Without the nearly pinpoint accuracy of the Global Positioning System (GPS), the margin for error was enormous. Most supercautious sailors like us would give a wide berth to waters known to hide ever-so-slightly submerged reefs. But with GPS, it was possible to *almost* pinpoint the location of the reef, as well as the opening to the anchorage. We already knew that charts for this part of the world needed to be used with care, and we could not assume the kind of accuracy we would need to find the passage. But finding the reef on a clear day, with good seas, was a snap. Entering the pass, Stephen was in the rigging as usual, calling out instructions to me on the helm.

These maneuvers required absolute faith in the guy in the rigging, and I never questioned—out loud or in my mind, at the time, or after the fact—Stephen's ability to see the correct course, to dodge coral heads, to keep our distance from the reef edges, and to guide us around these dangers.

By the time we had reached this juncture in the voyage, trust between us was absolute. It had to be; things wouldn't work any other way. Stephen's faith in my ability to wrestle with the helm had to be absolute as well. Situated up in the rigging, he could do nothing if I went astray—other than yell bloody hell. This teamwork through the reef passes was essential.

We did plan the visit to Minerva well. Conditions were mild, and Stephen, in the rigging, could see the reef, even submerged as it was, more than two miles away. We made the "reef-fall" and easily found the pass. As we rounded toward the pass, however, Stephen became nervous about the depth; it appeared to have gone very shallow all of a sudden.

"What's the depth?" he shouted.

"One hundred feet!" I yelled back, watching our depth sounder readout. The water was so clear, it seemed shallow; the details of the bottom were visible at one hundred feet! We sailed through the pass without incident, and found a patch of sand at a reasonable depth in which to anchor.

*   *   *   *   *

While Stephen made calls on the radio ("CQ, CQ, CQ, CQ, this is AA6LF"), I wandered the reef at low tide, when it was possible to walk safely. The reef teemed with colorful marine life. The algae were a vibrant maroon and peppermint green, lemon yellow, and sky blue. Tide pools caught polka-dotted puffer fish and crabs with red and white barbershop pole legs, as well as starfish of every color and shape—that is to say, star-shaped, but with thin legs and thick legs, thin middles and thick middles, and black, brick red, or cobalt blue. To me, this was magic. I spent hours at a time wading in water so clear that in my photos of the puffer fish you cannot tell they are in water.

*   *   *   *   *

Mellish Reef, off the east coast of Australia, was a very different piece of the world. The reef was half-moon-shaped and about four miles long, with a tiny island a quarter of a mile long pushed up in the middle. The island was mostly sand, with a few scraggly weeds on the top; at most it was three feet above sea level. The outstanding feature was the birds. The ratio of birds to humans while we were there seemed to be about ten thousand to one. There were boobies—masked, red-footed, brown—terns, and noddies. The noddies were very curious and would fly within inches of our faces—looking, looking. The birds were nesting on nearly every inch of the island, and curiously, the species intermingled. At least it was not clear to me that there were any noddy territories, separate from tern territories, separate from booby territories. There were young birds in every stage of growth, including some teenage booby gangs on one beachfront. I could tell they were youngsters from their immature feather colorations. The gangs flew together, landed together, and made loud noises together, just like a bunch of teenagers.

When we first went ashore I was worried about disturbing the birds. I didn't know if their exposure to humankind would be met with fear or awareness. I decided to try an experiment. I approached a noddy nest and got within a foot of the bird sitting on an egg before she flew away. I picked up the egg to examine it; it was comfortably warm. I replaced the egg in the nest and walked away. Within seconds the adult bird was back sitting on it, and maintained her brooding for the rest of our visit. Apparently my presence and my smell, even on her egg, didn't disturb her in any way. The egg hatched just before we left.

I wouldn't normally think of doing something so invasive as that experiment, but I was concerned that our presence might result in the birds' abandoning eggs, or in some way rearranging their habits. I knew that the birds had seen humans before; we had heard of one other boat that had visited the reef more than a year earlier. But the birds certainly didn't seem disturbed by our presence. If anything, we seemed to provide some amusement. The boobies, in particular, found fascination in the new toy (*Another Horizon*) parked in their front yard. Sitting on our stern pulpit was good fun, resulting in a huge mess all over the aft part of the boat. Most birds just plop their guano so it falls below their station in a singular glop, but boobies, bless their little hearts, lift their tail and *spray* their stuff with as much "wind" as they can!

*　*　*　*　*

Stephen's radio operation on Mellish was a success; he made contact with over 700 stations in more than sixty different countries. He was happy. While he hunkered in the tent he'd pitched to protect him from the sun and the birds,

I enjoyed watching the bird behavior and swimming. The fish species were beginning to change as we moved into the Coral Sea, and I saw many here I had not seen before.

I was mindful as I swam that I had no buddy. There were significant currents in some areas; I needed to be careful. Most of the time I kept the dinghy painter tied around my waist, so at the very least I would be able to get out of the water and use the outboard motor to save myself. Having the dinghy close at hand was also a defense against aggressive sea creatures. I could, you see, just throw myself into the rubber inflatable in a flash. Thinking back on that time, I declare that I was an idiot. As careful as I might have thought I was, the possibilities for bad things happening were large. But I never saw even a small black-tipped reef shark, and that may be why I'm here to tell this story.

In fact, I felt better on my walks along the island each day to see how the bird population was faring. I am not good at estimating numbers, but there is no doubt the number of birds on this island was in the thousands. Such a tiny space for so many birds.

I didn't actually talk out loud to them, but I'll have to admit that in my mind I carried on a conversation with several. While Stephen called stations around the world, exchanging messages over the airwaves, I was mentally (well, okay, sometimes out loud) talking to birds a few feet away. For the long hours Stephen called out into space, I had no one else to talk to but the birds and fish.

Not having any other people around was not unusual for us. We had already spent at least three weeks on our small craft with no land to walk on, let alone birds to commune with, but the fact that I was walking on land without any people made these reefs unique in our voyaging experiences thus far.

After reef-walking on Minerva and bird-talking on Mellish, I thought how lucky we were to see these reefs in their pristine condition. I'm not an especially political person, but experiencing a slice of nature like this and wondering how it could stay so untouched, I got a little steamed. Although Mellish was too much out of the way for most Pacific sailors, there were already a couple dozen yachts calling at Minerva every year. What havoc were we wreaking on that fragile piece of coral? There was no way, in Berkeley fashion, to post a sign: "Save Minerva! Don't anchor here." How could I, anyway, when we had already done so?

Enough sermonizing. The answer to the question, "What was your favorite place in all the world?" gets a generic "I loved them all." But in fact, these reef experiences were a couple of my favorites. I loved the isolation, the feeling of being in the middle of nowhere. Why I didn't get all anxious over this condition, I don't know. Good weather might have had something to do with it. If a storm front had come through while we were visiting either of these reefs, I'm sure I would have reacted as I had at the south end of Fakarava. But no front did come, and nothing went wrong with the boat or either of us—all conditions that I would normally fret about in such isolated situations.

It was also curious that at so many other times I had whined about being lonely. So why not here? The birds were such great companions, I didn't need the humans?

*   *   *   *   *

After leaving Mellish Reef we headed for Frederick Reef—much smaller, much rarer for DXing, but with far less protection from wind or wave than Minerva or Mellish. We picked out the reef in the early morning. Although not totally submerged, like Minerva, the visible land was tantamount to a postage stamp in that expanse of water. Not unlike Mellish, Frederick was horseshoe-shaped, and even as we approached from the north, we knew the reef would not be a good anchorage. The wind had veered to the north, and with the bottom of the horseshoe to the south, the winds and seas were pushing down into the anchorage. We would have no protection.

We did manage to anchor briefly, launch the dinghy, and land on the reef, but watching *Another Horizon* bucking in the swells, we were too nervous to stay more than a minute. I was disappointed—more than that, devastated—that we could not stay. Minerva was awash, but large and protected; Mellish was more isolated and full of bird and sea life. But Frederick was utterly unique: no humans, no birds, no plants, and no one we knew had ever visited this twenty-foot piece of sand. Who would want to?

Me ... very definitely me.

Dingoes and Didgeridoos

Australia

We were racing toward the east coast of Australia, trying to beat a strong weather front due to cross our path that afternoon. Our objective was Burnett Heads, at the bottom of the Burnett River, smack dab in the middle of that coast. We were approaching the buoys marking the outside channel to the river mouth, when we knew we were losing the race. We dropped the sails and turned on the engine seconds before the wind snapped to 40 knots, and the water was whipped into a froth of confused waves. A hideous line of black clouds swept down on us. We had only a mile to go.

And the engine died.

Why? We were low on fuel, but we knew for certain that there was more than enough fuel in the tanks to get us down the channel and into the harbor. What could be wrong? Stephen's hasty diagnosis was air in the fuel line. The fuel in the tank was low enough that as we were flung from wave to wave, the fuel intake could be briefly exposed and air sucked into the line.

We had extra fuel in jerry cans on deck that we could pour into the tank to raise the fuel level, but pouring fuel from jerries into a deck inlet without getting diesel all over everything is hard enough when the boat is still. As the deck heaved in the seas, we were unsteady in our task, and very soon diesel was sloshing onto the deck. To make matters worse, the wind was blowing the fuel away as it left the jerry can and before it reached the funnel to the inlet. Our legs and feet were quickly covered with the slimy, slippery liquid, and we carried it on the soles of our feet everywhere we stepped. Keeping our balance on a heaving boat was difficult at best, but on a heaving boat with a diesel slick it was nearly impossible.

At this moment the rain began. Torrential rain, stinging sheets of water, drenching us and now spreading the slippery diesel fuel *everywhere*. And then, as if on cue from the Warner Brothers studio, lightning and thunder added to the growing stress of the moment.

Just one mile to go, sails down, engine dead, an onshore gale pushing us toward the rocky headland ... *Shee-it,* I exploded, *what are we going to do?* It was a tossup: do we take the time to rig some sail and try to beat back out to sea, or continue to try to get the engine started as the boat was pushed slowly toward shore?

For better or for worse, we decided to try to get the engine started. Stephen went below to bleed the air from the fuel line. I was glued to the depth sounder, watching the depths become more shallow. At the last moment (of course), the engine took hold and we pulled ourselves back into the channel. Within minutes we were anchored in the river just behind the promontory of Burnett Heads. The storm continued to scream around us.

It was an inauspicious welcome to Australia.

* * * * *

Australia is the most American of any country we visited, including New Zealand. The TV news, advertising, food products, and urban lifestyles all seemed to ape American counterparts. Except for an occasional language lapse, Australia was the easiest country for us to fit into; of all the world's people, they seemed the most "like us." But if you look beyond the people, Australia is about as unique as they come. Isolated for millennia, Australia's flora and fauna, for instance, are unequaled.

Just south of Burnett Heads, we entered the Great Sandy Strait between the mainland and the west side of Fraser Island. Although touted as the largest sand island in the world, Fraser has decades of decaying vegetation covering the sand with "bush." We went ashore for our first Australian bush walk.

We climbed rapidly into the hills, passing innumerable species of gum tree (eucalyptus), listening for the kookaburras that are supposed to be laughing in them. We heard dozens of new birdcalls (but no laughing), and the rustling of many creatures in the "wallum" (low bush).

The trail came out of the woods, down a long dune, and deposited us on the beach, where we picked our way around the low-tide detritus. We felt, more than knew, that something was following us. A glance over our shoulders, and we spied the dingo prancing in our path. We stopped; he stopped, eyeing us warily. Dingoes, once domesticated dogs of the Aborigines, now run wild in the territory formerly inhabited by the Australian indigenous people. Despite being fed by well-meaning but ill-informed tourists, the dingoes are still careful around humans. Our friend was clearly looking for a handout, and he wouldn't be discouraged until we reached our dinghy and left him on the beach, staring after us.

Although there are plenty of parks and zoos where the fauna can be viewed at close hand, spying them in the wild was better sport. We walked for miles in Binna Burra, getting cricks in our necks looking for koala. We drove for hours in the interior looking for kangaroos of any sort—there are in Australia fifty species of kangaroo-like animals.

While hiking in the Lamington National Park we saw crimson rosellas and king parrots. Everywhere on the east coast there were huge flocks of rainbow lorikeets screeching at sunset, their noise slightly outdone by the gray and pink galahs, which were only slightly outdone by the shrieking sulphur-crested cockatoos. At Daintree we finally saw, and heard, a kookaburra, cackling in a gum tree.

In the waters off Airlie Beach, we came across our first humphead Maori wrasse. Although the name suggests New Zealand, and it is found in many tropical Pacific locations, this very shy fish is rarely seen anywhere. But when you see it, there is no mistaking it: four feet long, two feet high, a foot wide, with distinct, full, chorus-girl lips, eyes with a clown makeup-like look to them, and skin colors in a range of turquoise blues. It is a simply awesome fish.

Another imposing sight farther up the coast was the giant clam—the *giant* giant clam. These monsters are four to six feet wide, and three to four feet from the lip to the hinge. The lips enjoy a symbiotic relationship with algae that turn them (the lips) into glorious shades of blue, purple, green, and bronze, with spots and lines in contrasting colors. The orifices are so large (five and six inches across) that you can peer into the innards of the creature, where the tissues appear a phosphorescent orange, chartreuse, and blazing white. Like the Maori wrasse, these giants are not unique to Australia, but somehow the hugeness and the brilliance of the species in Australia made them seem singular.

North of Cairns we became more familiar with the Aussie crocodile. Granted, crocs are also not unique to Australia, but in Australian fashion they are given a unique status. Of the two species in Australia (salt-water and freshwater), the "salties" are by far the more dangerous (we were so happy to learn) *and* they are an endangered species in Australia. And let's be sure we have this straight: these were crocodiles, not alligators. We were interested in the crocs because they tend to congregate around the mouths of rivers, where we were finding our best anchorages as we made our way up the east coast.

To appreciate this creature adequately we paid a visit to a crocodile farm. Because the beasts were endangered, these croc farms came into existence to "take the pressure off the reptiles in the natural environment." Take the pressure off! What? They are so stressed-out that the Aussies felt compelled to provide sanctuaries for rest and relaxation, gourmet dinners, and special swimming pools? We were shocked. After a day of looking at these things, we wondered why couldn't we just let them become extinct? They are the ugliest, meanest, most dangerous creature I can think of—and except for their skin, they don't seem to have any social or natural redeeming value. And surely we can do without crocodile leather.

Along the Queensland coast, in our river-mouth anchorages, we scanned the shores carefully. You can be sure that we did not even putt around in our dinghy anywhere the crocs were known to be. We had heard of them swimming along and biting, and thus deflating, inflatable dinghies like ours. To be honest, however, we never saw a single one in the wild—at least on the east coast of Australia. There would be other places in the world where crocs, or alligators, would happily cruise in our midst. But in Australia, never mind ... there were other creatures to worry about.

Spiders—red-backed, white-tailed, wolf—more species of venomous spiders than anywhere else in the world. And sea snakes. At Ashmore Reef off the northern coast we spent a week swimming with the "world's greatest abundance and variety of sea snakes." Thirty-two of the world's fifty-five species are found on the reef; that's more species than anywhere else in the world, and almost half of these species are found nowhere else in the world. Ashmore is a national park with a resident warden, who told me the snakes were quite harmless. Their teeth, if any, are too far back in their jaws to enable them to bite any piece of the human anatomy, Ray said. "They are really quite friendly." Friendly!

Although not my choice of swimming companion, I could not resist looking for them. And they looked for me too. They were infinitely curious, it seemed, coiling about body parts (creeeepy) and looking into my snorkel mask, eye to eye. Still, I felt more comfortable with the reef shark that cruised around underneath me—not curious, and not interested in body parts, thank goodness.

*   *   *   *   *

In early December, moving south, we reached Brisbane, where we could berth the boat during our annual pilgrimage home for the holidays. In the weeks before our plane flight, we attempted to organize some boat work—the annual maintenance projects—that were essential to keeping *Another Horizon* fit. It was time to bring in the engine mechanic to give our engine its annual once-over.

Although Stephen was more than competent to check the engine for this and that, he was nervous about possible major parts about to go ping, or fittings or injectors about to go splat. He figured it was important to get a professional opinion, just in case. We didn't want pings or splats to occur six months later, out in the middle of nowhere.

It was true, in fact, that we knew there was something amiss. We had seen coolant coming out of the overboard exhaust when we started the engine, and for several months we had had to add water to the cooling system reservoir every time we started the engine—cursing when we forgot, because the engine would overheat in no time.

Enter our engine mechanic. He spent the first half hour of our well-earned money chatting with us about our travels. Where had we been? How did we like the islands? *How quickly can I tell you this in twenty-five words or less,* I said silently, *so we don't rack up too much time on your billing clock?*

We finally got him into the engine room, where we all agreed that our problem was more than likely in the heat exchanger. He would just "pop off" that "little baby," he said, and "whisk" it down to his workshop where he could test it, and we'd know "in a jiffy" what was wrong.

It was a bit disconcerting when the mechanic finally got himself folded into the engine room, snuggled up to our engine, and said, "Aye, never seen one quite like this."

"But you're the dealer for this manufacturer," we cried.

"Aye, but this is a turbo with a v-drive; never seen one quite like that. Do you have the manual for this one?" he asked.

The manual! The manual! We were thinking dark thoughts now, like, *We can read the manual ourselves—for free!*

He finally got down to removing the heat exchanger, grumbling that the nut wasn't metric and that he didn't have a "proper wrench." So we dug out *our* wrench for him. The little baby wasn't about to pop off, however, even with the proper wrench, and the poor bloke poured sweat (it was 88 degrees outside and must have been quite a bit more, folded up in our engine room) for a half hour before he got the nut off.

So, now he'd whisk it to the workshop, leaving greasy, smelly engine parts strewn around, in, and outside the engine room, which we wouldn't mind, would we—he'd only be a jiffy.

Three days later ("down a man," "wife ill," "emergency over in Wynnum") he announced that the exchanger *was* the problem, we'd need a new one, and that it would take only another day to get one from his supplier in Sydney.

We were at a disadvantage in all this because we didn't have a phone on which he could call us to say he was down a man, wife was ill, emergency and all that. We could, of course, walk a mile to the public phone box, or two miles to his workshop to place our query in person. But we resisted, knowing for certain that if we did leave the boat to walk or call, he would cheerfully appear at our marina berth while we were away.

So it was two days later when we discovered that his supplier (the only supplier for our engine in all of Australia) had just sold the last heat exchanger for our particular model of engine—which, by the way, did we know, the manufacturer was no longer manufacturing. The supplier would have to order the part from someone in Estonia … and it would only be a month—or two—and would cost, did we know, only $1,750 Australian.

Since we were by now on the eve of our departure for the States, we made a hasty call to our Stateside supplier, who said yes, they had one, for considerably fewer dollars, American. We could pick it up when we were home on our visit.

After the holidays we were back in Brisbane with the new heat exchanger in hand. Could we now continue our engine once-over, we asked the mechanic. It was Friday; he'd be over Monday. His assistant appeared on Tuesday ("down a man" on Monday) in the middle of the heaviest rainstorm of the decade. He stood in our cabin, dripping so much water through the cabin floor that the bilge pump went on—while we went through our life history, "loved the islands" (three words), and showed him the way to the engine room.

We went through the "never seen one like this" again, but we had the manual at the ready. Could he, we asked, check the other stuff that needs checking before putting on the heat exchanger? "Brilliant," he answered cheerfully.

"Noticed any leaks?" he asked.

Everything always leaks. What kind of question is that?

"Well, we should check this and that. Wouldn't want something to go ping out there in the middle of nowhere."

Right-ee-o. Couldn't take those pings—leaks, yes, but not pings.

Two hours later he was gone with half our engine loaded in a bucket to take to the workshop. The other half was strewn about the cabin along with *all* of our wrenches. The assistant, with a bit more honesty than we'd come to expect, said he'd be back when he'd be back. "The *rine*, you know."

Oh yes, we knew. The weatherman said it would *rine* for a week, so we could look forward to having either the mess and smell of a ripped-apart engine, or the dripping mechanic, or both, for some time to come.

* * * * *

With the engine back together eventually, we escaped Brisbane and moved north to the comfortable town of Mooloolaba (accent on the "loo"). We spent the hot, sticky summer months (the U.S. winter months of January and February) cleaning, varnishing, maintaining, provisioning, and in general getting the boat and ourselves ready for the long haul to the Mediterranean. For eighteen months we would not sit still again for so long a period.

At the beginning of March, with our work done, we began to move up the Queensland coast, continuing to look out for the uniquely Australian. Andy Martin on Middle Percy Island was unique, if not entirely unique to Australia. He had lived as a hermit on the island for over thirty years. We hiked three miles into the bush to find him.

As we approached his homestead we were greeted by a small herd of friendly goats that butted us toward Andy's home. A flock of sulphur-crested cockatoos screeched a warning of our arrival. Peacocks strutted across the yard. Ducks, roosters, and chickens scattered out of our path.

The ground floor of his home was wide open to the yard and housed his donkeys (and the chickens, and so forth). We called out a greeting and a distant voice yelled at us to come up the stairs. We climbed a bare staircase to reach his living quarters on the floor above. Although you wouldn't say this was primitive living (his house was well-built with modern materials), Andy was clearly isolated. There were no other persons living on the island, and it was plain that he enjoyed living off the land. Imagine our surprise, therefore, when we entered his living room to find him standing behind an enormous Canon photocopying machine.

"What is that for?" I asked.

"My work."

"Are you writing a book?"

"No, nothing like that."

"We thought you might be writing a book about your life on the island, like ..." and I named a couple of other hermits on Pacific islands who had written quite successful books.

"No," said Andy. "I'm not a good liar."

"What do you mean?"

"Your life might be the basis for the story, but to make it interesting, you have to ..." He was looking for the *mot juste,* I thought.

"Embellish a bit?" I suggested.

"No, lie is what I really mean. To tell a good story you have to be a good liar."

So there you are: How to tell a good story, by Andy Martin. (It eventually came to light that he was copying pages for some sort of philosophical tract he mailed to a following on the mainland.)

After some congenial conversation, Andy let it slip that he had just baked some of his famous bread. We had heard that he sold bread, fresh eggs, honey, and other products from his homestead to passing yachts. Would we be interested in the bread?

"Absolutely." He sold it by weight, he said, Aus$3.50 a kilo (2.21 pounds). Would that be all right?

"Gracious, of course," I replied, rummaging around in my pack for the money purse. It appeared I would have enough; I mean, how much does a loaf of bread weigh? Well, I tell you what: Andy's loaf of bread weighed a ton—nearly two kilos (over four pounds)! Digging deeper in the coin purse, I found enough also to buy some orange-lemon marmalade and a quart of the best honey I've ever tasted. Andy may be a hermit, and not interested in telling lies, but he was one amazing entrepreneur. And since someone had to keep him in Xerox paper, it might as well be us.

* * * * *

The northern half of Australia's east coast is protected by the Great Barrier Reef, another Australian phenomenon. The world's largest barrier reef, it provided us with weeks of protection from the ocean swell, while predictable trade winds provided the power for us to sail fast—faster than we would sail anywhere else in the world.

At Lizard Island we climbed a hill where there was a spectacular view of the outside reef. From the crest of the hill we could clearly see Cook's Pass, a break in the reef wide enough and with water deep enough to pass through into the open sea. Captain Cook had made the same hike, to the same crest—Cook's Look, it is now called. He saw the same opening in the reef, a great relief to him since he did not believe that the reef could protect his passage much longer. Without charts, to say nothing of GPS, Cook probably made the right decision. But we continued inside this marvelous reef all the way to the top of Cape York and the Torres Strait.

* * * * *

Turning west, we crossed the Gulf of Carpenteria and came to the Northern Territory, where we at last found the Australian people who are *not* "like us": the Aborigines. Bill Bryson (*In a Sunburned Country*) calls the Aborigines the planet's invisible people. He was mainly describing their lack of historical reference, but in fact, the Aborigines are just about invisible in Australia too. Packed into the Northern Territory or on reservations in Queensland, they are an out-of-sight, out-of-mind people. I believe the Australian government has tried, and is trying, to reconcile decades of mistreatment, but looking around, it is evident that the Aborigines are not in the mainstream of Australian life.

You don't see them as drivers of the tourist boats along the reef, for instance. Or as waiters in Melbourne restaurants, or selling groceries in

Brisbane. Or even as workers in the bauxite mines of the Gove Peninsula in the Northern Territory. And certainly not as officers of companies in Sydney, or owners of real estate in Adelaide. There are exceptions, of course—many notable exceptions. But on the whole, the Aborigines are stuffed into central Australia and the Northern Territory, there to figure out how to balance their ancient culture with modern-day demands. Although time breeds change, the Aborigines are still a very private people, many of whom would prefer to be left to their own way of life.

In their quest for privacy, the Aborigines of the Northern Territory require a permit to visit their property—the Arnhem Land. We were reluctant to try to obtain these permits ourselves, so we looked to an organization of local yachties for help. The Gove Yacht Club, on the east side of the Gove Peninsula, had for years arranged for yachts to move as a group "over the top" of Australia, stopping a number of times in Arnhem Land. GYC obtained the necessary permits, and over the years had secured the friendship of the Aborigines—sufficient to bring them down to the beaches, to mix with a fleet of yachties from all over the world. Although we generally steered away from group jaunts like this, joining a rally of yachts along this part of the Australian coast made sense to us.

In Refuge Baym we sat with one Aborigine clan around small sand pits of red-hot coals and made damper bread together. A simple mixture of flour, water, and baking powder, damper is kneaded thoroughly, spread into a flat round loaf, thrown into the sand, and then covered with hot coals. The shy women smiled as I tried to make my bread gooey enough to stay together in the fire. We shared the baked result, which tasted wonderful and, incredibly, had few ashes or sand particles attached.

At Echo Island we went ashore in the late afternoon and were joined by the Benthula Settlement, with a preponderance of children. There was a teenager who was a passable didgeridoo player, and as he played, other young ones began to dance. They had applied a white, chalk-like substance to their faces, arms, legs, and clothing. They danced the movements of the animals they found—and worshipped—in their lands, as their ancestors had for thousands of years.

We reached "the top" of Australia and slid down to Darwin in early July. We called our business agent at home as soon as we landed. We had been out of touch for weeks and just hoped that we still had money in the bank and that everyone was doing well. Penny told us to call our daughter Holly immediately. It could be anything. It was July, so not college. Probably money, but she had a job. Scenarios went whirling through my mind.

"Pop," Holly said. "He fell, and broke his hip. They set it, but he isn't doing well." Holly suggested calling my brother and sister who were with him and my mother in New Hampshire.

Pop was failing, and failing fast. He was already beyond knowing who was around him, my brother told me. "You can come now, but he's not going to know that you're here. He will not last much longer."

I was devastated. In Australia I could not be farther from the East Coast of the States. Although Darwin had a decent airport, nothing went to the States directly from there. I could fly to Japan and across the North Pole; I could fly to Hawaii and stop in California; I could fly to Sydney, then to Los Angeles, then to Boston. I could not do it in less than three days, or for less than $3,500 on such short notice. I called New Hampshire again at the next opportunity, given the nine-hour time difference. Pop had died in the early morning, just as I was trudging back from the travel agency.

* * * * *

Not long before leaving on the voyage, I had spent several days with my parents, trying to assuage my guilt over leaving. My father was philosophical.

"You are already 3,000 miles away (San Francisco to Boston); a few more thousand won't make much difference."

I told him we would be coming home once a year, and we'd be sure to take a swing by Boston, coming or going.

He told me he wouldn't expect me to return for funerals. "Doesn't make sense. It doesn't do the dead any good, and the living are going to carry on whether or not you are there. Don't worry."

I told him I didn't expect to have to worry about that in any case. He and my mother were still hale and hearty (even though that wasn't quite true).

My brother and sister were anxious to bring closure to this passage in our lives. I didn't blame them. While I was out sailing over the top of Australia they were watching Pop slip away. And they were dealing with my mother and her severe dementia, not knowing that the man she had lived with for sixty years would not be there for her anymore. My brother and sister were tired.

"Manage it however you wish," I said. "I will have to join you in spirit."

The next few days were dispiriting and guilt-ridden. I had made my peace with Pop, but it still hurt. We are forever our parents' children, and when they die, even in old age, we feel abandoned. Despite good friends all around and a sympathetic, loving husband, I felt incredibly lonely.

I am often asked, "What was the most difficult aspect of the voyage?" My questioners are looking, I suspect, for something like storms, small spaces, or querulous foreign officials. But I tell them it was the remoteness from family. Other than Stephen, family were so many thousands of miles away. At best we could talk in civilized places with a long-distance phone service—and at great expense ($10 a minute from Tahiti, for instance). We could mail letters, but it would be weeks before they reached their destination, and we would not receive mail coming to us for months. (E-mail was not yet available to us.)

We observed over the years that voyagers stopped sailing more often than not for two reasons. The men were tired of trying to keep their vessels seaworthy and safe. The constant barrage of repairs and maintenance wore them out. For women, it was family. Since a majority of our fellow voyagers were at or near retirement age, many had adult children who were getting married and having children—grandchildren. Women wanted to be around their children and grandchildren. This is not to suggest that the men didn't; it just wasn't quite as significant to them.

In the time we were at sea both my parents died; Stephen's mother died (his father had passed away years before I met Stephen); a son, a daughter, a niece, and two nephews were married; and four grandchildren were born. And Holly graduated from college. These were all important family events. We managed to find a way back to the States for a few of them, and the closer we sailed back toward the States, the easier it was to manage. But for many of the occasions, we had to swallow hard and let them go by. Separation from Holly and missing family gatherings were my biggest regrets of the eight years.

*   *   *   *   *

From Darwin we made one last sojourn into the interior of the great island nation. Southeast of Darwin, almost 100 miles by "bitumen," we came to the entrance to Kakadu National Park, an Australian gem. It holds acres of Australian uniqueness: billabongs teeming with 77 fish species and 25 frog species; dry grasslands and flooded plains supporting 50 species of mammals, 280 types of birds (one-third of which are found only in Australia), 1,000 plant species, and 4,500 insect species! There are lizards, turtles, snakes, pythons (only just discovered in 1977), 25 species of bats, kangaroo, wallaby, wallaroo, and yes, crocodiles—along the Alligator River! But the finest image of Kakadu for me was the Jabiru stork, a huge bird with long red legs and a heavy, long bill. It stands four feet high—regal, enormous.

Kakadu is not only home to an abundance of Australian natural life, it is also home to the origins of Australia's native people. Evidence of their past can be seen in over 5,000 sites of rock art, some as old as 20,000 years, some as recent as 1960. There are still a few Aboriginal groups living in the park, and (can it be?) over half of the park rangers are Aborigines.

Looking back at Australia, we have come to realize that although we once thought of the country as a lot "like us," its dingoes, didgeridoos, and damper; crocs and cockatoos; "rine" and 'roos; and the Aborigines' art, music, dance, history, and way of life are all as unique as anything we experienced anywhere else in the world.

Dragons and White Monkeys

Indonesia

We left the north coast of Australia, where the population was 195,000, and overnight arrived at West Timor, where the population was 1.2 million. Indonesia, with 200 million people, is the fifth most populous country in the world. Its land mass is less than 1.5 million square kilometers spread over 13,700 islands, only somewhat larger than Australia's Northern Territory. A majority of the 200 million people, however, live on five main islands, including Timor. The contrast of the wild, sparsely populated Northern Territory of Australia with the teeming shores of Timor was shocking.

Even before we went ashore at Kupang, we could hear the sound of an Asian city: the incessant bleating of car horns. And within minutes of embarking on the shore we were engulfed in essences of Asia: hot, humid, sticky, sweaty; the pungent smells of sewers, rotting vegetation, and hot-oil cooking; the jostling of throngs on the streets; the curious stares of locals at the "great white monkeys." Even at five feet, three inches I felt as if I towered over everyone as I walked along the streets. And even with our tropical tans, there was no mistaking our paleness—and in my case, blondness. The "monkey" part, I was hoping, applied to all of humankind, not just us.

Getting legally checked in with all the officials in Indonesia was not going to be easy, we had been told. Indonesia is notoriously bureaucratic, and we had heard all sorts of horror stories about negotiating the labyrinth of offices, paying unofficial "fees," and filling out stacks of forms. Our alternative was to find Jimmy, an agent who would take care of everything for us. Fortunately, Jimmy appeared at our side the instant our dinghy ground ashore.

Our permit to visit Indonesia in our boat was for only two months, not nearly enough time to see all parts of the country, so we had to choose carefully. We would sail more than 2,000 miles in those two months, and visit only twelve of the 13,700 islands.

Our route began with the more sparsely populated southern island, Savu, just west of Kupang. Seba, the "capital" of Savu, was really a village of ramshackle shops lining a two-block length of dirt road before spreading out into small thatch-roofed homes. In the middle of the village stood an old Dutch colonial home, the only remnant of Dutch occupation. It was now the home of the queen of Savu.

Although Islam is the dominant religion in this part of Indonesia, animist traditions still prevail, especially on these more remote islands. We had heard that there was an animist ritual site in a village near Seba, and we asked directions to it. Frankie, a friendly fellow with surprisingly good English, said he would be happy to take us there. At the outskirts of Seba we began walking through dried-up rice paddies and peanut gardens, over dry creek beds that Frankie said were overflowing in the wet season. We found the village of Namata clinging to the side of a hill. We sought out the chief to get permission to see the ritual site.

The chief was away in a neighboring village, we were told, but a second chief would receive us. A small, slight man, the second chief was anything but welcoming. He was scantily dressed in a sarong wound about his thin hips and a scarf wound about his head. His milky eyes suggested cataracts; his sunken jaw suggested few teeth.

There was a long argument among the second chief, a woman whose function we could not determine, and Frankie. It soon became apparent we were not to have access to the ritual site, but … perhaps if we bought some *ikat,* we could. This was the suggestion of the woman, I felt sure. At our assent, she escorted us to a house close by, where we bought several small pieces of this distinctive Indonesian cloth. Ikat is produced with a technique of tie-dyeing the threads *before* weaving, giving the woven patterns an unusual softness. I didn't mind buying the pieces; it was very good ikat.

Back in the dusty street, we tried to make better friends with the second chief and asked if we could take a Polaroid photo to give him. After another argument, he relented. I had Stephen poised behind me to take a second picture with our regular camera at the same time. I gave the second chief the Polaroid and a 1,000 rupiah note. He pocketed the bill and refused to look at the photo. And we still could not see the ritual site.

More rupiah were needed, Frankie suggested. We started to argue and then saw the futility of it. Another 5,000 rupiah were handed over. Five thousand sounds like a lot, but at the time that computed to about $2.50 U.S. I tried again to get the second chief to look at the Polaroid photo. I asked Frankie if his eyes were good enough to see it.

"Oh yes," said Frankie. Finally, I grabbed the photo out of the second chief's hand and pointed.

"Look! It's you!" I exclaimed, jabbing my finger at his image. Finally, he looked. A very, very faint smile crossed his lips for just a second. We could look at the ritual site.

Now understand that the ritual site was a mere 50 feet from us, and we could look at it anytime we wanted during this encounter, but we weren't supposed to. We did, surreptitiously, while waiting for various segments of the argument to be settled, but what I really wanted, of course, was to take a photo of it. I asked, and the ikat woman said I could. I started to, and the second chief became very angry, waving his stick in front of my camera to ruin my picture. The pictures of him waving his stick are extraordinary. Quite a bit more interesting than the ritual site, really, which was just a group of large rocks with curiously smooth rocks on top of them.

So the second chief continued to try to protect the sacredness of the site. He might have been distracted briefly by rupiah and Polaroids, but just in the nick of time he apparently remembered that it was not right, in his mind, for us to take photos.

Throughout the world we tried to be responsive to local sensitivities with regard to picture-taking. Some people are worried that their soul will be snatched away by the camera; some are worried that an evil eye is in the lens; some are afraid they'll end up in a travel book, unreimbursed for this exposure; and some (like our second chief, I think) just went after the camera out of some principle. The women who had gathered around us apparently felt that we had paid our dues (we had bought their ikat) and that it was okay to take a picture. Perhaps they did not adhere to the rules of this sect, and the old man did. It was difficult for us to know, and Frankie's English failed to reveal the issues clearly enough, so we just retreated, trying to suggest that we did not wish to offend. The whole event was edifying, and only the beginning of our sojourn into the complexity of Asian culture.

On the way back into Seba we stopped at an "antik" store filled with old animist carvings. In addition to ceremonial animal sacrifices (at the rocky "altar" we had just not seen), animists are also interested in ancestral spirits. The carvings at this store were offerings to the spirits. Some, if we were to believe the shopkeeper, were quite old—"two generations," he said. How old is that? "One hundred twenty years." What constitutes *old* in anyone's mind is often curious. On another Indonesian island we found a shop that advertised "antiks made to order."

From Savu we moved to the next island to the west, Sumba, stopping at the relatively large town of Waingapu. When we went ashore in the late afternoon we found a parade under way. The marchers appeared to be drill teams from the local schools. They were in their school uniforms, and each team marched to its own cadence. *Satu, dua, tiga, 'pat, kiri ... kiri* (one, two, three, four, left ... left). A few did some fancy footwork every once in a while to show off. There were 57 teams, with exactly 18 students each, from all over the island.

We were trying to walk to a hotel about a mile and a half from the waterfront, and the only way we knew to get there appeared to be along the parade route. So we made our way up the street, trying to walk discretely behind the parade watchers that lined the pavement, four and five people deep. It was soon evident that we were just as interesting to the parade watchers as the drill teams were. We nodded and exchanged greetings. *Selamat siang.* They giggled. *Selamat siang.* No, I do believe they were laughing. At one corner we had no choice but to move into the street to make our way. We were not alone; others (locals) were doing the same. But we were an event. Children were calling out all the English they knew: "Hello mister, missus. How are you? Where are you going? Good-bye. I love you." We tried to find a way off the street, but to no avail. Then one of the young men watching us started to chant. *Satu, dua, tiga, 'pat, kiri ... kiri.* Everyone laughed. We got into the spirit and began to march ourselves, chanting *satu, dua ...* They loved it. They clapped and we waved. Number 58 drill team. Americans. California. Distinctive. White monkeys.

From Sumba we sailed overnight to Rinca, a small island in the Selat Lintah, the strait between Flores and Sumbaya. The strait is a maze of islands and reefs, and is known primarily as the home of the infamous Komodo dragon.

This creature is not really a dragon but a monitor lizard, a particularly large, ugly, carnivorous beast of which legends are made. Rinca is one of two islands on which the beasts live. Our first anchorage on Rinca was representative of the wild, desolate area. Steep hills dropped precipitously to the sea and were covered in brown-gray grass with a few gray-green shrubs. It hadn't rained there in months. Where the hills dipped into vales near the beaches there were dry creek beds with just enough moisture to sustain some palms, brambles, and sand grass. In these little oases lived innumerable monkeys, deer, feral pigs, cranes, and Komodo dragons.

The "dragons" are to me akin to crocodiles and alligators—that is, they have no redeeming value, they are ugly, and they are dangerous. I was happy that they occupied just these two small islands in all the world, Rinca and Komodo. Nevertheless, we had to confirm my opinion, and we went ashore late in the afternoon to stalk the dragon. We carried our dinghy oars as we walked, in case we came upon a dragon that was interested in fresh meat. For a time I felt as if we were on a snark hunt, peeking in bushes, peering behind rocks, and carefully studying the ground around trees, our dinghy oars at the ready. (How ridiculous did we look?) We finally saw some tracks, distinctive claw-like tracks with a squiggly line between them—the slithering tail. We followed the tracks to the edge of the bushes, and there in the dim shadow of the hedge was a baby Komodo, almost cute at about two feet long. It took one look at us and skittered into the bushes. Our dinghy oars sagged at our sides.

The light was fading by this time, so we vacated the beach to head back to the boat. Looking to the beach as we rowed we saw monkeys suddenly appear and roam the sand in droves, searching for food. Another little dragon came along, and the monkeys rapidly scattered. Even baby Komodos command some respect.

We sailed up the west coast of Rinca to the Komodo Park, where the dragons are "protected." Stephen went ashore to check out the scene, and to see how we could get a guide to show us around. He landed on a small dock. At the head of the dock was a sign, "Welcome to Komodo Park," and underneath was what appeared to be a model of a Komodo dragon. Quite a good likeness, Stephen thought. And then it hissed and whipped its forked tongue out at his ankle. These tongues are long and somehow enable the lizard to overwhelm prey which, by expanding their mouth cavity, they are then able to eat whole.

Late in the afternoon, with Stephen still in one piece, we found our guide as arranged. He was a serious young man, short and slight of build. He wore boots, long pants, a rugby shirt, and a Crocodile Dundee hat with a red tassel—a worthy outfit for a dragon hunt. As we turned to the trail, we passed a rack of sticks, each about four feet long with a small fork at the end. Our guide picked one from the rack—his defense against the dragons, he said. I thought this ludicrous. How on earth could this 100-pound man with a little stick fight off one of those monsters?

We walked for an hour and a half through dry savannah and then up a steep hill that overlooked the anchorage. The area wasn't exactly beautiful, but it seemed exotic somehow. Monkeys, a water buffalo, and beautiful wild ponies roamed across the fields and into the scrubby trees. We didn't see that many dragons, but the ones we saw were worth the walk.

One big mama was atop a mound with an indentation in the top—her nest. She was guarding her egg, our guide informed us. I'm not sure we understood everything our guide was telling us (the accent was tough), but I think I understood him to say that it took nine months for the egg to hatch.

Farther along, a stench reached us that was truly awful. "I'm sorry," our guide apologized. "There is a good sight here, but it smells." We didn't have to understand that; the smell was gagging. "Beyond the bushes," Sutan said, "there is a rotting wild buffalo, and the dragons are feeding on it." Okay … smelly, but maybe interesting. On Sutan's instruction, we crept ahead to peer through the bushes. It was one of the most bizarre and disgusting sights I have ever experienced. There was not much of the buffalo left, but enough that three dragons were attracted. One of the smaller ones was inside the rib cage, tearing small bits off the bones. Okay … smelly, briefly interesting, but really disgusting.

On a path to a dry creek bed we came across the monster of the day. Twelve feet long, this behemoth looked as fierce as any monster could. His clawed feet, at the end of his stubby powerful legs, were at least twelve inches across. The guide was very nervous and commanded that we not get too close. We, of course, were trying to get as close as possible for some photographs. At the first turn of the dragon's head, however, we heeded the guide's words and sought refuge atop a rocky ledge until the monster went on his way—back along the path we had just been walking.

* * * * *

Although Indonesia is the largest Islamic state in the world—in terms of numbers of Muslims—there are parts of the country that are decidedly Hindu. The island of Lombok (next to Bali) is one of those.

Our first anchorage at this island was in front of a deserted beach backed by some scrawny trees. As usual, Stephen insisted we anchor as close to the beach as we dared, to gain the best protection from wind and wave. He needn't have worried; the night was very hot and very still—humid and sticky. I bedded down in the main salon, leaving Stephen the stateroom—a much smaller space with less "breathing room." I was sleeping fitfully when I felt a sharp jab on my arm. Jolting up out of my restless slumber, I looked at my arm and found an enormous cockroach making his way to my elbow. It didn't take long for my soggy brain to realize that the huge, ugly, brown, crunchy bug had bitten me!

I flew to the galley and scrambled for some roach spray and blasted that sucker to bits. Blaaach. Now the cabin smelled of roach spray. It took me long minutes to calm down, fan the spray away, and resume my sweaty tossing and turning. I couldn't keep my eyes closed for long, though. Where there's one, there's bound to be more. Right on. There came another of the hated insects creeping along the cushion of my makeshift bed. Jeez-zus. Spray, spray, spray, blaaach, blaaach! And there was another one. I realized that these huge, brown, crunchy, icky, horrible insects were everywhere in the main cabin.

I retreated to the stateroom (Who cared about breathing room?), only to find them crawling the walls in there as well. Stephen slept, blissfully unaware of my trauma and his peril. But they were not crawling on his arm. And why not, for heaven's sake?

Morning came none too soon, and I learned that these creatures were not, in fact, cockroaches, but palmetto bugs. They look like cockroaches but they are capable of flying some distance, and they are huge. We were parked so close to shore that the bugs were flying from the palm trees to our cozy-looking craft, landing on deck, crawling through the ports, and bee-lining for the galley (where they might find tasty crumbs)—right over my body lying in the way. I convinced Stephen that we *must* find another anchorage. We moved a little west. It wasn't as good an anchorage (some swell made it rocky), but I could toss and turn in the sweaty night without getting bitten by ersatz cockroaches.

From our new anchorage we found a congenial fellow to take us on a tour of the island. We arrived on the beach dressed in our respectful clothing—long pants for both of us, shirts with sleeves to the elbow, closed-toed shoes and socks. All of this cloth lying next to our skin was hot and sticky, but we learned to live with it. Appropriate dress was important, especially in Indonesia, and especially as we pushed out into more remote neighborhoods.

We drove through lush countryside, visiting villages where everyone made crafts for the tourist shops of Bali, each village specializing in one craft only. They saw us coming down the road, and they were ready for us as we pulled into the center of the village. We were soon loaded down with carvings, baskets, weavings—it was hard to resist.

As we drove between Sade and Remblan, a flood of people in the road stopped us. Our driver pulled aside to let them pass.

"It's a wedding," Made (pronounced "Ma-day") said.

"And very clearly a Hindu wedding," Stephen whispered to me.

Made described the occasion to us: "The villagers are accompanying the bride and groom from her village to his." In the center of the throng a gold umbrella was held high over a very solemn-looking couple.

"They don't look very happy," Stephen said.

Made explained that it was important that they *not* look happy, especially the bride. She was leaving her family to join his, and it would be an insult to her family if she appeared happy about that. In contrast, the villagers were raucous, smiling, laughing, and dancing to the cymbals and drums of musicians preceding the betrothed couple.

The costumes of the principals—bride and groom and musicians—were colorful, but in some cases looked a little ill-fitting.

Made read our minds. "The clothing belongs to the village and can be used by anyone in the village who marries," he said. That would explain the too-long sleeves of the groom's embroidered jacket. And why the bride held her head slightly forward and had not just a solemn look, but an expression of decided worry. Would her elaborate headdress stay on? A fan of gold spanned the back of her head; more gold—crowns and dragons—sat precariously at the top of her forehead, tied to the fan by thin strings of beads. Long pigtails of red and white flowers fell from one side of the fan over her right shoulder. It looked heavy and awkward, and I had no doubt she couldn't wait to take it off.

The musicians were decked out in fuchsia pink shirts over a variety of sarongs in equally loud colors of orange, red, and turquoise. Wide gold and black headbands completed their uniforms. The color of this procession was in sharp contrast to the plain, neutral colors of the clothing we had seen on Indonesians thus far—the difference between the somber Muslims and the gaiety of Hindu custom.

Our anchorage for Bali was in a long, narrow harbor. It seemed safe in terms of the anchor holding and protection from the elements, so that we could travel to other parts of the island. One night, following a day of inland travels, we were awakened by a jolting thud against our hull. We sprang from the bunk and rushed on deck to find a 50-foot steel hull lying alongside us. The crew, a German couple, looked as shaken and anxious as we felt. Within minutes we determined that the German boat had dragged anchor, and we could not see any damage to either boat. With profuse apologies they gathered in their anchor and chain, in order to reanchor. Stephen and I stood on deck, still a bit unnerved but also puzzled by the incident, because the wind was not so exceptional as to cause an anchor to drag. But as we looked around us, we were flabbergasted to see boats everywhere in the anchorage, zinging and zanging all over the place.

Stephen looked into the sky. No clouds, but a full moon—a spring tide, maybe, he said. And so it proved: there was a confluence of exceptional tides that night, and as the tide ebbed, it ran against the wind. The eddies and countercurrents that were set in motion through the narrow harbor sent yachts skating across the anchorage, pirouetting on one side of their anchor line range and sliding back to the other side. Because of the erratic movement of the water, the boats were not moving in their normal unison. Sterns faced sterns, and bows were at right angles to broadsides. We skated while our neighbor slid, and we were close enough to pass the Grey Poupon®. There were numerous "kissings," and the anchorage was soon alive with crews on deck struggling to maintain a safe position. We remained on deck for the rest of the night.

By dawn the tide had changed again and the currents had gone slack. We could relax, and I went below to put on water for coffee. I felt a dull ache in my lower face. My teeth had been clenched so hard for so long that my jaw trembled for several minutes as I tried to get my body to calm down. It did not take us long that morning to decide it was time to leave Bali and continue our trek through Indonesia.

*   *   *   *   *

At the rarely visited island of Bawean, we walked several kilometers to the main town in search of a market. Indonesian markets sell a plethora of fruits, vegetables, and every imaginable plastic, wooden, and glass article "made in Indonesia (or Malaysia, or China, or the Philippines)." Our purpose that day was to replenish our fresh food supply, and once again it appeared that our walking along the road was providing more amusement than the locals had had in some time. The women in particular were curious about us, feeling the cloth of our shirts and passing a finger over my blond-haired arm. And they were intensely interested in what we bought, often pawing unabashedly through our bags to take an accounting of our purchases.

Soon after our visit to Bawean we crossed the equator again, back into the Northern Hemisphere. Everything that was upside-down righted itself, and everything that was backward turned itself forward again. It was seriously hot then, as it had been for most of the last six months.

In fact, the single overarching memory of those months is the unceasing heat and humidity. We went to bed sweating and we woke up sweating. Heat exhaustion was a serious threat every day. And it was not as if we could retreat to an air-conditioned hotel. Cooking over the hot stove was almost impossible. Our cabin fans were running constantly, and we thought of the fog flowing in through the Golden Gate, enveloping everything in the Bay Area in cool, moist clouds. Lordy, that would have felt so-o-o good.

Although our course through Indonesia to Singapore was an easy route as far as islands and reefs were concerned, we had not anticipated the boat traffic we encountered, especially at night. The area was swarming with fishing boats, with an occasional freighter to add to the excitement. And by this time we were sailing through the notorious South China Sea.

Just mention the South China Sea, or sailing anywhere through Southeast Asia, for that matter, and we are immediately asked about pirates. There had been no reported attacks on small yachts in this area for several years. Commercial ships were occasionally boarded and robbed of the considerable cash kept for wages and harbor fees, but we were too small to bother with—so we were given to believe.

Why then were we so nervous as we tried to keep clear of local craft, and *they kept following us*? We would change our course, and they would come after us. They would aim right for us at a great rate of speed, before veering off just a boat length away. Scarrrry. And if not pirates … what?

Over time we came upon two explanations for this odd behavior.

If the fishermen believe they have a bad spirit on board (perhaps they hadn't caught any fish for several hours), they attempt to rid their boat of that spirit. Bad spirits can't turn corners very easily, you see, so if the boat burdened with a bad spirit can get close enough to another boat (preferably a "white monkey's" yacht) and then make a sudden right-angle turn at a great rate of speed, the spirit might be flung from their boat onto ours.

At times, however, it appeared that their chasing us was just a water version of what we found on land: infinite curiosity. Indonesians want to look at you and see how you live—up close and personal. Thus the peering into our market bag to see what we'd purchased; and the bumping into us, without apology, to feel our clothing; and the asking of incessant questions (what's your name, where are you from, etc.) were all part of their wish to find out about us. So, on the water the fishermen were getting as close as they could to see what we, and our boat, looked like. But did they have to approach at such speeds? It was an unnerving practice, regardless of the reason.

Although certainly not men from Mars, white Westerners were rare enough in parts of Indonesia. We had been warned about this intense interest, especially as we came along in our relatively lavish yachts, with expensive equipment and bountiful food and clothing, the likes of which tried the imagination of the average Indonesian. Still, it was disconcerting to be peacefully anchored, and down below in our cabin, cooking, eating, or reading … and hear whispering voices. Looking up, we'd see half a dozen faces peering in through the cabin ports. There were even a few occasions when some of our visitors came aboard uninvited. That was not rude, if there was even any distinction, because the outside of the boat is the outside of our home, and it is not inconsiderate to come into a neighbor's yard. I don't know about gazing into a neighbor's windows though.

We looked on these visits as opportunities to get to know our neighbors better, however, sharing some food and talking a little if we could. Indulging their curiosity was indulging ours too, when you come right down to it. And when we tired of the encounter, we could always say that it was time for us to go below to say our prayers. Saying prayers crosses cultural lines, and it was understood to be a private activity. Our guests unfailingly left us quietly so that we could practice our form of religion.

This seemingly insatiable prying into our lives took some getting used to, some patience, and at times (as they careened toward us in the straits) grim tolerance. But it was understandable when you think about it: if a white monkey appeared in your neighborhood, wouldn't you be curious?

Saffron and Serene

Singapore to Thailand

"It would be suicide to cross Singapore Strait at night," we were told.

"And *why* would anyone in their right mind do that?" we asked.

"I don't know," our friend said, "but it would be suicide." We had better ideas about doing away with ourselves, so we started across the infamous strait midmorning, in broad daylight.

Singapore is now the busiest port in the world. Even if ships don't stop there, they go through the strait to save going through the multitude of islands to the south.

Now it is one thing to have an 80-foot Indonesian fishing boat swoop down on you for a look-see, and quite another to have an 800-foot tanker bearing down on you, with no way to miss you if you are in the way. These vessels do not stop or even change course for some little 40-foot sailboat, so it was up to us to dodge around them. In the three hours it took us to cross the straits we encountered more than one hundred freighters, container ships, and super-tankers. They came galloping out at us from all directions. We were gasping from the effort of estimating speed and distances, clipping the stern of one to hop across the bow of another. And wouldn't you know it, there we were right in the middle of the strait when a rainsquall hit, reducing visibility to nearly nil. We turned to dodging blips on the radar. We might as well have been cross-ing at night. If not suicide, it was the most nerve-wracking passage of the voy-age thus far.

Once across the strait, we turned north to go up the west side of Singapore—only to find that we had to thread our way through a "petroleum anchorage," with some sixty-odd tankers and supertankers at anchor, on moorings, or milling about looking for a place to light. We had no choice but to motor through this area, at times coming within yards of some of the ships. They were huge. We had never felt so small.

As if all this weren't enough to rattle our nerves, as we made our way out of the petroleum anchorage a flotilla of Singapore Coast Guard boats came charging at us, yelling for us to divert our course. They were in the middle of a *live* firing exercise and we were in the way! And *where,* we asked, should we go? "Not this way." We throttled back to a standstill and waited. The SCG was still agitated, so they came close enough alongside that we could decently communicate. We told them where we were going; they told us how to get there—without getting shot. *Thank you,* we bowed in gratitude.

We spent two weeks in Singapore, mostly doing chores on the boat, including getting it hauled out of the water to put on some badly-needed bottom paint. The weeks were punctuated with forays into town.

Singapore is a relatively small island with a population of four million. To accommodate the high population density, everyone lives in high-rise apartments. And for these apartment dwellers, the most prized pet is a songbird. On Sunday, it is the duty of a male member of the family to take the birds out for some fresh air and some communal singing with other birds, something like taking the dog for a walk, or perhaps taking your preschool kids to the park for some peer socialization.

One Sunday morning we went to the corner of Tiong Bahru and Sing Poh roads to see, and hear, the birds sing. On the street corner we found wires strung between trees with numbered hooks on which to hang your birdcage. Numbered, because this particular corner was for only one kind of bird, all of them in identical-looking cages, and the only way to tell which one was *your* birdcage was to remember your number. Other such cafés for other kinds of birds were located on practically every corner of this neighborhood.

While the birds hopped about and sang to each other, the guys got a coffee and chewed the fat with their buddies. There were 250 hooks on this corner, about half of them filled when we arrived at 9 AM. But as we walked away up the street, we saw men laden with birdcages streaming from nearby buildings and pouring out of buses. Those hooks would be filled in no time.

*   *   *   *   *

After two weeks, our Singapore transit permit had expired, and although it was renewable, we decided to push on up the Malacca Straits. The straits are bounded by Malaysia on the east and Sumatra, Indonesia, on the west. This would be our chance to see a bit of Malaysia, so we stuck to the east side. We had decided that we would do no night sailing in the straits. For one thing, this was another pirate territory. But we were more concerned about all the local fishing activity, complete with nets, traps, lines, and other paraphernalia designed, so it seemed, to ensnare white monkeys' yachts.

There are no natural anchorages on the east side of the straits, but the waters near shore are relatively shallow, with a good, sticky mud bottom. Our strategy was to buzz along this water highway until sunset, pull over to the "shoulder," and "park" for the night. This was good strategy until the sumatras struck.

Sumatras are small, intense storms that whip across the straits (from Sumatra), packing high winds, torrential rains, thunder, and lightning. On the east side, we had no protection from a storm from the west. Fortunately, the storms were short-lived—one or two hours at most. Unfortunately, they always occurred just after midnight, leaving us sleepless for the rest of the night.

Although we were traveling only by day, and therefore could cover only 50 to 60 miles a day, we seemed to be streaming past Malaysia. When we reached Port Klang, however, we forced ourselves to stop, go ashore, and sample a little Malaysian culture. A railroad line from Kuala Lumpur came out to Port Klang and made it easy for us to reach Malaysia's capital.

In our prevoyaging days, Kuala Lumpur always sounded like an exotic destination. Asian, of course, and so mysterious. It's now a huge Asian city, however, not unlike Hong Kong and Singapore. Their economy was booming, and they were building bigger and better high-rises, more and more fashionable shopping malls, and one grand hotel after another. They were just finishing the Petronas Twin Towers, at that time the tallest buildings in the world.

By contrast, Port Klang was filthy—a paradox, because the Malaysians personally are spic and span. Their clothes were always spotless and well-pressed; the women's hair meticulously groomed, their skin clear and bright. How could they stand such filth around them?

Despite the garbage and the accompanying smell, I enjoyed wandering the streets, because often there would be something unusual happening. One day a ferry from somewhere arrived at the wharf with a Chinese funeral procession aboard. The casket and mourners were ushered up the wharf into several truck-type vehicles, with much chanting and drum beating. Mourners were decked out in costumes and headdresses. Along with all the other dockside observers, we gawked.

Near the end of the Malacca Straits we came to Pulau Pinang. This island, with a history of Dutch, Portuguese, and British rule, has come through it all with a predominantly Chinese culture. Doss houses (essentially good-luck temples), clan houses (meeting halls for the highly influential clan leaders), herbal medicine, and mahjong are all part of the everyday life of the island. Equally enthralling were the Buddhist temples—resplendent in gold ornaments, with thousands of Buddha statues in every yoga position, standing and reclining. Despite the preponderance of Chinese, there is a large Indian population too, so throw in a Hindu temple or two and you see Pinang as a truly multicultural place. Of course, we were still technically in Malaysia, a predominantly Muslim country (Islam is the "state religion"), so there were a few mosques serving the island's Malaysian population.

As one might imagine, the food was magnificent: Chinese spare ribs, Indian murtabak (a kind of omelet in a sort of crepe), curries to numb your lips, rice and noodles cooked in every way imaginable, and all so cheap you couldn't afford not to eat out. It all made Pulau Pinang a most exotic, energetic, and eclectic island.

* * * * *

At the end of the straits we came to the south islands of Thailand and enjoyed lazy days of short sails from island to island, swimming, and wandering ashore to sample the marvelous, fragrant, spicy Thai cuisine. The real meat of our Thai experience, however, was the time we spent in northern Thailand, in Bangkok and the area around Chiang Mai to the north.

Bangkok is a sad city, sinking slowly into its polluted waters. It was once called the Venice of the East, with canals graced by golden temples, colorful rice barges, and produce boats moving around the city with ease. But now many of the canals have been filled in, the city is clogged with motorized vehicles, and there is no smog emission law here.

All of Thailand is temples, it seems, and some of the most magnificent are in Bangkok, including the huge Wat Phra Kaew. The façade of this temple is a mosaic of millions of pieces of colored glass and gold leaf. When the sun was out, the sight gave new meaning to the word "dazzling." Another favorite shrine was the lingam (phallus) shrine, which has ended up on the grounds of the Hilton Hotel. A fertility shrine, it sports hundreds of very realistic phalluses, up to six feet tall!

* * * * *

Chiang Mai is the center of northern Thailand, and it has become a tourist mecca. From there we drove north to the Golden Triangle, where the Thai, Laos, and Myanmar (Burma) borders meet at the confluence of the Mekong, Sai, and Ruak Rivers. What used to be fields of opium poppies have now been turned into golden fields of rice, so they say.

The border between Thailand and Myanmar had just opened a few months previously, and streams of Thais and Burmese were crossing the bridge hourly to purchase on the other side items not available in their homeland. We crossed the border ourselves by surrendering our passports and forking over

$10 U.S. (no other currency accepted). Conveniently, there was a bank nearby that had ten-dollar bills all ready to go.

On the way back from the border we stopped at several hilltribe villages, where formerly nomadic tribes from China, Burma, Laos, Vietnam, and Thailand have begun to put down their roots, send their kids to government schools, and raise rice and tobacco instead of opium. Their costumes were beautiful, their crafts unique, and their smiles broad. They also charged twenty cents for every photograph we took, aggressively sold their wares, and clearly were out to get their cut of the tourist trade.

The only trouble with Thailand is its language. We had an easy time in Indonesia and Malaysia. The languages of the two countries are almost identical, and they are extraordinarily simple: no verb tenses, no articles, and the same word order as English. By the time we left those countries, we could carry on a simple conversation on the street or in the marketplace. Thai was a wholly different matter. There are forty-four consonants and forty-eight vowels, and it is a tonal language, with five different tones. A single word can have five different meanings depending on the tone applied. Thus, *kar* can mean "to dangle," "a cooking spice," "to trade," "to kill," or "a leg," depending on the way you say it.

If the spoken language is a problem, the written language is impossible. It is a script for which roman transliterations are difficult and not consistent. There are no spaces between words, and no punctuation marks. Vowels appear to the left, right, above or below the consonants they accompany, and they often appear in clusters. Clusters of vowels—I didn't even know how to imagine this.

With this language problem, my greatest frustration was grocery shopping. Unless the product had a label with a picture, I didn't have a clue what I was buying. My best bet was to keep the phrasebook at hand and point to a relevant phrase. That was good for our side of things. How to translate what came back to us as a long, enthusiastic stream of forty-four consonants and forty-eight vowels was something else again.

All of Thailand is Buddhist, and everywhere there was the flash of golden robes as Buddhist monks made their way—with hoes, baskets, shoulder bags, cameras, or briefcases. There are 32,000 monasteries in Thailand to accommodate the men in orange. At one we peered into a small *viharn* to see a monk sitting crossed-legged on the floor, eating with his fingers from a number of bowls surrounding him. A dozen or so Buddha images looked on—while the monk watched television! I don't know why that should have surprised me, but watching TV seemed so unmonklike.

I was fascinated by the Buddhist culture, and in particular by the monks who were everywhere. It turns out that men of the Buddhist faith can become monks any number of times in their lives. Most become monks at least once,

some many times, and a few permanently. The young boys were an anomaly—
hair shaved close to their heads, orange robes twisted and wrapped again and
again as they learned how to manage them. I have a photograph of one young
man, about sixteen or seventeen, standing curbside in his orange robe on a
busy street, talking to another youth of about the same age. The posture of the
teenage monk suggests the youth that he is—slightly arrogant, slightly impatient, slightly frustrated. Facing him is his friend in regular Thai teenage dress
(black shirt, black pants) … on a motorcycle. There is no question, looking at
this photo, that the teen monk would really, really rather be the fellow on the
motorcycle.

Traditionally, young Thai men "take the robe and bowl" (to receive alms)
when they have finished school and before they begin their adult life. But more
recently it has become socially prestigious for a family to have a young son
(under twenty years old) enter a monastery as a novice, which explained why
there were so many children in orange. Like taking piano lessons for some of
our Western young boys, being a young monk in Thailand must be endured.

* * * * *

The orange robes turned up in bus stations, at tourist attractions, at
monasteries and temples. I have a photo of two young monks fixing their
robes in front of a huge billboard advertising feminine lingerie. Another
image has a pack of monks visiting a temple. In my photo they are grouped
around a Polaroid just taken, seriously watching the image emerge. In another
there is a man in orange striding purposefully down a busy street, with a very
businesslike briefcase in hand.

Walking through the brambles of a temple ruin in the north, we saw the
golden flash off to our left. "Monks over there," I said to Stephen.

"But this is a ruin," he said.

"Perhaps they come here to meditate," I countered.

"Seems unlikely," he asserted. "Nowhere to sit."

I was too fixated on my monk-watch to be deterred. I turned onto a trail to
the left, walking stealthily. The orange flashes grew large and strangely unhu-
manlike. Pulling branches aside, I came to a clearing next to an old compound.
There, drying on clotheslines tied from tree to tree, were several pieces of
orange cloth—large, oblong pieces of orange. Monks' robes, flapping in the
breeze.

Just to the west of Chiang Mai is a fourteenth-century forest temple and
monastery, Wat U Mong. The quiet of this monastery and temple complex was
remarkable after the roar of Bangkok and midcity Chiang Mai. The old chedi

was sprouting weeds, the brick wall sagged, and the heads of several abandoned Buddhas lay quietly in the brambles. Saffron robes walked quietly among the trees. This place was how I remember Thailand—uncomplicated, devout, blessed, golden, antique, and serene.

Tigers and Saris

The Subcontinent

On our first night in the tiny harbor of Galle, Sri Lanka, we settled down for a good night's rest. It would be our first full night of sleep following the ten-day passage across the eastern half of the Indian Ocean. But deep into the night, we were suddenly awakened by a tremendous explosion. It sounded close by; it had the dull thud of being underwater; and although it was odd that we felt no thump of impact, I was certain we had been hit by something.

I was out of our bunk in a flash and into the main cabin, flipping up the floorboards, expecting to see water pouring into the bilge. But it was dry. I looked at Stephen. "Perhaps these are the detonations we read about," he said, and the light dawned. Of course.

There was an active civil war going on in Sri Lanka between the disenfranchised Tamils and the majority Sinhalese. The campaign for an independent Tamil state within Sri Lanka had turned ugly in recent years with a pattern of violence, killings, and reprisals. Scores of people were killed and wounded even during our time in the country. But except for the odd terrorist attack, the fighting seemed to be limited to the north and east of the island, the disputed Tamil territory. Galle was located in the southwestern corner.

In the past, however, Tamil Tigers, as the extremists are known, had swum into Galle harbor at night to attach explosives to the hulls of navy ships docked only a dozen yards from where we had anchored. To discourage this activity the Sri Lankan navy set off underwater explosives during the night. Every night. They detonated up to a dozen of these explosive charges at random times, and I was convinced they timed each one to the moment we were just drifting off to sleep, again and again.

Sri Lanka hangs like a teardrop appendage off the east coast of India. Formerly the British colony of Ceylon, the island lived earlier under the influence of the Portuguese and Dutch as well. Although Sri Lanka's independence was contemporary with India's, and far calmer, the struggle between the Tamils (who are Hindus) and the Sinhalese (Buddhists) was just as bitter as the

142

Muslim-Hindu conflict in India. Although partition ostensibly resolved India's problem, nothing had yet resolved Sri Lanka's conflict.

* * * * *

The timing for the end of a 1,200-mile ocean passage, like the one to Sri Lanka, is difficult to calculate, and the timing of our landfall at Galle just at sunset was not perfect. Our approach to the harbor appeared to be right on course. We could see a freighter hovering at the entrance to the channel. "Good, follow that guy, full speed ahead," Stephen said. Except at the last moment we realized the freighter was actually a *wreck* on the rocks we were trying to avoid.

A little frantic searching in the GPS revealed that one of us had absent-mindedly put into the GPS the *same* coordinates for two *different* locations in the harbor entrance. Although I used to be amazed at the news stories of groundings of large ships (presumably with all the sophisticated electronic gear one needs to avoid such calamities), I am no longer. It's called human error. It happens all the time.

Once the error was discovered—and we aren't saying whose it was—we were fine, we thought. But by now it was almost dark. There were buoys for the channel, as the chart indicated, but none of them was lighted, and they were not *exactly* in the charted spots—close, but "Uh-oh, why are there *two* buoys just ten feet apart?"

"What does that mean?"

"Does a depth of eighteen feet jibe with the chart right here?"

"Where is that 'wreck, conspic.' on the chart? It can't be that freighter. 'Wreck, conspic.' is supposed to be here, and that wreck is over there!"

We called out these comments to each other, frantically trying to sort out what was on the chart and what was real.

"Christmas! Is that a fishing boat?" I yelled. A small outrigger manned by three oarsmen was desperately trying to cross our bow. We swerved, and they waved. The light had really faded. Hoping to avoid becoming another "wreck, conspic.," we crawled our way into the harbor toward a seawall, watching the depth sounder very closely.

"Oh heck, let's just dump the anchor here; it's probably okay." Stephen suggested.

"Yes, we are getting a little close to the street with cars on it just ahead."

Stephen jumped to the bow and "dumped" the anchor. We were tired.

With the anchor set, another successful passage had been completed, half an ocean had been crossed, a new country was at hand, and there were new sights to see. But now it was time for a shower to wash off the passage grime before we fell into our bunk for a well-earned full night's sleep. Just as I was toweling off—stark naked—there was a thump … bump against the hull. Had the boat swung and bumped into something (like a street with cars on it)? Voices. Someone had bumped into us.

"Moment," I called, and grabbed a pareau, hurriedly wrapping it about me.

"Madame."

Damn, they were looking in through the port! "Moment!" I gasped, desperately.

"Sri Lanka Navy," a voice from a dark face in the port called out.

"But the Harbor Control said you would come tomorrow. It's sooo late now," I wailed.

"We come now." A very definite command.

"Okay," I said resignedly. I donned more clothes, looking to see if anything was showing that shouldn't be showing. Finally with a decent amount of clothing on, and Stephen in a T-shirt and shorts at least, we invited our visitors to come below.

They looked about. "Where's the bedroom?" An unusual opening gambit.

I showed them. "Very small," I said.

"Mmmm … small," the inspector scowled slightly, probably trying to imagine how we managed. The navy captain spied some videotapes.

"What?" he asked.

"Movies," I said.

"Tapes?"

"Tapes."

"What?"

"American tapes."

"See!" Another command.

Another sigh, "Yes," and I started to drag out the VCR and TV.

Stephen whispered, "Whatever does he want?"

Me (sotto voce): "To see if they are X-rated." (Many countries forbid pornography to be brought into the country.) As I started to haul out the equipment, the navy captain must have decided it wasn't worth the effort, if I was actually going to show him.

"No, okay," he said. "See you tomorrow."

So—once-naked white woman, with small bedroom and videos of who knows what, passes inspection.

Off they went, leaving behind scratches and gouges on our port side, but hey, who cared? They were doing their job, and rather cheerfully at that. They were good-natured, and maybe even cute. And *now* we could get a good night's sleep.

Enter the underwater depth charges.

* * * * *

It didn't take long to decide on a car trip inland, to have a few nights away from the navy's nocturnal pyrotechnics and to see some of Sri Lanka, the island Marco Polo called the "finest in the world."

We hired a car with a driver, because we had been warned that the roads were narrow and twisting, especially in the mountains. We could see more if someone else was doing the driving. What we hadn't been warned about were the drivers, our own included. They drove fast, with what appeared to be little regard for other living things in the streets—goats, chickens, even *children,* for heaven's sake. We had to ask our driver, more than once, to please slow down because he was scaring us. There was no other way to explain to him how worried we were about the children walking along the edges of the road.

Although not a careful driver, Martin was careful about where we were going. He listened religiously to the morning news to see if there were any "concerns" in the areas we planned to visit that day. There were numerous police patrols along the roads, and at strategic spots we were stopped at checkpoints. It did not take long for the guards to see that we could hardly be Tamil terrorists, so we were never detained.

Travel in countries at war was nothing new to us. We had spent time in Northern Ireland years before. We knew that if you exercised good judgment and listened to where locals advised you to go or not go, you were unlikely to get into trouble.

Nevertheless, I would characterize those detonations in Galle harbor as heart-stopping, and we did ask Martin very seriously if it should worry us that 134 police were killed or wounded in the northern city of Jaffna the day before.

"No," he declared, and off we drove at breakneck speed. Perhaps the question I should have asked was how many people had been killed or wounded in cars on the roads in Sri Lanka the day before.

Sri Lanka is well-known, of course, for its tea. The tea plantations covering the hills of the interior were bright green, spotted with the colorful headscarves of the women picking the leaves. We stopped to visit a tea factory and discovered that we could never have imagined what went into producing the tea bag we so casually dropped into our cup. Plucked, wilted, crushed, fermented, dried, and sorted, the tea leaves of our future made their complicated way from these luxurious fields.

We came across a few of the tea-picking ladies, who, between posing for our photos, showed us how they picked only the shoots with one rolled-up leaf and two to three unrolled leaves. As they moved through the fields, they carried their large baskets on their backs by a strap across the top of their heads. And for this backbreaking work, they were paid all of twenty cents an hour. Martin explained that it was a good job, that they were lucky to have such a job, and that they earned more money than the average Sri Lankan. Twenty cents an hour. I wondered if Martin's defensive explanation was given because he thought we would be outraged by the low wages. I wouldn't argue with him, but the tea-pickers certainly didn't make in a *month* what we were paying him for our four-day tour.

We visited a Buddhist temple with a four-story-high Buddha, and painted on the walls, a comic strip of Buddha's life. Another temple was called the Temple of the Tooth, because it allegedly contained a tooth of Buddha. The temple was so important to Buddhists that it was heavily guarded, and we had to submit to a frisking. The thing is, the tooth is so well hidden (and we don't really know if it is the real tooth or a replica) that it would have to be more trouble than it was worth to get into the vaults, or whatever it was that they hid the tooth in. But this was definitely a place where terrorists could do their thing and get a lot of mileage from it. In any case, I was fine with the frisking, as I am with all security checks anywhere in the world today. If it keeps the locals safe, the monuments intact, and me alive—body search away.

We passed by fishermen balancing on stilts, casting their lines in the surf along the coast. We saw the Kandyan dancers performing their rigorous, athletic dances, in such contrast to the subtle and genteel dancing of Thailand. There were monkeys everywhere, and evidence of elephants roaming (crushed trees, footprints, and dung). We didn't actually see any elephants, however, until we reached Pinnewala Elephant Orphanage.

Outside the elephant orphanage, there was a small monkey riding a tiny bicycle, tended by an elderly man hoping to supplement his income with tourist tips. The monkey obviously enjoyed his game, wheeling up and down the street like some kid after school. What threw me for a loop was the cigarette hanging from his lips. He stopped cycling now and then so he could put his fingers to the butt and take a puff! There are kids that do this after school too, I know, but watching this little guy I was simultaneously amused and appalled. The rascal was so, well, *human-like*.

*   *   *   *   *

In the fifth century AD, a certain King Dhatusena of Anuradhapura was overthrown by a man named Kasyapa. But old Kasyapa was afraid of the king's revenging family, so he built what he hoped would be an impregnable fortress on the rock of Sigiriya, smack dab in the middle of Sri Lanka.

The rock is 600 feet high and can be climbed today by way of a modern stairway. Arduously, we headed up to Kasyapa's summer palace at the top of the pinnacle. On the way we passed an art gallery, the walls of which were plaster made from limestone powder, termite clay, bee honey, egg white, and tree sap—not a recipe easily duplicated. The paintings on the walls were frescoes of Kasyapa's concubines, all 500 of them.

In the sixth century, after all the vengeful family fighting was over, some "tourists" came and admired the gallery of concubine frescoes. The walls of the gallery opposite the paintings had been polished to a reflective shine, and on this wall the visitors found the perfect place to express their feelings regarding the paintings: sixth-century graffiti. One of these reads, "The ladies who wear golden chains on their breasts beckon me. As I have seen the resplendent ladies, heaven appears to me as not good." (Poor chap.)

Another century later, a bunch of monks came along and turned the fortress into a monastic refuge. The monks didn't care for the pictures of women in various stages of undress, and they destroyed all but twenty-two of the lovely ladies. These paintings were above the main gallery, and at the time were inaccessible to the pernicious hands of the religious. On our way up the modern staircase, however, we had a good view of these extraordinary paintings—the oldest nonreligious paintings in Sri Lanka. The color is still lustrous, and the images and character of the women are clear.

There were 1,200 steps to the top of the rock and the palace, which was an attractive sight, but not nearly as captivating as the commanding views of the countryside surrounding Sigiriya.

* * * * *

Later, as we drove through the mountains of the central island, we stopped along the road now and then to sample the wares that the locals were proffering. How about buffalo curd? Quite delicious with a sweet tree sap poured over it. Or some sugar candy—quite like maple sugar, only, well, *different*.

As we were winding our way down the mountains, we came across a young fellow who was selling flowers. He waved and waved, pointing to his bouquet. We had no use for a bunch of flowers, so we waved back but drove on. A few minutes later, we came across another youth selling flowers. More waving. We continued to have no use for flowers, and drove on down the mountain switchbacks. A switchback or two later, here was *another* youth with flowers—but wait … he looked familiar. Indeed, he was the same young man for the third time running—literally. He had been careening straight down the hill while we had been traversing the switchbacks, meeting us at the curves in the road below. The fourth time we met him, with his beaming face and waving bouquet, well, what the heck ... flowers would be great. We couldn't resist rewarding his industry, especially when we realized he would have to climb all the way back *up* the hill to find his next victim—ah, customer.

Back in Galle we found that the depth charges continued and that the navy patrol boat weaving through the anchorage during the night now had a mounted machine gun. Perhaps it was time to leave. But I had hoped to mail a couple of letters before departing, so I took the dinghy ashore and walked to the Galle Harbor Post Office Substation to purchase the necessary stamps.

The substation was located in a small building (about ten feet square) that was either in the throes of construction or destruction—it was difficult to tell. I entered through an opening in the front façade—no door—walking into a dimly lit room with an alcove to the left, where the postmistress sat behind a rickety wooden table. She had before her a scattering of folders and a basket or two of dispatches of some sort. There were cubbyholes behind her, housing miscellaneous documents of some importance, I was sure. Although English is supposed to be the "uniting" language of the country, experience had suggested that I needed to use a lot of physical gestures for clues.

"I need stamps," I said, pointing to the upper right-hand corner of my envelopes.

"One and two," she said, with a waggle. Sri Lankans have a peculiar habit of moving their heads from side to side—not a nod, not a shake, but a waggle. This is a means of expressing not yes, not no, could be, no problem, I agree, I don't agree, maybe.

"Two," I said, making it clear I had two letters.

"One and two," waggle.

I shrugged; we were losing something here in waggles or hand gestures.

"No stamps," waggle waggle.

"You have no stamps?"

"No," waggle.

"Can I get stamps for these letters?" (Just to make sure.)

"No stamps," waggle; "one and two," waggle; "come back tomorrow," waggle waggle.

At this moment she flipped open her folders, displaying sheets of stamps.

"You have stamps," I exclaimed.

"No," waggle.

Scrutinizing the stamps in the folders, I finally got it. She had only one- and two-rupee stamps. The number of these stamps I would need for my letters would cover the whole face of the envelope, obliterating the address.

"You'll have more stamps tomorrow?" I tried.

Waggle. We were planning to leave in the morning, but for a chance to check this out, I hoped to convince Stephen to delay our departure.

And the next morning as promised, waggle, she had the stamps I needed, waggle. Would the letters arrive in the States any time in this century?

Waggle.

*   *   *   *   *

And so we departed Sri Lanka, bound for Cochin on the southwest coast of India. We sailed around the Horn of India with a full moon. It was the kind of moon you would expect to see over India—veiled, mysterious, a hot and sultry moon rising over the subcontinent.

I was just getting into this romantic vision when a small fishing boat— about eighteen feet long—came alongside. There were five men in the narrow, open boat. They appeared to be subsistence fishermen—very poor and most likely, as they indicated, very hungry.

But we had been listening to radio chat the last few weeks about "problems" in this part of the world—pirates, boardings, ugly encounters—all the sorts of things we had hoped to avoid. So when these fishermen approached us with five on board, we knew we were outnumbered, and we wondered if we should take their pleas at face value. Not that we had much choice. By then they were firmly attached to the side of our hull.

We gave them some food, and what seemed even more important to them, some fresh water. They departed. But a few minutes later another boat approached, and they had the same requests. We couldn't refuse. We had food and water, they did not. It wasn't long before several more came alongside. We were beginning to feel a little desperate. This all seemed legitimate, but how many of these fishermen were there, and could we satisfy them all?

As it turned out, no.

The next boat seemed to have a different attitude. They demanded every-thing from beer to shirts to cigarettes, as well as food and water. I gave them some food. It wasn't good enough. I gave them some water. It wasn't enough. I gave them some cigarettes and said that was all I had. They became aggressive, banging into the side of our boat. They finally made me angry, and I started yelling at them. I dare say they couldn't comprehend my words, but maybe they got the gist of my ire. There was some ranting and raving from their side.

"All we have," I yelled as emphatically as possible. Muttering. "That's it!" (Was I screaming by now? It's possible.) Off-watch and asleep, Stephen was awakened by my loud voice. He came topside to see what the trouble was. There was some grumbling from the fishing boat, and then, thankfully, they went away. Was it the appearance of a man, or my screaming that did it?

We had been traveling ten miles off the coast. The fishing boats, only eighteen feet long and barely two feet wide, seemed fragile for the open ocean. "Perhaps if we move farther offshore," Stephen suggested. We changed course, and soon found ourselves in a shipping lane with large freighters and container ships. This was not my favorite position, but bingo—no more fishing boats. Shipping lanes were not their favorite position either, apparently.

It took me hours to recover from the fishing boat confrontation. Although I was furious with the manner of the last of these fishermen, I couldn't help but sympathize with their perceptions of us. Here they were: poor, wallowing about in the seas, trying to eke out a living. And here we were in what appeared to them to be a golden vessel, carrying more food on board than they might see in a year, enough drinking water for an army, clothing for many families— riches beyond belief. Why shouldn't they ask for water if they had none, food if they were hungry, clothing if they needed it?

And thus began our lesson in Indian poverty, and our struggle in dealing with the issue. As "wealthy" as we were, we could not feed the multitudes, clothe the throngs, or supply fresh water to every being in this country. We had to make choices, harden our hearts to some pleas, continue our visit with a mind to understanding, and decide how we would make amends. A contribution to Mother Teresa's charity was recommended as a way to do something meaningful, and in the end we made that our way of helping.

*   *   *   *   *

Our landfall in India was at Cochin (also known as Kochi) on the southwest coast. It is a complicated harbor, with a narrow entrance and several islands that break up an elongated expanse of water inside. It's a little like a miniature San Francisco Bay, except there are few bridges; instead, ferries move people and goods around the harbor, as in Hong Kong. The entrance, between two peninsulas, is so narrow that we were forced to wait for a freighter to depart before we entered.

Our anchorage in Cochin was in a tight little space between Bolghatty Island and the northern end of Ernakulam, the main town of Cochin—a good anchorage where we felt it was safe to leave *Another Horizon* and take a trip inland.

We spent several days in Cochin just deciding how to approach this vast country. It's like landing in Boston and trying to decide how to experience the United States in a few days. After a long discussion with the local American Express Travel Bureau, we put together a triangle tour in the northwestern corner, the points of the triangle being Jaipur, Agra, and Delhi. To continue the U.S. analogy, it was a little like going to Portland, Spokane, and Boise, except in India we were close to a desert instead of an ocean.

Jaipur is rich with sights, sounds, and smells: red forts, silver palaces, spice markets, camel carts, snake charmers, monkeys everywhere, green and yellow fields of mustard. Jaipur is called the "pink city" because every building is supposed to be painted pink. In Rajput culture, pink is the color associated with hospitality, and one of the Maharajas had the entire town painted pink in honor of a visit by the Prince of Wales. The color is actually light and dark shades of coral and salmon, and it is stunning.

It is said that you can tell which part of India a woman is from by the way she wears her sari. In Rajasthan, Jaipur's state, they wear very simple single-colored saris that are wrapped around the body and then extended into a shawl over the head. The colors are bright—vermilion, saffron, turquoise, lilac, lime, mandarin. In the monochromatic rural areas, where everything is the dusty color of the earth, these women were brilliant flashes of color walking along the paths through the fields.

I found it curious that so many Indian men, particularly in the urban areas, have chosen to wear Western pants and shirts in shades of beige and gray, but nearly every woman wears her traditional dress. I never grew tired of examining the fabrics, the patterns, and the colors of these glorious saris.

We were driven from Jaipur to Agra in a tiny car along a narrow and very busy road. It was memorable for the local life we observed along the way. My favorite was a "camel rest stop," where we too had stopped to stretch our legs. It was like a truck stop, but for camel carts, the camels eating and drinking by the side of the road while the drivers drank coffee and traded gossip.

The drive to Agra was reportedly "only three leisurely hours"—but I think something was lost in translation. What must have been meant was that it was leisurely for the *first* three hours. Then darkness fell, and the journey turned nightmarish. Indians, like Sri Lankans, drive with wild abandon, no matter what they are driving—overloaded trucks, cars, motorcycles, camel carts, or tuk-tuks (motorized rickshaws). In addition to these varied vehicles, we shared the road with the usual cows, pigs, and pedestrians. If any of these vehicles or beings had lights (and most did not), it didn't really matter. There were as many lights broken as there were working.

Was this single light in the middle of the road bearing down on us a motor-cycle, or a car with only one light working? And since it was in the middle of the road, was it the left light or right light? Or was one light or another out of whack, and thus shining off to the side of the road? Or worse, off into the middle of the road and into the eyes of our driver. What followed our three leisurely hours was another three hours through a black tunnel of horrors.

* * * * *

Agra is the Taj Mahal. Nothing prepares you for the size of the monument, on the one hand, and the minute intricacy of its ornamentation on the other. Built by Emperor Shah Jahan for his wife, who died in childbirth, this stunning vault took twenty-one years to build (1632 to 1653). The marble is intricately carved and inlaid with silver, gold, carnelian, jasper, moonstone, jade, lapis, and coral. We arrived at the Taj about midmorning, and standing at one end of the reflecting pool, we could barely make out the huge building only yards away because of the air pollution.

The smoke from iron foundries and the locals' cooking and heating fires, burning through the night, cast a thick haze over the area. We first learned of the problem when our driver dropped us off *a mile* from the entrance. Motor vehicles were restricted in the immediate area, he said. Bad exhaust, he said. As the day wore on, however, a light breeze stirred, the haze lifted as a veil, and the sparkling magnificence of the monument appeared.

The third leg of our journey, to Delhi, was accomplished by train in the early evening. We had first-class tickets, for which we were rewarded with rock-hard seats in a long, open car; the smells of everyone else's dinner brought on board; and cockroaches. It was fortunate that American Express saw fit to have us met at the train station in Delhi. The crush of people led by porters with two and three huge suitcases piled and balanced on their heads, the noise of so many people trying to get the attention of so many other people, and the jostling of the throngs were overwhelming. We sat by the train track and waited for our escort to find us. It couldn't be hard, with our white skin and my long blond hair.

* * * * *

Delhi and New Delhi are the old and new of India. Old Delhi is a walled city built by the Mughals in the seventeenth century; New Delhi is a modern, planned city with wide streets and boulevards, built by the British in 1931 as the new capital. The best part of Delhi was our guide. Lalit had a remarkably mature personal philosophy for a man only in his early twenties. We asked if he were Muslim or Hindu, to which he answered, "I was born into a Hindu family, but I no longer believe." In a country where religion is so inextricably entwined in all aspects of people's lives, Lalit must be like an alien. Despite his religious indifference, he obviously revered Gandhi, and our visit to Gandhi's grave was like a pilgrimage.

Lalit was no starry-eyed, invincible youth, but a fellow who looked around him and realized his life in this country of economic, geographic, and social extremes was going to be no easy haul. In just the day we spent with him, we came away sympathetic and ever-so-slightly optimistic that Lalit would realize his dream—to be a politician.

* * * * *

In all of these cities—Jaipur, Agra, and Delhi—we visited a number of tourist attractions, and as a result we were exposed to hordes of touts selling everything from fake marble boxes to exquisite textiles. More difficult was the swarm of beggars who surrounded us at every stop. Our guide in Agra told us that some families deliberately deform their children in the hopes they will garner more money. One young boy scooted himself around on a board with wheels, using his hands to propel himself, his legs folded on the board at impossible angles. Could this be? It was so pitiful.

At one stop, as we alighted from the car, Stephen slipped a small coin into the hand of a young girl carrying a tiny infant. As discreet as this action was, in a second there were half a dozen more of these unfortunate women with tiny babies-in-arms surrounding us, pleading for a similar pittance. Our guide was embarrassed for us and angry with the women. He hustled us through an entrance gate where the beggars were not allowed.

We discussed this incident for days. We acknowledged a mistake on our part—giving the first woman a coin—realizing that our experience with the offshore fishermen was similar. The first boat we gave bread and water to had obviously rowed back into the pack and passed the news.

By the end of our visit to India, our whole outlook on begging had taken a strange turn. We looked at a beggar in India and finally had to accept the sight as part of that country's culture. We observed, absorbed, and compartmentalized this condition—something of which we were aware, but over which we had no control. We remembered, however, that we thought the beggars on a street corner in our hometown, Berkeley, were an eyesore, irritating, and even shocking in the sense that they still exist in a town where there seems to be an excess of everything—even beggars. In a city, a state, a country with so much material wealth, how is it we still have beggars? In Berkeley, beggars are a sorry sight. In India, beggars are a cultural phenomenon.

*   *   *   *   *

Back in Cochin, we stopped by the American Express office to tell Sanjeev, our friend there, how much we had enjoyed the trip he put together for us. He was pleased with our compliments, and returned them by asking us to his home for dinner the next night.

Sanjeev and his bride of just three months lived in a rabbit warren of bungalows near a Hindu temple. They greeted us at the end of the lane that led to their home. Sanjeev wore his workaday clothes, Western pants and shirt in beige and gray. His wife, Alpana, was lovely in a pale green sari laced with white and gold threads. Her jet-black hair was a sharp contrast to the lightness of her dress. She was a vivacious but serious woman, and a good cook. She served us food typical of Kerala, the state in which Cochin is located. Alpana had learned the recipes from Sanjeev's mother, she said, because she herself was from northern India, which has a much different cuisine.

There was fish dipped in spices and fried (spicy hot), potato curry (hot, hot), beans and coconut, rice papadams (deep-fried bread), and garlic and mango chutneys (hot, hot, hot). A cooling dish of sweet-milk noodles and curd was served for dessert. About halfway through our meal, Sanjeev disappeared momentarily and returned with several candles, which he lit and distributed around the already very warm, low-ceilinged room. The windows were closed to keep out the bugs, but there was a ceiling fan that at least moved the warm, steamy air around.

"Why the candles?" we asked.

"The electricity is about to go off," he explained, and at that, it did. The ceiling fan stopped turning and the lights went out.

"It is a conservation measure," Sanjeev said. "Every night, from eight to eight-thirty, we have no electricity."

So there we were eating hot hot food, in a hot hot room, with hot hot candles burning, in our conservative, covered-to-the-ankle, hot hot clothing. I was afraid to look at the floor for fear of seeing pools of sweat around my chair. I looked at Alpana instead. There was not a drop of moisture on her brow. She looked so sweet and sincere—in her cool green sari.

Qat and Camel Insurance

The Arabian Peninsula

On the way westward from India we crossed longitude 58 degrees, the antipodes of the longitude of San Francisco. We had sailed halfway around the world. We were in the middle of the Arabian Sea.

One night in the middle of this passage, I was down below donning my safety harness, preparatory to taking my watch, when I heard some familiar joyful squeaks. The underwater noises were audible through the hull of the boat. Climbing out the companionway, I looked out to see some splashing dolphins. We didn't often encounter dolphins moving at night. I don't know why. Perhaps they usually sleep at night too. But this night they were moving, and playing, and creating one of the most fantastic sights of the sea: the dolphins were streaking through phosphorescence. The algae that cause this iridescence in the water were especially thick that night. The dolphins were like so many phantoms as they raced to and fro, leaving ghostly trails of their wake in the phosphorescence. They came from a distance, fluttering white streamers, gathering speed, shooting toward our hull like wavering pelagic comets. They frolicked, jumping into the air with starlit bursts, puffing for air with little twinkles of light. It was magical, utterly magical.

At the end of this passage, at the other end of the Arabian Sea, we came to our first Arab country, Oman. Our harbor was in the southwest corner, at Mina Raysut. Oman was once the wealthiest country in the world, because by some quirk of nature the trees that produce frankincense grow only in that particular spot. Frankincense was one of the most sought-after substances in the ancient world; in fact, the frankincense offered to the baby Jesus was far more valuable than the gold.

After a period as an imperial power, with colonies in the Arabian Gulf, the Indian Ocean, and along the coasts of India and East Africa, Oman gradually became more isolated. Early in the twentieth century, the country was almost hermetically sealed off from the outside world. There were no paved roads, no hospitals, and no schools. The current sultan, however, has transformed the

155

country from the near-feudal state of his father's day to a modern culture. Free education, medical assistance and elder care, new roads, hospitals, and schools were just some of the many innovations of his regime, which was just twenty-five years old at the time of our visit. Everything we saw in this remarkable country was positive, clean, and seemingly prosperous. The people appeared to be quite happy with their lot in life, in part perhaps because they have been slow to allow any Western influence to creep into their lives. Oman had been open to tourists—and foreign yachts—for only a few years.

In town we hired a car and driver to show us something of the countryside. Letief drove us west along the coast and up into the mountains, where we saw Bedouins tending flocks of goats, and some of the fabled frankincense trees. The trees grow wild in *wadis* (river beds that are dry most of the year). Scrawny trees, they do not have the look of wealth, and these days they seem to have little value to anyone.

The people we met along the way were friendly but reserved. The men were tall and handsome in long flowing caftans, or *thobs,* and loosely tied turbans. Women were scarcer than grass in the surrounding desert, but when seen, they looked like specters of death. They walked swiftly through alleyways in their long black robes and mysterious black veils covering everything, even their eyes.

In one village I spotted a small group of men, resplendent in white thobs and colorful turbans. I asked Letief if he thought they would allow me to take a photograph of them. Letief looked doubtful.

"Could you ask?" I pleaded. "Tell them that I want my friends at home to see their native dress, if you think that would appeal to them." Letief spent a few minutes talking to my subjects while I stayed at a respectful distance.

I could understand Letief's reluctance to ask my favor. Oman is a conservative Islamic country, and as we had already observed, women were rarely seen outside the home. They wore their burqas everywhere. They had no place in the streets, shops, or anywhere else outside their homes. Although I was dressed in my dreary black pants and white long-sleeved shirt, with long black socks and closed-toed shoes, I was still out of place with my uncovered white face, long blond hair, and white hands gripping a *camera.* I didn't hold out much hope.

After many minutes, Letief returned to us and told me that the men had decided I could take a picture of one of them, to show my friends about their clothing, but that was all.

"Fine, wonderful," I said. "That's all I want." Because the designated subject was in the shade, I motioned for him to move a few feet into the sun. He did so, and I fussed around posing him, getting my camera set, the right light reading, focusing. "Okay, ready." And there in my viewfinder were *four* men standing together, hands on each other's shoulders, smiling. I could have burst out laughing. They couldn't resist. It was too much for just the one to be so prized. I took several photos, moving my telephoto in for some close-ups. It was over in a few seconds, and I don't think they realized I had taken a half-dozen photos instead of one. I asked Letief to thank them, to tell them how pleased I was. I really was thrilled. And they looked so happy to accommodate me!

This reluctance to be photographed was the norm in Islamic countries, and I never wanted to go against their wishes. I always asked permission to take a photo, and I was turned down about half the time, mostly by women. Quite often, however, my experience was much like this one. The men and women were hesitant, but if just one of them said yes, others were quick to follow. This was not a place where there is concern for one's soul being snatched away by the camera, or that the camera is an "evil eye." Mostly the people were simply so conservative, and shy, that having their photo taken made them uncomfortable.

In the Raysut area of Oman there were about as many camels as there were people. The vast, flat, brown plain we drove along was studded with them. Like cows in India, they roam freely, even down the middle of the highway. As Letief drove us back into town late that afternoon, we watched as some internal clock seemed to signal the camels that it was time to migrate from the beaches on the south side of the highway to the wadis on the north side. One moment they were on our left, and the next moment the whole herd began streaming across the road in their slow, ambling gait, intent on their goal but in no great hurry to get there. Their progress brought the normally whizzing traffic to a comparatively slow pace.

"It's not good to hit one," Letief said. The camels all belong to someone, he explained, and if you damage this property you must compensate the owner. "If you kill one, it costs about five thousand dollars." (*Let alone the damage to you and your car,* I thought). "Of course, your insurance will take care of it," he added. Ah, we mused, a new concept in car insurance: do you have camel coverage?

* * * * *

We left Oman, sliding down the south end of the Arabian Peninsula, into the Gulf of Aden, and on to Aden, Yemen. Yemen is one of the oldest inhabited regions in the world, with a history dating back to the dawn of humankind. In modern times, it has been occupied by the Portuguese, the Turks, and the British. Even with independence after World War I, it remained a suppressed culture. More recently there had been a series of seemingly unending wars between the north and the south sections of the country.

As we turned into the harbor we could see forts, bunkers, and gun emplacements on every promontory of land. Even from a distance, the rubble and bombed-out, abandoned buildings were depressing to see. The two Yemens were united in 1990, but the armies of the north and south continued to battle it out until 1995, when the southern area around Aden defected. The wars devastated the economy, the countryside, and the people. Partly as a result, Yemen is one of the world's poorest countries.

We had been looking forward to seeing some of the ancient sites in Yemen, but several incidents of tourists being kidnapped quelled our enthusiasm. We contented ourselves with a little tour of Aden instead, again hiring a car and driver.

As we settled into the car for our tour, Hassan held up a small branch with bright green leaves. "Qat," he said. I had read about this plant. It's like kava in the South Pacific and betel nut in Southeast Asia—a mild narcotic. It's chewed something like tobacco, in the pouch of the cheek. As the afternoon wore on, more and more leaves disappeared into Hassan's cheek, until the accumulation looked like a huge growth. And the more leaves that went in, the slower his driving became. Toward the end of the afternoon I began to wonder if we would make it back to the wharf—going five miles an hour!

Like addictive drugs in other cultures, qat has become a menace in Yemen. As unemployment has grown, qat use has as well, and it is not a cheap treat. Like alcohol consumed by our homeless, it costs money that the men do not have. In many cases more than 25 percent of a qat chewer's income may be spent on the plant. At last back at the wharf, we left our driver with the fervent hope that he used *some* of his financial gain from us that day to provide for his family.

In the following days we attempted to prepare ourselves for the Red Sea. Our two anxieties for this transit were fuel and food. In order to mitigate the fuel problem, we decided to top off our tanks in Aden.

We took the boat over to the fuel dock at 8 AM, the time we understood it to be open, and tied up. We waited. Nothing happened; no one appeared. Around 8:30, Stephen decided to scout around. He found a man, also wandering around, who pointed him to a building toward the street. Stephen wandered the halls of this building, eventually finding the office of the Assistant Director of Bunkering (ADB). The ADB asked Stephen how much fuel we needed—in imperial gallons. Forgetting, if he ever knew, what the conversion from imperial to U.S. gallons is, Stephen returned to the boat to look it up. (One imperial gallon equals 1.2 U.S. gallons.) Back to the ADB, whom he found gazing out the window. Without turning around, the ADB told Stephen to return to the boat. Another half hour passed.

Frustrated, Stephen began the trek back to the ADB office. On the way he met a friendly taxi driver (FTD) we had met the day before. The FTD went with Stephen to the ADB, and a rapid conversation in Arabic ensued. Finally the taxi driver turned aside to Stephen and said quietly, "He wants backsheesh." Of course! We would not be served until this "tip" was proffered. How stupid of us. Stephen whisked out a five-dollar bill.

The ADB wrote out a note with our boat name, nationality, the number of imperial gallons we wished to purchase, and a bunch of other numbers that meant nothing at the time. The FTD took Stephen to yet another building, where they found the financial office to pay for the fuel—in advance. More forms were filled out—with six carbon copies—and Stephen paid in American dollars. No other currency was acceptable. Stephen and the FTD returned the financial forms to the ADB, who gave them to a typist to prepare yet another form and once again commanded Stephen to return to the boat.

It was nearly 11 AM by the time the fuel pump attendants arrived. The three of them stood around talking in confusing streams of Arabic. The tone of their voices suggested a problem. The FTD finally informed us that the pump was locked and none of the attendants had the keys. They would go get them. More waiting. A half hour later the attendants returned without the keys, smashed the valve open with a rock, and proceeded to fill our tank. We watched. Even if we could have commented on this action, we definitely would have remained silent. Never question ingenuity when it is producing something you want.

Unfortunately, the tanks were full at less than the amount Stephen estimated we would need. So we had paid too much.

"We have to go back to the offices," our FTD told us. At the office of the ADB another form was filled out with the amount of fuel "delivered" in metric tons, specific gravity, delivery temperature, viscosity, and flash point. Stephen signed the form and returned to the financial office, where an assistant signed a receipt and gave him his change. Stephen handed it all to the FTD. Although backsheesh is usually given *before* the event, and although it was clear the FTD wasn't expecting any compensation for his time (a rare event itself in the Arab commercial world), it was also clear that without this smiling, amiable person, we would never have managed the transaction. He was worth all the dollars Stephen had in his pocket.

Back at the fuel dock, I greeted Stephen with the news that the fuel dock attendants were requesting backsheesh as well. We should have known. This backsheesh business would become commonplace, and we would learn to ante up right away if we expected anything to happen anywhere. That was the way it worked.

Westerners often balk at the backsheesh game. It doesn't seem right to us to give a tip before the service is rendered. But we didn't mind. It was part of the culture and we were happy to comply. It was just hard to remember.

With our fuel tanks full, we went off to town in search of fresh food. Our travels in Oman and Yemen made it quite clear that we were near a desert. Only 200 miles north of Oman is the Empty Quarter, so positively uninhabitable that no one goes there, and the countries that abut the area don't even care who owns it. There are no border wars here—the borders are "undefined." There is nothing about the Arabian Peninsula that suggests green leafies, ripe tomatoes, or even real potatoes or onions. Dates, maybe?

"Oh yes," another FTD informed us, "let me show you," and off we went to the date market.

I always thought dates were dates. How uninformed was I. There are Yemeni dates, Omani dates, Saudi dates, Iranian dates, and so on, and they do not look (and especially do not taste) anything like one another. Size, color, texture, sweetness, and tenderness (or lack thereof) vary enormously. We set about tasting. The date guy was very patient, letting us sample one from every country. I chose to buy some from Yemen (which seemed only fair), some from Oman, a small batch from Saudi Arabia, and a handful from Iraq (because they were the sweetest). Dried fruit lasts forever, and dates, date cookies, date bars, dates on cereal, dates and coffee would do very nicely as we made our way up the Red Sea.

"Other fruit?" I asked the FTD hopefully.

"Of course," and off we went again to a fruit and vegetable market. Despite the Empty Quarter and excessive dry heat, lack of water, and wretched soil, the wadi valleys to the east are somehow successfully cultivated to the extent that Yemen is known as the "green land" of Arabia. The variety of fruits and vegetables in the market was more extensive than I had been led to expect. I happily put eggplant, figs, melons, carrots, avocados, peppers, garlic, and cabbage into our canvas grocery bag. But there was no lettuce, spinach, or tomatoes. We could forgo these delicacies for another two months. As in the South Pacific, we grabbed what fresh food we could, and hoped that over the many months, the vitamins, minerals, fibers, and whatevers would distribute themselves in some healthful way. To tell the truth, I never thought about whether we were eating healthfully or not. We simply ate what was before us.

Contrary Governments, Friendly People

The Red Sea

We had long anticipated that the charge up the Red Sea would be the most difficult part of the circumnavigation. Contrary winds and seas swoop down its length, and contrary nations line either side. The weather we figured we could handle; it was the ever-changing political climate that worried us. The moment the first yacht began this transit, our radio was abuzz with stories: boats were being detained, boats were being asked to leave, boats were being boarded by the military, boats were being shot at.

We already knew that Saudi Arabia was not friendly to foreign yachts, and that was quickly confirmed by the first yacht that tried to sail up the east side of the sea. The yacht put into a Saudi port and was asked to leave immediately. They asked for 24 hours to put on fuel and get some water. They were refused. International maritime law says that any vessel can stay in any port for 24 hours for emergencies. This yacht had no water and had no means of obtaining any, but they were told they couldn't stop in Saudi Arabia for any reason. So our strategy was to hug the west side, going as far and as fast as we could while we had southerly winds. But first we had an important stop to make.

* * * * *

Eritrea, a long, thin country that lines the southwestern shore of the Red Sea, had been at war with Ethiopia for thirty years, a war that ended with Eritrean independence just four years prior to our visit. The year before our visit, the crews of two yachts had been arrested and detained in Eritrea for nearly two months, apparently because they had not checked into the country properly. To avoid such an incident we stopped at Assab, the southernmost port, to report to the authorities.

But the officials didn't know what to do with us. We couldn't tell if it was a case of new personnel who didn't know what they were doing, or whether there were some new regulations with which they were grappling. We insisted we needed some kind of document that would make us safe while we traversed their coastline. They kept saying it wasn't necessary. We were not going to leave, we said, until we had some paper spelling out that it was all right for us to travel along their coastline and to anchor in their bays. We ended up with a "transit visa" that was good for only seven days and wasn't supposed to be good for anywhere but Assab. Since as far as we could tell it didn't say anywhere on the paper that it wasn't good for anywhere else, we had to hope that it would be protection enough.

That night the winds came up from the southeast, and our anchorage was unprotected. We spent a hideous night bucking in choppy water and wishing for daylight, so that we could leave. Although the southerly winds were uncomfortable in the anchorage, they would be favorable winds for our passage along the coast of Eritrea—we would be flying.

In the morning as we sailed north, however, the southerly wind strengthened, and ten-foot waves came up directly behind us. The trick in these conditions was to maintain a speed to keep pace with the waves and ride with them—just like surfing, if you will. But every once in a while the rhythm changed and we got caught under the lip of the wave, and the crest of water came on board. On one such occasion the wave came horizontally into and across the cockpit, down the companionway, and into the cabin, drenching the on-watch person on the way. Unfortunately, the cockpit port to our sleeping cabin was open, and a portion of the wave flew through, drenching the snoozing off-watch person in the bunk as well. There are few things worse than being awakened by a bucket of water, but one of them is finding yourself in a salt-water-soaked bed.

We stopped the next day in an anchorage behind a small, flat island. There was no protection from the wind, but the water was calm. I hung out the soggy bedclothes, which the hot desert wind dried in minutes. We were both upset by the rough passage, and pissed about the errant wave drenching us. It was the first time in months that sailing had been "bad."

"Oh, all's well that ends well," I postulated.

"I'll be happier when we are secure in Israel," grumbled Stephen.

"Yeah, yeah, but I tell you what: we've got a *long* way to go before we see Israel."

The opening paragraph of the weather section of our Red Sea pilot manual reads, "The Red Sea is notorious for its weather. Headwinds, rough seas, poor visibility, sand and dust storms, mirror calms, rapid and unpredictable changes; something for everyone to hate." We would experience every one of these conditions over the course of our passage. We were hating it already, and we'd only been in it two days.

We next put the anchor down in the northernmost port of Eritrea: Massawa. In Massawa the ravages of the Eritrean war of independence were fully evident. There were dozens of bombed-out shells of buildings, and walls spotted with bullet holes. Enough of the old town was left, however, to sense what a beautiful place it once was, with a combination of Moorish and Italian architecture. Eritrea, and some of the surrounding area, was an Italian colony through the Second World War, and we could still get a cup of real cappuccino in any one of the dozens of cafés that lined the streets. Cappuccino in Africa!

It had been weeks since we had had a meal off the boat, so when we heard of a restaurant along the waterfront where the food was passable, we went ashore to try a little of the local cuisine. And I made a stupid mistake. I ordered the "green" salad. It sounded, and looked, so good—fresh lettuce, tomatoes, carrots, onions … But I forgot: never, *never* should one have any fresh food that isn't peeled or cooked to a pulp in a country where sanitary conditions are suspect. Never, *never* should one have fresh food that might have been washed in the local water.

I was sick for days, and I hated myself for being such a fool. I put it out on the radio: watch out for the green stuff. But others were suckered in just as I had been. Even with my warning, they forgot, their eyes gleaming at the sight of fresh green leaves. One after another they were felled. If I hadn't known how awful they felt, I might have been amused.

*   *   *   *   *

The border between Eritrea and the Sudan, to the north, was still in dispute, and our cruising notes advised us to stay at least five miles offshore in the border area so as not to cause the naval patrols of these two countries any anxieties. We decided to double that five miles, to be on the safe side. We kept the radar on, which outlined the land on the screen and made it possible to keep an accurate course at least ten miles off the coast. We were traveling in the company of two other boats and traveling at night, when we thought the military would be less likely to be out and about.

Wrong. About midnight our radio crackled to life. The boat two miles ahead of us reported that they had been approached by a "heavily armed" Eritrean military boat and had been boarded, but that the encounter was "friendly enough." (It was not possible to interrogate our friends over the radio as to what "friendly enough" really meant. You never knew what might be heard, understood, or misunderstood, or by whom.)

Just at that moment we picked up two unidentified blips on the radar, half a mile from us and closing. Looking out over the water in the direction of the blips we could see no lights, but on the radar we could easily see that one of the blips was heading for the boat close behind us, and the other one was coming our way.

Suddenly, the boat behind us by a mere quarter of a mile flipped on its masthead strobe light—a signal of distress. We called them on the radio. Were they all right? "We are being shot at." The tension in Stan's voice was palpable. We asked Stan if he could tell if the guns were in the air (perhaps they were just trying to get his attention) or leveled at him. He said he had turned on his spotlight briefly and the guns were aimed at the boat. His decision was to keep going, full throttle.

"We'll stand by," we said, as we watched the radar blips. There was one still coming at us. How could we know whether this would be a "friendly enough" encounter, or whether guns would be leveled at us too?

Stephen and I discussed the possibilities as calmly as if we were discussing where to anchor, but I could detect an edge in his voice, and my mouth had gone cotton-dry. I did not fancy imprisonment in this country, and I was not prepared to have guns leveled at us. I did not think we wanted to take the risk of allowing a heavily armed boat without lights to get close enough to us to determine if its crew was going to be friendly or not. But would we have a choice?

I looked again at the radar to check our position. We were twelve and a half miles offshore. This wasn't supposed to happen here! But it wasn't the first time that we experienced a change in the "rules." *Contrary climates,* we said, and we were not talking weather.

Suddenly the "lightless" blips on the radar turned aside and headed back toward shore. A half hour later we were north of the border and into Sudanese waters. We surmised that our pursuers were not interested in encountering any Sudanese "blips." And although we kept a constant watch on the radar, no other blips of any sort appeared. We breathed a sigh of relief as dawn began to light the sky. I don't know why, but somehow heavily armed boats in the daylight were easier to contemplate that those lightless blips in the black of night.

We learned on the radio that morning that the Eritrean military authorities were asking vessels to stay *thirteen* miles offshore, information that was a day late and a half-mile short for us.

And so, in the end, it did not appear that we needed the transit visa we had spent so much energy acquiring in Assab, but who cared? We felt safer, and we worried less—except that last night. If we had been boarded, would the paper have helped? Who knew? And we were thankful not to have had that matter tested.

*   *   *   *   *

If there were any country where we might have worried about our reception, it would have been in the Sudan. In addition to their border war with Eritrea, the Sudan was in the midst of a civil war between the non-Muslim south and the ruling Muslim north. The fighting had uprooted millions, brought farming to a standstill, and caused the disintegration of whole communities and towns. Famine and disease were rampant. For whatever reason, the United States had been supporting the rebels attempting to overthrow the government. And to put the icing on this situation, our Secretary of State, just days before our arrival, gave an inflammatory speech, broadcast on the Voice of America, lambasting the government of Sudan for harboring terrorists and for their deplorable human rights violations. All of this was true, and her speech was no doubt good policy, but we wished she had waited until *we* were somewhere else.

Furthermore, we had just heard that the American Embassy in Khartoum had sent home its staff, that airlines were canceling all flights to the Sudan, and that any casual visiting of the country had come to a virtual halt. Why would we run any further risk? Hadn't we had enough the night before along the border?

The radio the next morning was abuzz. Calls were zinging back and forth about the military encounters. Since we were generally ahead of the main pack of boats making the passage through the Red Sea, our experiences were helpful to those behind us. Thankfully, we were not at the very head of the pack, however, and we found that two American yachts were in the port of Suakin (in the Sudan) already, and had found a friendly reception. We would carry on—no reason not to, right?

Suakin was once an important commercial center, and in the nineteenth century it was a major slave-trading port, the trading having ended, so we were told, in the early 1950s. Only weeks after our visit here we read articles about the Sudanese slave trade continuing in other parts of the country. There was a group from the States actively "buying" the young women and children in order to return them to their villages and freedom—only to discover that the same women and children were being sold again a few weeks later.

As we entered the port, the ruins of the old city were on our right. The entire city had been built of coral blocks, a lovely, light honey beige color. Arched doorways, wrought iron grillwork, tiles, and carved lintels still stood amid the rubble.

On our left, in stark contrast, was the new commercial port, where huge ferries from Jedda, Saudia Arabia, landed. The ferries transported the Islamic faithful from East Africa on their pilgrimage to Mecca, just inland from the Saudi seaport. One ferry had just disgorged a throng of returning pilgrims with huge piles of baggage: bedding, pots and pans, tents, and all the other paraphernalia of their journey.

We were so enthralled with what we were seeing, left and right, that we almost ran into a sand spit that nearly closes off the tiny small-boat harbor beyond it. Just in time we pulled to the right and squeezed between the sand spit and the edge of the ruined city, with only a couple of feet to spare on either side. We anchored, but decided to remain on board to rest and recover from the short, but exhausting passage. I couldn't resist taking up the binoculars, though, and peering at the activity onshore. I thought I was looking through the wrong end of a spyglass.

Everything I saw came from another century, another time—oh, say, about the time of Jesus. There was Mary—can you believe it?—in her blue robe and white headscarf. And who was that riding the donkey down the dusty street? He was leading another donkey whose back was piled high with kindling. I had it all wrong, of course. The Muslim minaret peeking up over the town ruins was enough to tell me that.

The next day we hopped ashore. We walked the dusty streets, met "Mary" and "Joseph" and several shepherds, all in long beige robes (Mary notwithstanding) and dusty turbans. If I had been even slightly more observant, I would have noticed that there were no women except for "Mary," who turned out to be a young girl with a white shawl completely covering her head and shoulders, her olive-skinned face peering out. The men and "Mary" were in a market area selling vegetables, coffee, wood for kindling, and dried beans. They watched us—somber, not offering their wares to us, somehow knowing we wouldn't be buying.

And then we crossed some invisible line and found people as different in appearance as I could imagine. Black-skinned—not tawny, coffee, mocha, or any of those other colors we associate with Blacks, but truly *black* black. The men wore loose pants and shirts, and jaunty hats; the women were in gaily colored patterned-cloth dresses with bare heads, or with a bright color-coordinated scarf worn loosely over the top of the head. All were in marked contrast to their neighbors across the street. These colorful folks were members of nomadic tribes who had come from the desert to buy and sell their wares too. The faces of the men were scarred, according to their tribal tradition; they rode camels and they carried long, lethal-looking swords strapped to their waists. They all smiled and laughed, gesturing expectantly to their wares, which as far as we could tell were exactly the same stuff as on the "other side."

Along with many other anomalies in this place, Suakin was unusual for the Arab Muslims and the South African Blacks coexisting—separately, to be sure, but still on the same turf. We bought beans and eggplant from both sides. But only on the tribal side could we bargain for a souvenir sword, encased in a beautifully tooled leather scabbard.

*   *   *   *   *

Along the west side of the Red Sea there are a number of *marsas*, small bay-like cuts in the sand and rock that are beautifully protected from the seas, although the wind blows across them off the flat coastal plain. Small passes through rocky reefs supply entrances to these havens. Marsa Fijab, 60 miles north of Suakin, was such a place. It was peaceful enough that we decided to rest there a day or two.

The surrounding terrain was desolate, dry, and brown—definitely camel country. The coastal plain ran dozens of miles inland to the mountains in the distance. There were nesting ospreys, egrets, and ibis along the shore. The wind was blowing hard (no more reason needed to rest a day or two), but the water in the marsa was utterly flat.

About noon of the first day we heard a thump on the hull and a tapping. Topside we found Sharif, a twenty-something Sudanese who spoke remarkable English. He was paddling on an old surfboard, broken in several places but pieced together with some twine. We invited him on board.

He handed us some fresh eggs. We were astonished. "I just wanted to give you something," he said quietly, a little shyly.

Was there something we might have that we could give him in return? we asked.

"Coffee? Flour?" Of course, we had plenty to share.

Sharif was a camel herder in the winter and a fisherman in the summer. We could just make out his camels on the far shore. Somewhat surprisingly (to us), it wasn't long before our conversation turned to governments. "Everyone hates the Sudan government," Sharif confessed, "which makes things difficult for the Sudanese people." As good as his English was, we weren't sure we could get into the fine points of why other governments "hate" the Sudan government. I decided it would be best to say that people were different than governments, and we could be friends. Sharif beamed. Contrary nations, perhaps, but very friendly people.

*   *   *   *   *

Contrary winds, however, had been giving us a hard time. We tried to leave our anchorages at first light—before the wind had a chance to build—scurry as fast as we could for a few hours, and tuck into another anchorage before things got too rough. In the northern half of the sea we were motoring most of the time against the wind and the seas, and it was becoming a long slog. Suddenly, as we neared the Sudan/Egypt border, we got a break: no wind and absolutely flat seas. We revved up the engine, crossed an area that was usually like its name (Foul Bay), and just as the high winds and seas returned, put down the anchor. We were in Egypt, which was friendly with the United States—wasn't it?

We anchored near a military base, and a small horde of young men came out to check our papers. It took about a half hour to sort out our clearances from Yemen, Eritrea, and Sudan, together with our Egyptian visa, which did not look familiar to them. The process was protracted because they kept trying to read the papers upside down. We passed around a bowl of popcorn, and taking the papers as they grasped the bowl, we flipped them right side up before giving them back. In the end it didn't seem to matter. A couple of *shukrans* (thank-yous) and a cigarette or two, and they were all smiles. We had read that these military outposts are manned by the Egyptian youngsters who have more recently joined the service. And yes, they were so young, and trying so hard to do their job right. At least they were not sporting any weapons.

*   *   *   *   *

About 210 miles south of the Suez Canal is a medium-sized town called Safaga, which has a growing tourist trade for European scuba divers. It was a convenient stop for yachts going up the Red Sea to get some fresh provisions and, more importantly, to replenish the fuel supply. It was also the closest spot on the Red Sea for us to reach the upper Nile Valley. We took advantage of this with a trip to Luxor, Karnak, and the Valleys of the Kings and Queens. Such extraordinary sights! Tombs of pharaohs, temples of queens, temples within temples, where the inner temples are large enough in themselves to house Notre Dame Cathedral. The reliefs and paintings, hieroglyphics, cartouches, sarcophagi, and obelisks were pages of ancient history leaping out at us. For a change of pace we engaged a felucca, the distinctive Egyptian sailboat—heavy, wooden, and awkward-looking, with a tall lateen rig and an enormous rudder.

We set sail on the Nile. Could we have imagined years before that we would sail on the Nile?

The unique part of this trip to the Nile Valley was traveling in a convoy of cars, trucks, and buses—mostly tourist buses. As a result of terrorist attacks on tourists, the Egyptian government had set up the convoys, escorted by armed military personnel, to give tourists some semblance of safety as they traveled to the tourist sights. It was very clear to us that any band of terrorists could just as easily wreak havoc on the convoys, especially since the escorts kept falling behind or breaking down. But we decided to put that out of our minds and enjoy the scenery. The desert, as we traveled south, had its own peculiar beauty, and the transition to the fertile valley of the Nile came with startling suddenness. And I tell you what: there are one thousand minarets between Safaga and Luxor, and as we drove back at night they were all lit with neon lights. Since little else was electrified, the towers pierced the darkness like glowing pickets.

* * * * *

We returned to Safaga and our dreadfully dirty little floating home. The salt content of the Red Sea is extraordinarily high, and the boat was caked with it. The lines were so stiff with salt that they would no longer bend, except by force. On top of the salt were layers of fine grit (dirt and sand) that had blown off the desert. If there was any moisture in the air at all—and as weather fronts occasionally moved through the area, there were brief moments of humidity— the salt absorbed the moisture, turning the grit to mud that we would track all over the boat as we moved around. We longed for a marina with abundant fresh water. It would take bathtubs-full to leach the salt from the lines, but just to wash the boat ... sigh, we had to wait.

We finally arrived at the southern entrance to the Suez Canal in the middle of April. All in all, we called our passage up the sea successful—notwithstanding a few lightless blips, errant waves, and a sandstorm or two.

* * * * *

Cairo was within easy reach of our Suez anchorage, so we took a short inland trip to see the city and the pyramids of Saqarra, Memphis, and Giza. Another day we wandered in "old" Cairo. We passed through Bab Zuweila, one of the original gates of the old walled city, built in 1092, and walked along the narrow streets where people were weaving, sewing, caning, making furniture and tents as they had for centuries. The perfumes of the spice market were intoxicating. Walking along the streets with us were men and women carrying everything imaginable piled on their heads—jugs, furniture, even room-size carpets. One fellow came along on a bicycle, with a board at least as long as he was tall and about four feet wide balanced on his head, and piled high with *hundreds* of small loaves of flat bread.

Within minutes of entering the old Cairo, Hussan came to our side. He was about twenty, nicely dressed in Western clothing, and his English was excellent. He would like to guide us through the markets, he said.

"We don't need a guide today, thank you," I said.

"What are you looking for?"

"We're just wandering," I said.

"I want a kaftan," Stephen said. Well, that did it. "Kaftan" was all Hussan needed to hear.

"I know the best places for kaftans. I'll take you."

"No, that's all right. We're just wandering," I persisted.

"But the tailors are not here," Hussan persisted too. "I'll show you where."

"We'll find them ourselves, thank you." I kept on walking.

Stephen was agitated by my resistance. "Oh, come on, let's go with him," he murmured. Two to one, so I gave in. "But only the kaftan," I said.

Hussan was eager: "I'll show you everything in the market."

"No, only what we want to see." I was trying to be adamant.

"Oh, yes, madam, only where you want to go."

He did take us to the tailors for kaftans and to the spice vendors, and to the tent makers and the fabric places, all places I confessed I wanted to see. But he also took us to his brother-in-law's inlaid box "factory," and his favorite lunch place (where I'm sure he got a kickback for bringing us). But we ended up buying him lunch, because he really was a nice fellow—engaging, smart, with a nice sense of humor. I ended up liking him, despite the inlaid box factory—where I bought four.

Later in the day, after Hussan had left us, we shopped in the markets for more gifts. One stall had a handsome display of hammered metal objects. I picked out one wastebasket-type item in pseudobrass, and began the bargaining process. My adversaries were two youths not even in their teens. I decided that Papa had left them in charge while he went for coffee, or some such fantasy. I bargained hard, talking them down from $10 to less than half that. It was probably not worth even half the price I paid, but I felt we'd done the ritual, and I was pleased enough with the result.

The young shopkeepers wrapped the item in newspaper and presented it to me with a great flourish. "*Shokran* (thanks)." And then the elder of these boys held out his hand, palm up, and brushed the thumb over the tips of his fingers (universal sign for moolah, or in Arabic—backsheesh). I was incredulous!

"You've got to be kidding! I just paid you a good price for this piece of gold-colored tin," I exploded. "I don't owe you any more! You haven't done me any service!" I was mad. The boys dropped their hands and backed up a pace or two. I don't know if they were truly abashed—that it wasn't right, their asking for more—or whether they were simply taken aback by my aggressive manner. But this was the first time we had ever encountered such a request, and I just figured it was kids being kids—let's see if we can get a little on the side. Later I felt stupid about the exchange. What were they asking for? Sixty, seventy cents? And I realized that I still didn't fully understand the intricacies of backsheesh, and decided I probably never would.

*   *   *   *   *

So here it was mid-April, and the Son of the Prince of the Red Sea came to tell us that there was a holiday in the next few days, so they were stepping up our transit of the Canal. The Prince of the Red Sea Shipping Agency made it their business to take care of the small-boat traffic transiting the Suez Canal from the south. They saw to our customs clearance, pilotage dues, security clearance certificate, and tonnage certificate; deposited our transit fees in the appropriate bank account; obtained the necessary Egyptian insurance policy; paid the port dues; and, most importantly, hired and assigned the pilots necessary to take us through the Canal. The Prince was now aging and preferred his son, Heebi, to do all the running around.

Heebi informed us we would start through the next day. We were taken by surprise. We hadn't done anything about food, water, or fuel, and we were running low on all three. But we looked carefully and realized that if we were prudent, we wouldn't have a problem. The canal transit would be two days, and we hoped to carry on to Israel in the following two days. So, four days.

We always had enough vittles on board that we wouldn't starve—rice, flour, beans, lentils, that sort of thing, were in abundance. The fresh fruit and vegetables we had hoped to take on, we'd have to forget. We could manage the water; there was always the watermaker once we were out of the Canal. Fuel. Now *that* we worried about. Whenever we started a passage, especially if we knew we would have to use the engine for extended periods, we wanted to be sure the tank was full. Heebi came to our rescue and brought several cans of diesel that gave us some assurance, even if it didn't fill the tank.

Several yachts would make the transit with us, and in the morning the air was thick with anticipation as we all adjusted lines, pulled up our dinghies, looked at the wind indicators (hoping for something light), and waited for our pilots to show up.

There are no locks in the Suez; it is just a ditch, not quite 100 miles long. Large vessels can accomplish the transit in a day, but at our more limited speed it would take two days, with an overnight stop at Ismailia. It is obligatory to have a pilot on board in the Canal, and we had heard horror stories about their greed and incompetence: pilots who took over the wheel, ran boats aground, and overtaxed engines by going too fast. Stephen prepared his sternest "I am captain" look as we welcomed Abdel on board.

We were pleasantly surprised when Abdel turned out to be a wonderful pilot. His watch over our movement along the Canal was interrrupted only at the appropriate times by his prayers. He went forward to the foredeck, the only place with enough room to get down on his knees, and facing east he brought his forehead to the deck and said his prayers.

The pilot for the second day was not so religious and not so gentlemanly. He was loud, boisterous, and flamboyant. He guided us through to the end of the Canal well enough, but he seemed more interested in what videos, cigarettes, and U.S. dollars he could extract from us.

We asked Ahmed about the "third pilot" that we had heard might try to board us at Port Said.

"No need," Ahmed said. "I will make sure."

"We are not stopping at Port Said," we made clear.

"Okay, I will take care of the third pilot." Ahmed discreetly extended his hand palm up. We deposited a few dollars to ensure we would not have to deal with the third pilot. At that moment the pilot pickup boat came alongside, and Ahmed jumped aboard, loaded to the gills with our cigarettes, videotapes, and dollars.

We powered ahead toward the channel through the Said waters, confident we could proceed unhindered. Another pilot boat approached. We kept our course. They came alongside, calling for us to stop. "No pilot," we yelled.

"Yes, must have pilot here."

"No, no pilot" (and where was Ahmed—with the extra dollars to "take care" of the third pilot?). We tried, but we could not outmaneuver them. Even while we continued apace, the pilot boat kept at our side and the third pilot leaped on board.

"We don't need a pilot here," we kept reiterating.

"Yes, if you go through Port Said, you must."

He was wearing us down. "How much?" we relented.

"Twenty dollars will be enough, but some pay me fifty."

The audacity! I was getting close to another explosion, but this was not a couple of kids in the market. And what were we going to do with this guy *on* the boat? We were *so* close to making our way into the Mediterranean. So, with four crisp, new five-dollar bills (our last) in his hand, we dumped the guy back onto the pilot boat.

My conclusion about our experience of the last few weeks was that Egyptians are really quite admirable and friendly people, even if they are always trying to fleece you.

Free of the Canal and Port Said, we turned right and set our course for Israel.

The Watchers

Israel

It was just daylight when over the VHF radio we heard, "Any sheep, any vessel that is 35 miles west of Ashkelon, please call Israel Navy." Sheep? Could that be us? Well, we were 35 miles west of Ashkelon. And it's possible that "sheep" and "ship" were one and the same. We responded.

We were asked a number of questions: vessel name, description, country, number of people on board, and where we were headed. Later, 17 miles off Ashkelon, an armed navy ship came by, circled around us, and hailed us on the radio. They asked many of the same questions. The radio operator apologized. "I know you have been asked these questions before. I hope you don't mind." Heavens, no, whatever you need. In a few minutes he said that was all. "Welcome to Israel," and they sped away.

It was a curious introduction to a very curious country. Straight up front we were dealing with a country possessing what must be a very powerful, tall radar to be able to detect our relatively tiny presence 35 miles offshore. That's over the horizon, at sea level. And then there was a face-to-face inspection far enough offshore to be sure that our relatively tiny presence didn't suggest any huge threat to their coastline. My thinking at that moment was something like: *one look at us and you have to know we don't pose a threat.* My thinking on this matter was very naïve.

We squeezed through the narrow entrance to a new marina development at Ashkelon and tied up at their arrival dock as instructed. Within seconds, the marina manager greeted us and asked us to please remain on board until the "bomb squad" came to inspect our vessel. The bomb squad turned up shortly, in the form of a young uniformed man who stepped aboard, shook our hands, and said, "I'm sorry. I'm sorry we have to do this."

"No need to apologize," we said, *and in any case we are quite used to military inspections.* His inspection was swift—not exactly thorough, but not exactly superficial, either. (We heard later that less tidy yachts were given a longer and more careful inspection.) The more time we spent in this country, the more we realized the importance of their vigilance. They could not afford to accept *anything* at face value.

The military presence was all-pervasive; evidence of the Israelis' vigilance was everywhere. We saw schoolchildren on a field trip, escorted by parents, just as we would chaperon our children on such a trip—but these parents were armed with rifles. The schools keep the weapons in their closets, as our schools might keep soccer balls, to "outfit" their chaperons. Every Israeli adult knows how to use guns as a result of the two- to three-year military service required of men and women alike. The country is swarming with young people in their khaki uniforms—in the streets, on the buses, in the shops—carrying their automatic weapons as you and I might carry an umbrella. It seemed at once reassuring and very scary.

Twenty-four hours into our Israel visit we were calling it an "intense" experience. Superman radar, bombs inspection, ever-present military, gun-laden schoolchildren chaperons. I suppose some might say that's to be expected, but *everyone* we saw seemed furtive and watchful, almost (but really not quite) suspicious. And *that* is what made its mark on us.

*   *   *   *   *

We had arrived in Ashkelon with a broken television on the boat. We hadn't cared about the fact that it was broken. It wasn't something we could have used much for the last year, anyway. However, now that we were approaching places where we might understand the news, or where we might get a cable TV wire, or where we might have enough electricity to watch a taped movie, we decided to get it fixed. The marina folks told us about Schmuel, close by. "He repairs things in his garage."

We found Schmuel and his wife Rachel in a comfortable home a few blocks away. After fixing the TV—in his garage, as advertised—Schmuel asked if we would come the next day for Shabbat, the traditional Friday night dinner. We were delighted with the invitation. It was a memorable evening of good food and fascinating conversation. We cataloged our observations of Israel so far, and Schmuel and Rachel helped interpret what we were seeing, feeling, and wondering about. "Israel is not an easy place," Rachel commented.

Schmuel and I found a shared passion: violin music. It had been so long since I had talked music with anyone. He played a number of his favorite CDs. We talked performers, composers, and pieces of music. I was enthralled. Music goes everywhere in the world, and for some reason I had forgotten that. We hadn't heard much music in the last year. Correction: we had heard music everywhere we went. In fact, we enjoyed the refined sounds of the Indonesian

gamelan bands; the haunting modal tunes of the Middle East; and the twang-
ing sitars, droning tamburas, and thumping tabla of India. It was Western
music we hadn't heard, and as much as I was fascinated with the Eastern tonal-
ities, instruments, and musical forms, I nearly wept hearing Itzhak Perlman
play the Brahms Violin Concerto.

Rachel talked a little about the Persian Gulf War (1990–1991), the gas masks
that they kept at the ready, and their very real fears. "We live with this war
[Israel and Palestine] every day, but in those months, it was different," she said.
"We were truly afraid."

"And you are not afraid now?" I couldn't help asking.

"Not immediately. We are safe here where we live." I didn't know whether to
comment that they were not many miles from the Gaza Strip. I decided not.

Rachel is originally from Hungary, and Schmuel from Romania. "Everyone
in Israel, except the little ones, is from somewhere else," she quipped. We knew
that many of their neighbors came from Russia because we heard some of
them speaking Russian.

It shouldn't have been a surprise, all things considered, that we found little
English spoken. I had expected to hear it spoken and see it "on the street" in
signs and ads. But Israel was making a concerted effort to maintain Hebrew as
the national language. The lack of English didn't matter a whole lot. We had
been doing without for a long time. I had just thought things might be easier
here.

* * * * *

Well-situated in the Ashkelon marina, we felt that the boat was safe enough
that we could make a journey to the most historical of cities, Jerusalem, where
the currents of political and religious feeling swirl about you day and night.
Everything about Israel is crammed into Jerusalem: history, conflicting beliefs,
religions, people, military, antiquities, and outstanding sights.

Jerusalem is one of the most photogenic cities I've seen. The old city was
crowded with buildings, walls, mosques, churches, and archeological sites that
span the centuries—hundreds of beautiful photo opportunities. My shutter
finger developed cramps.

We walked the ramparts of the old city, looking down into the streets,
schoolyards, gardens, and out over the rooftops to the Temple Mount and its
golden dome, which even on a cloudy day shone with brilliant light. The
Temple Mount is sacred to Jews, Christians, and Muslims alike. Originally the
site of a Jewish temple, it is now dominated by one of the most beautiful
mosques we had seen. In the center of the mosque is a large rock that is

believed to be the place where Abraham offered to sacrifice Isaac, *and* from which Mohammed began his Night Journey. This is the place, sadly, where Israelis and Palestinians cannot coexist. It is so beautiful to look at, and so deadly in its conflict to the people who surround it.

That all of Jerusalem is significant to the central religions of this region was nowhere more evident than at the Jaffa Gate of the old city. We sat in a sidewalk café by the Gate and watched a parade of people, many dressed in the "costumes" of their different religions. There were Orthodox Jews wearing yarmulkes; Hasidic Jews with long black coats, fedora-like hats, and earlocks; Armenian, Russian, and Greek Orthodox priests in black robes, colorful overcoats, and distinctive tall, flat-topped hats; Roman Catholic nuns and priests in gray habits and white collars; monks in earth brown robes with chains and heavy crosses worn about their waists; Muslims in long thobs and bishts with red and white ghutra headdresses, the women in black veils; and Protestants of different stripes murmuring prayers and singing hymns on their way to the Via Dolorosa and the twelve stations of Christ. And yes, there they were, representatives of another "religion," the tourists in their costume—shorts and T-shirts.

In a rented car we drove in a wide circle to the Dead Sea and back to Ashkelon. After visiting Jericho, the lowest city in the world (820 feet below sea level), we drove about looking for the road back toward the Dead Sea. After a bit we were conscious that our surroundings had changed. We saw camps, tents, and cookfires on hillsides. The countryside seemed untidy, the villages in a jumble. The people looked different, but we weren't sure how. We wandered into a small town, and suddenly realized what had happened. We were informed by the flag flying from one of the buildings. We were in Palestinian territory, one of the disputed pieces of land on which Arabs were trying to establish an independent Palestinian state.

Should we be there, we wondered? We had crossed no border that we saw, and no one seemed to pay us any mind, but this was an area of earlier disturbances, and we weren't sure if there was any risk. We stopped in the town for a few minutes without incident, but we drove on with some haste, eventually finding our way back to the Dead Sea road. We were as puzzled as the Israeli border guards as to how we had erred. The border guards were polite—as we found all Israeli military or officials to be—but they suggested we continue south *directly* to our destination.

Later that afternoon we took the requisite swim in the Dead Sea. Weird. The high salt content makes it impossible to submerge yourself, and depending on where your body's center of gravity is, you roll to it. Keeping our balance was a trick.

The most important site in this part of Israel is Masada. A fortified complex atop a mountain of sheer cliffs, it was captured from the Romans in the first century AD by a group of Jewish Zealots, starting what is called the First Jewish Revolt. After some time the Romans decided to recapture the site, and they built an earthen ramp up one side of the cliffs for the soldiers to climb to make their assault. The Zealots—967 of them—believed capture was inevitable, and they committed suicide rather than become Roman slaves, or worse. We stood at the top edge of the fortified mountain looking west, the ruins of the Roman camp still visible below us. And there, slanting up the cliff, was the ramp. It sent chills down my spine. It was not hard to imagine how terrified those Jews were, watching the ramp getting higher and higher, closer and closer.

*　*　*　*　*

In the middle of our stay in Israel we returned to the States. One son was getting married and one daughter was graduating from college, events not to be missed if at all possible. That was why we had come to Israel in the first place: we thought we would have a better choice of flights and would get to Israel in plenty of time to make our travel arrangements. And so, in the middle of May, we went to the airport outside Tel Aviv to fly home. We were surprised to be met at the *doors* to the airport and asked where we were flying. We were then escorted to the appropriate line, where we were to wait to be interviewed.

The interview was lengthy and complicated, with our explanations of why we were in Israel, and why we had so many stamps in our passports, including Egypt. Our young interrogator was looking at our plane tickets. "Why are you coming back to Israel?"

"Our boat is here. We live on our boat. We travel on our boat."

"Why did you go to Egypt?"

"We were on our boat. We are sailing around the world [why was this such a hard concept to absorb?] and we came through the Suez Canal. You have to go to Egypt to do that."

"Did anyone get on your boat in Egypt?"

"Yes, we had to have pilots in the Canal."

"Did they give you anything?"

"No," (*but we gave* them *a lot*).

"Why are you in Israel?"

"We wanted to see some of your country."

"Where are you staying while you are here?"

"On our boat."

"A boat?"

"Yes, our sailboat," (we should have had a picture).

"And you must come back to Israel?"

"Yes," (*you remember ... please*) "to continue sailing on our boat."

"Why did you come by boat?" *Oh, oh, oh.* "Why are you going to Boston?" (That, at least, was easy.)

And so it went for over half an hour before our interviewer was satisfied that she understood our intentions, and that despite our visit to Egypt, we were no threat.

And then the examination of the baggage began. Our checked luggage was scanned by x-ray—while we were standing at the x-ray machine. I watched our hair dryers (looking like guns) and shaving razors pass inspection. But when the twelve-inch Sudanese knife (a birthday gift for a teenage grandson) came into view, my heart sank. At the very least it would be confiscated; at worst *we* would be confiscated. But not a blink of an eyelash. Checked luggage, I guessed. The knife didn't matter there.

What *did* matter was the computer printer that we were toting in our carry-on bag, taking it back for repairs. Stephen was ushered into a private room, where he was asked multiple questions about the printer. "Why do you have it?" "Why are you taking it back to the States?" And then they took it apart, bit by bit. Another half hour later, he returned and we proceeded to the body search. We were separated—men one way, women another—and patted down, very thoroughly. In privacy booths, we were asked to remove some clothing.

Another hour and a half and we had passed all the tests. We were exhausted and hadn't even boarded the plane. Suddenly I had this thought. I looked around to verify my observation. I whispered to Stephen, "There are no military, no guards, no armed personnel here. I haven't seen one since we arrived at the airport."

"None that you can see," replied Stephen. Ah, yes, there was that. But still, I thought it was curious—no visible deterrent to terrorist activity. In Frankfurt, Germany, where we changed planes to continue to Boston, there were guns walking everywhere.

∗   ∗   ∗   ∗   ∗

Israel exhibits its history well. We were delighted by the creative ways of hanging art and displaying such jewels as the Dead Sea Scrolls. The Museum of the History of Jerusalem, in the Citadel, was a marvel of exhibition techniques: models, computerized graphics, holograms, videos, and dioramas. There was hardly an "ordinary" exhibit. But the Advat Caravansary in mid-country took the prize, in my mind. Advat was once a stop along the spice route between

South Asia and Europe. The ruins have been carefully reconstructed. You can tell what was original and what had been restored. And what was that on the ridge overlooking the site? Arabs in robes and turbans, as well as camels, donkeys, and dogs, all walking along the trail leading to the caravansary, just as they had so many centuries ago. The two-dimensional metal figures were ingeniously situated on the ridge to appear as silhouettes to the visitors in the ruins. It gave a "feel" to the site that we probably would not otherwise have had. It was clever.

But then, Israelis are clever people. They have learned to live in what many might have assumed to be a godforsaken piece of earth. They have managed to grow some of the most delicious vegetables and fruits, and beautiful flowers, where none should normally grow. And they appeared to have unlimited water, both for irrigation *and* for filthy sailboats that have just spent a couple of months in the Red Sea. I will be forever grateful for the water that we poured over our dirt-coated rigging, sand-blasted decks, and muck-encrusted cabin in the Ashkelon Marina.

When it came time to leave Ashkelon, we spent a day readying the boat. Everything seemed set, except the engine. We ran it for awhile to check its readiness, but it started overheating. I ended up going over the side to check the seawater intake—perhaps it was clogged. I found a small fish stuck halfway up the pipe, impeding the water flow. Poor little fellow. And fortunate it was that I made this dive, for I also found that the propeller and prop shaft had grown three-inch-long weeds. Like vegetables, Israel grows seaweed exceptionally well, and we hadn't been sitting in Ashkelon that long.

We left in the late afternoon, in order to time the passage to Cyprus for a morning arrival two days later. And we heard them on the radio all night. "Any sheep, any vessel that is 30 miles west of Haifa, please call Israel Navy." We heard them calling on the radio for nearly 24 hours. But as long as our bow was pointed away from Israeli shores, they appeared to pay us no mind. We were not called, we were not buzzed, we were not followed. But we knew they were watching ... Israel is always watching.

Muezzins and Discos

Turkey

In Datça the anchorage was so still we could hear conversations at the restaurants on shore—not just murmuring, but real words. "This meat is tough." "Ach, ist bin wunderbar." "...[something in Turkish]." We pretended that our cockpit was an extension of the restaurants. "Wow, this goulash is exquisite!" Stephen exclaimed.

"It is not," I retorted. "It's hash with the remains of our fresh veggies, and I do mean *remains*."

As the sun set, we retreated below decks and prepared to hit the sack. Just as we were ready to doze off, the booming music from a disco began, pulsating out over the anchorage and continuing through the night. I slept fitfully, feeling the boom-boom of the music as the hours crept on. At 5:30 AM (I was wide awake), the town's muezzin launched into Islam's first call to prayer for the day. This competition between muezzin and disco produced a cacophony of sound that characterized all of our Turkish experience: the old and the new, the religious and the secular, the conservative and the modern, all trying to break into the twentieth century.

The disco was a scourge to me—mindless, pounding music, so loud, and with that horrible bass beat. It was creeping into my inner being, giving me headaches, making me cranky, and keeping me sleep-deprived. Even if you couldn't hear the music, you could feel that insidious beat that pounded the air. And what really killed me was that quite often there was *no one* in the disco, yet the music boomed on until dawn. In the United States, we'd be suing for noise pollution. In Turkey, the disco represented tourism, money, flash, and Western ways. The noise trumpeted their success.

Much more pleasing were the Turkish anchorages watched over by ruins of the past: castles on capes, towns on islands, tombs in cliffs, churches on beaches, most of them unattended, unrestored, and unexcavated.

We anchored near the town of Üçağız and went ashore to have a look. The buildings along the shore were all made of beige-colored local rock and featured red tile roofs. Most of them had the crumbling look of "old." Brilliant flowers and vines covered some of the crumbling, so that they looked even older and more charming.

Along the waterfront, which was about half a city block long, there were a half-dozen restaurants with long piers extending out into the bay. At each one, the proprietors' young sons were on the docks waving to us to come and tie up at their dock—hoping, of course, that we would then eat at their restaurant. Hassan's son had the biggest smile, so we maneuvered our dinghy to his dock.

Behind the restaurants, the rest of the town consisted of a row of shops where men sat drinking tea and women swept, or wiped tables, or cleaned windows. It was quite serene. We walked the length of the village of Üçağız in two minutes. At a rise in the path at the far end we found a couple of dozen Lycian sarcophagi—dating from the third century BC—lying about, *just lying about.* Many were overturned, with the lids half on, half off; many of them had tumbled down the hillside into the water. They were almost identical, looking a little like stone houses, the lids making peaked roofs. Weeds grew up around them, and prickly bushes made it difficult to approach. There was no entrance stile, no ticket to purchase, no sign prohibiting this or that—there was no sign at all. There was no graffiti, no trash on the ground, nor empty squashed soda cans tossed inside the stone relics. They just sat there, tumbled there, rested there—quiet, unprotected, and unnoticed, except by the occasional visitor like us. *Third century BC* sarcophagi!

With scratched legs, but enchanted by this sight, we returned to the village and Hassan's restaurant to eat a fresh and fragrant fish stew.

They say that Turkey has better ruins than Greece. I would not want to be the one to decide this argument, but there is a range of ruins in Turkey that seems to outdo the scope of ruins in Greece. In Turkey, some ruins were magnificent, as at Didyma, and some were unique, as was Ephesus. But in Greece the ruins were better preserved, restored, or exhibited, and the magnificence was on a higher scale. How could anything be grander than the Parthenon. But then again, how could anything be more pleasing than walking alone among weed-entwined sarcophagi of the third century BC?

The most perfect of Turkey's ruins is at Ephesus. Once the Roman capital of Asia Minor, as many as 250,000 people had lived there. About one-third of the city has been excavated, and some remarkable buildings have been uncovered. Quite the best is the Library of Celsus, the façade of which has been restored. There are two grand stories of arches and columns; it is of classical proportions, and breathtakingly beautiful. Some 12,000 scrolls were housed there, including the *Iliad* and the *Odyssey.*

Although we made our first visit to Ephesus in late September, it was still such a popular tourist sight that we were afraid we might be disappointed because of the crowds. But the city originally had thousands of citizens, so it was really quite appropriate for hundreds of people to be wandering along the marble streets and visiting the marketplace, the swimming pool, the baths, the brothel, the library, and the remains of the terraced homes. We were anything but disappointed.

On another visit to Ephesus, we had the privilege of seeing the ongoing restoration of the terrace houses, the homes of Ephesus' elite. The homes had been renovated two or three times into contemporary styles, just as we do today. There were mosaic floors over tile floors; frescoes over frescoes over mosaics on the walls; marble carvings plastered over; interior walls erected and torn down. A team of archaeologists was peeling away layer upon layer to reveal the marvels beneath.

Besides Ephesus, there were still more ruins within a day's drive of Kuşadası (where we berthed for the winter)—the 2,000-year-old hillside town of Priene; a superb 15,000-seat, first-century amphitheater at Miletus; and best of all, the enormous fourth-century Temple of Apollo at Didyma. With an exterior porch of 120 columns some 6 feet in diameter and close to 100 feet high, the Temple of Apollo would have been one of the wonders of the world, if only it had been completed! Although only a few columns remain standing, it was not difficult to imagine the colossal grandeur of the original.

Farther along the coast, in another wide bay, we anchored behind a half-mile-long island covered with the ruins of a complete Byzantine town: houses, storage caves, tombs, a small theater, baths, a surprisingly large basilica, a watchtower at the top of the island, and a wall surrounding the peak, part of which was an intriguing tunnel where the villagers must have hidden when there was threat of attack. Although there were small boats bringing visitors across to the island for a fee, there were still no tourist site trappings—no kiosk selling plastic replicas of the church, or badly reproduced drawings. Turkey appeared to be still discovering its tourist trade, and it hadn't yet cottoned on to all the wonderful ways to grab the tourist dollars.

*   *   *   *   *

One of our dreams was to see some more of Turkey than just the coast, and so on a comfortable fall day in late September, we picked up a rental car and began a drive into the interior. Although friends advised us to drive carefully and defensively, and to expect the unexpected, we were not prepared for the wild driving on Turkey's roadways. As a people, the Turks have not been driving motorized vehicles for very many years, and their rules of the road seemed to be different from ours. We were not unfamiliar with wild driving—in Sri Lanka, India, and Yemen, for example—but in those places we had been chauffered. I'm still uncertain whether it is better to be in the car of a wild driver, or to be driving yourself, facing scores of them on the road. The scenario in Turkey was the latter, and we soon regretted our stubborn independence. Although we drove defensively, carefully, and tensely, with our eyes darting in every direction, we were constantly nervous. The driving rapidly exhausted us.

Our goal for this trip was Cappadocia, a region of Turkey just about in the center of the country. The history of the area began several million years ago with the explosions of three volcanoes that spread a thick layer of volcanic ash over the district. The ash then hardened into a porous stone called tufa. Over time, the stone has eroded into a Disneyland of weird and whimsical shapes—cones, mushrooms, castles, chimneys, and phallic, um, things. In human history Cappadocia was the center of the Hittite Empire, then an independent kingdom and later a Roman province.

The soft, porous tufa was easy to work with primitive tools, and caves were readily dug out of the cliffs, providing excellent shelter. Whenever invaders appeared, the Cappadocians dug deeper, creating entire cities underground. Built on many levels, with air vents to the surface, these subterranean cities housed thousands of people at a time. We walked through one, following a maze of tunnels eight levels down into the ground, hunched over much of the time (these folks must have been very short) and feeling a trifle claustrophobic.

When early Christians arrived, they carved elaborate churches from the stone. When marauding Arabs appeared in the seventh century, the Christians also retreated into the caves, moving stone doors across the entrances. These early churches illustrate a curious chapter of Christianity in this now-Islamic state.

The cave-cities' inhabitants are referred to as Troglodytes (cave dwellers), which seems to be an appropriate-sounding name, from the look of the area. From the inverted cone-shaped hill caves, I expected to see little gnomes with peaked caps come bounding out singing "Hi Ho." Troglodytes—in fact, ordinary (maybe shortish) people—lived in these stone caves until the early 1950s, when finally everyone realized that the erosion was continuing and that most of the cave dwellings were really unsafe. You can see in places where the face of a hillside has fallen away, revealing the interior of the dwellings carved inside.

On the way to and from Cappadocia we traveled through one beautiful valley after another, filled with apple orchards and fields of cotton. Between the valleys we drove along a high plain, every inch of it cultivated. There were pumpkins and potatoes, almonds and olives, figs, pomegranates, tomatoes, cucumbers so tender they didn't have to be peeled, and cabbages more than two feet in diameter. Turkey is one of the few countries of the world that is a net exporter of food. Along this route it was easy to see how that could be.

The huge fields on this plain were oddly spotted with trees that had to be a nuisance when plowing and harvesting. In the States we would have chopped them down and dug up the roots. But the Turks revere trees. It is illegal, so they say, to cut down a tree without permission, even on your own land. And everywhere we had seen hills, even whole mountainsides, densely planted with trees in meticulously even, horizontal rows. This was the work of the military, apparently, when they were not engaged in watching the Greeks across the channel. The planting was at the behest of Kemal Atatürk, who wished to see his countryside reforested.

Atatürk was the father of Turkey—his name means that, in fact. One of Atatürk's many reforms was to require the Turkish people to have last names. Up to that time (1935) family names were optional, and usually not used. Atatürk himself was known only as Mustafa Kemal until that year, when he proclaimed his name to be Kemal Atatürk—"Father Turk." From 1928 until his death in 1938, Atatürk went about completely redesigning Turkish society. He outlawed polygamy and the fez, which he thought was a symbol of cultural backwardness. He separated religion and state, removing Islam as the state religion.

Here is the difference between Turkey and Iran, for instance, where Islamic law is the law of the land. Kemal Atatürk had a vision of Turkey that wedded, and melded, and separated (if all those things are possible at once) religion and state in what purports to be a democracy. It is not perfect, this democracy, where state and religion are one and not the same, especially as more years separate Atatürk and his country's future. But it remains a phenomenon in mideastern politics—a government like no other.

As part of his reformation, Atatürk brought in a team of linguists in 1928 and asked them to recreate the Turkish language. The Arabic alphabet was replaced by a Latin-based alphabet, and a more logical and simple language was constructed. At least, the Turks think it is more logical and simple. Although we took Turkish lessons and worked hard at learning as much as we could, our best efforts were still mostly two-word declarations and one-word questions (e.g., "Ne zaman?" When?).

Atatürk is revered by the Turkish people; his likeness is found in every art form everywhere. The reverence is well-deserved, for he brought his country out of the dark ages and shaped it into a secular state, economically stable and able to stand on its own. On November 10th, the anniversary of his death, there is a full five minutes of absolute stillness throughout the country starting at exactly 9:05 AM, the moment of his death. Although sirens and horns are blown and flags are lowered for this period, the people all stand stock-still in utter silence—a very eerie event we experienced while in Kuşadası.

Unlike some other countries, the population of Turkey occasionally does what it is told *en masse*. The anniversary of Atatürk's death is one instance when all the people make this silent obeisance, even noisy children, talkative rug merchants, and loud construction workers. Another instance of incredible quiet and compliance comes on census day. On this head-counting day, there is no averaging, extrapolating, or guessing. Every individual must remain *in* his or her domicile for the *entire* day, so that the census-taker will find them there. That way you can't be counted twice, or not at all. Even though we didn't count, so to speak, we were remanded to the marina. We were not to go out into the street, especially. There were special police everywhere to make sure that the population remained where it should. I did venture far enough through the marina gate to experience the unusual personless, carless, remarkably silent street. It was as if the War of the Worlds had been announced, and everyone had fled.

* * * * *

On the way to Cappadocia we stopped in the town of Konya, the home of the whirling dervish. The dervishes are a sect of Muslims that Atatürk argued should be contained to Konya, their peculiar whirling rite to be restricted to their monastery there. Dervishes are the Muslim equivalent of monks and have many different orders, of which the whirlers are one. There are regular dancers who have mastered the dervish whirl and can be seen performing all over the world, but as a religious rite the whirling ceremony is performed now only in Konya. The Mevlâna Müzesi (Mevlana Museum) is the former monastery of the Whirling Dervishes. It is not just a museum, but a shrine that more than a million Turkish Muslims visit each year.

In Kuşadası, where we were berthed for the winter, and all along the Mediterranean coast of Turkey, tourism was the major industry. In these tourist areas, Turks have adjusted their attitudes to accept tourist idiosyncracies (as well as their dollars)—such as wearing shorts and bathing, even nude, on the beaches. But inland, in towns like Konya, it was a different story. While visiting mosques, the Mevlâna Müzesi, and other important buildings, we wore our most conservative clothing: long pants and long-sleeved shirts. I had a scarf to wear over my head too. But as we walked back to our car, which we had left sitting in the baking sun, we began to sweat in the hot afternoon. Just the thought of our oven-like car drove me to remove my outer shirt, leaving just my short-sleeved top. Stephen soon followed suit. A man passing us just at that moment gave Stephen a glare of naked hatred. I was stunned by his expression. Since I was standing there already in short sleeves—and a *woman* in short sleeves, at that—it was apparently the act of disrobing that so disturbed this man. As we reached the car, he looked back with what can only be described as an evil eye.

* * * * *

In early May we rode a bouncy bus to the nearby town of Şirince. This is a lovely town with old brick buildings and narrow cobblestone streets. As we walked along the main street, a taxi driver slowed as he came alongside us. He leaned out the window and called, "Hello lady, you from marina." Uh-oh, you know you've been around too long when taxi drivers 30 miles away know who you are! But the next week, when we cast off from Kuşadası, I was sorry to be departing. I regretted leaving the town where, indeed, so many of the locals knew me—the baker, the clerk in the grocery store, the cheese merchant who knew it had to be goat cheese, the guy in the market who had the best broccoli, the portly lady selling vegetables downtown. But we had been restless for several weeks, thinking about the months ahead.

* * * * *

With perseverance and patience we reached the Dardanelles, the huge crack between the continents—Europe on the left and Asia on the right. We then began a long haul against a flow of water that *starts* high in the Black Sea. There are innumerable European rivers (most notably the Danube) that empty into the Black Sea, a body of water that is landbound except for a southwest outlet, the Bosporus. The Bosporus, a short and narrow strait, rushes past Istanbul into the Sea of Marmara, a small, almost landbound body of water with a westerly outlet, the Dardanelles. All of this water flowing south and west is making its way to the Aegean Sea. The currents are especially strong at the narrow end of the Dardanelles, where the water is bursting forth into the Aegean. Although our cruising speed was six knots, in the strait we were often reduced to less than two knots actual speed. There were a few moments when I wasn't sure we had the power to push our way through.

Midway in the Dardanelles, the strait narrows to just a few hundred yards. On the south side is the town of Çanakkale, where we put into the town wharf. On the north side is the peninsula of Gallipoli, where a disastrous World War I campaign was fought. A movie of the same name, *Gallipoli,* was Mel Gibson's first notable starring role. We took a tour of the battleground to learn a little more about this piece of geography and its history.

Our guide was a Turk whose grandfather had fought and died in the battle. All the other people in our tour group were Australians, many of whom had relatives who fought on the other side as part of the Anzac troops. It is a very emotional story, this nine-month battle, which ended with the Anzacs and the Turks becoming unseen friends from trench to trench, in some cases not more than a few yards apart.

The battle was astonishing for all the blunders by the British—such as getting lost as they approached the peninsula by sea and landing at the wrong place—and for the number of deaths. More than half of the men engaged in the battle were killed. The final retreat by the Anzacs was accomplished without a single casualty, because the Turks refused to shoot their friends in the back. Although as Americans we have, remarkably, no association with this battle, we were both moved by the stories and stood incredulous in the midst of the fields, imagining it all. We later saw the Mel Gibson movie, a heartbreaking story and as near the truth of the event as you'll see. It was at Gallipoli that Turkey's "father," Atatürk, began his meteoric rise to fame.

*   *   *   *   *

They say there are 2,000 mosques in Istanbul, and we started our explorations of this ancient city with one of the grandest, that of Suleyman the Magnificent. Suleyman's mosque is huge, with lofty minarets, mushrooming domes, and magnificent stained glass windows (fashioned by one Ibrahim the Drunkard). In the mosque's graveyard, many of the stones had hats on them. This practice of topping gravestones with fezzes or turbans was one of the many customs outlawed by Atatürk in the 1930s, as part of his attempt to modernize the life of his subjects. Another of his reforms, changing to the Western calendar, was evident in the dates on some of the stones—"born in 1422, died in 1943," for example. These graveyards have become relics of the old Turkey.

With so many mosques in Istanbul, there is an unearthly sound at prayer time as the many muezzins get going, calling the faithful to prayer. First one, then two, then three voices in some sort of wild counterpoint, then six that you can hear in any part of town where you are standing. Aside from the strange melodic intervals, it is the *insistence* of the sound that makes one pay attention. Even in this supposedly secular state, it is a dominating feature, not just of their Islamic culture, but of their daily life, Muslim or not. And there are precious few "nots" in Turkey—less than 1 percent of the population.

Everything about Istanbul seems beautifully old, from the twelfth-century walls that surround the city to the narrow, eighteenth-century wooden houses that line the streets. Although it is possible to walk through, around, under, and over dozens of sights, the two that dominate the city (as well as our memories of Istanbul) are enormous architectural wonders: the Blue Mosque, taking its name from the blue tiles lining the walls, and the Aya Sophia, starting its life as a Christian church in 548 and now overlaid with the trappings of a mosque.

It was not just ruins and architectural phenomena that occupied our time in Turkey, however. The people had their days too. From our marina just outside Istanbul, we rode the train to the heart of the old city, and inevitably a number of hawkers came on board to join us. These were genial young men with a fast-paced sales patter, roaming the aisles of the cars and plying their wares: double-A batteries; toothbrushes; dust mops; cheap plastic toys; various sorts of food, of course—and beach balls. Beach balls? There isn't a beach within hundreds of miles of Istanbul. But these guys could talk you into anything. They reminded us of the ubiquitous Turkish rug merchant: "You like this one. This one *perfect* for you."

In the mountains east of İzmir we came across rug merchants of a different kind. In the village of Karakaya, they make rugs of deep navy blue and "drunken cherry" red, the village's special colors. We wandered among their homes, watching shy women and young girls at their looms. The men quietly unrolled before us rugs of exquisite beauty. No sales patter, no pressure. How could we not buy one? We bought four, small ones that would fit the floor of *Another Horizon*'s cabin. The woman whose rugs we chose was beside herself with joy. A round face framed by a proper Muslim scarf, a mouth full of steel teeth, and two deep, dark eyes were all bursting in smiles with her luck.

Ali, our guide through Gallipoli, was another of our favorite people. He had been a sea captain in both the military and the merchant marine. He was fascinated by our journey, and at the end of our day-long tour he invited us to his home for dinner. "Does your wife know we're coming?" I joked with him.

"Oh, she'll be enchanted," he said. ("I bet," I whispered to Stephen.) I didn't dare ask if he did this often—bring home stray tourists for dinner, unannounced.

We certainly were enchanted with Aiten, Ali's wife, who welcomed us with grace, charm, and a delicious dinner. They were not a typical Turkish couple, we decided. Their home was large, comfortably furnished, and with the gadgets of someone with plenty of disposable income. They did not act like a typical Turkish couple, either. They were openly affectionate with one another, and they drank beer and wine.

It was perhaps Fatih who best represented to us the Turkey of muezzins and discos. He was young, a schoolboy really. We sat next to him on the train from

Istanbul to Atakoy, where we were berthed. "What is your name?" I asked in Turkish.

"Fatih," he said, "and I speak English, a little. May I practice?"

"Of course," I said, "especially because I can already tell that your English is better than our Turkish." Fatih was fifteen, still in school and hoping to go to the university, to prepare for a career in computers. He was new to our Turkish experience. Fatih was a city kid getting a good education, with prospects of doing something other than selling rugs, cheese, or beach balls. After a little time I realized that we had passed his train station. "You forgot to get off!"

"No, no ... I come with you." *Oh dear,* Stephen and I exchanged glances. *What did he mean?* "I practice more." He was like a stray puppy following us.

Haltingly I explained to Fatih about how we lived, and that it wasn't possible to take him to our home. Well, of course it was, but it was pouring rain, and early evening already. We were tired, and he was fifteen and ought to be doing his homework, in his own kitchen, where his mother would know that he was safe and sound. I took his address and promised to write. "You can practice reading English, then," I suggested feebly. He was pleased nevertheless. It seemed certain that he would somehow struggle to make his way into the twentieth century, just in time for it to be the twenty-first.

I just hoped that he'd stay out of the discos, and if it pleases Allah, that he'd become a Turkish computer genius.

Sailing Past Byzantium

The Black Sea

I woke at 4:30 AM to the haunting sound of muezzins. There must have been six of them singing their melancholy melodies, their phrases beginning and ending at different intervals, like a round. It was the last time we would hear that sound, so evocative of the East.

From our marina just west of Istanbul, we battled our way through the Bosporus, fighting the current and dodging ships coming and going, as well as a plethora of ferries crossing from one side to the other. Sailing along the waterfront, we had a grand view of the city. So many minarets piercing the sky. So much granite, marble, and stone piled into huge, magnificent shapes. So many veiled visions as we coursed this channel. I had a hard time concentrating on the ship traffic, because the scene off our port side was mesmerizing.

At the end of the seventeen-mile channel, we made one final push against the current and popped out into the Black Sea.

* * * * *

There was little wind, and we motored almost all day and night to Bulgaria. During the night it was so still the water reflected every star in the sky as in a mirror, a very rare occurrence at sea. Although sailing with a gentle breeze on the beam would have been nice, I'll have to admit that I was perfectly happy with this motoring bit. We had been warned of "terrible" weather in the Black Sea—"gnarly," they said. But the passages were short, and the sights in our ports of call were wonderful, so it would be worth getting through the ugly seas, they said. Motoring instead in flat, dead-calm seas was just fine with me, and extraordinarily beautiful too. The light of the sky reflected in the sea made the ambient light very bright, even when the moon had not yet risen. But what was that smell?

I asked Stephen when he came on watch at 4 AM. It was a musky smell, like peat or rich compost, an earthy smell, but we were 25 to 30 miles offshore. It

191

seemed like a long way for earthy smells to be reaching us, especially with no wind.

In the morning I came on deck for my watch, and Stephen pointed out all the insects we had collected during the night. Good heavens! Every species of moth, fly, nits, and gnats had come on board—in the hundreds. They covered the sails, the deck, the lines—ick! … everywhere. Again, I thought it odd that we were having these land things going on so many miles offshore.

Midmorning, another land thing arrived on deck. A small, brown insect-eating bird appeared. He flew about, landed, flew about, landed, and then began eating. He stayed with us for nearly 30 hours, gobbling away. I asked him if he could call up some of his friends to join the feast; we had enough insects for a hundred of his kind. But, alas, no other feathered creature appeared to join the fun. And the questions persisted: Land smells? Land creatures? But we could not see land, and we knew for a near fact that land was far away.

* * * * *

Our port of call in Bulgaria was Varna, where we found the Varna Yacht Club in a tiny corner of the harbor, boxed in by breakwaters and piers. ("Yacht clubs" in this part of the world are really sailing centers, not the boating and social clubs to which we are accustomed—and at that, they are also rather primitive.) There was no room for us to turn around in the marina, so the club manager showed us a length of pier where we could tie alongside and avoid any maneuvering. We had just secured our lines when the port officials were dockside, asking to come aboard. Their promptness flustered us and made us anxious.

We had purposely left Istanbul for this Black Sea venture without any visas, since we had been given to understand that the countries we intended to visit would issue us transient or visitor visas for a short stay. This suited us just fine, because our days in the Black Sea would be limited.

The Bulgarian officials, all smiles, greeted us with the news that Bulgaria and the United States had just ten days previously ratified an agreement that allowed us to stay in Bulgaria up to a month without any visa at all—and no fees. "Three cheers for diplomacy," we said, inwardly sighing with relief. "If only we could stay the month," we declared.

The immigration man filled out a couple of forms for us, and we all shook hands as they cheerfully departed. It was the shortest—and perhaps the friend-liest—checking-in process of the whole voyage.

A walk through the old city of Varna showed us a town that was charming, if a little run-down. There was a variety of architectural styles—eighteenth- and nineteenth-century buildings just crying out to be refurbished. But there was also energy; it appeared that there was interest in turning the city around. In the evenings we walked the main boulevard, where there were busy restaurants and bars, and plenty of people-watching. The younger Bulgarians liked to promenade in their smart clothing, greeting friends in the various sidewalk cafés. There was a certain façade of prosperity. We knew from our reading that, as in the Soviet Union, once the Communist regime in Bulgaria fell, tiers of haves and have-nots quickly emerged. The latter were clearly not among our promenaders on Slivnitsa Boulevard, and to judge by the number of people we encountered trying to eke out a living on the other streets, the have-nots were in the majority.

We could not judge all of Bulgaria by Varna, of course. As a city on the Black Sea, with some tourism and an edge of agriculture to fall back on, the citizens of this city seemed to have more hope than the rest of the country.

One day we engaged an energetic and enterprising taxi driver to take us on a little tour into the countryside. He showed us the palace of the last Romanian queen (1931), a monastery carved into the cliffs of a mountainside (fourteenth century), and the latest resort hotel (1994). But the really interesting part of the day was Asen himself.

He crewed on a tugboat four days a week, he said, and drove the taxi the other three. Asen was married to Constantina and they had one child, Martina, and he was very serious about trying to make a better life for his family. "It is so hard," he said. "I cannot afford to take any days off or I will fall behind my goals." He counted himself lucky, he told us, because he owns his own house, thanks to his father and grandfather who managed to accumulate property when it was affordable, before collectivization in the early '50s. Asen said he could not hope to acquire such wealth today.

By comparison to the average Bulgarian, Asen considered himself wealthy, and yet he had to work two jobs, seven days a week, all year, in the hope of making a change in his way of life. Given that unemployment in Bulgaria was hovering around 25 percent, Asen was lucky to have good work.

At the end of our tour, as we said good-bye, Asen asked where we would go next. "Constanța [Romania]," we said.

"Watch out for the gypsies," Asen warned. "Very bad, the gypsies."

"Okay, we'll be careful," we promised.

The handicraft of Varna was tatting, or crochet. Women lined the streets with tables laden with their creations. The women selling it, crocheting all the while, were charming, but a little aggressive in their attempts to get us to buy *their* products, not their neighbor's. Still, they were very gracious when I said "No thank you"—and they fell all over themselves when I bought something. There were enough crocheted objects in this town ... well, they couldn't hope to sell half of them in their lifetimes, and yet they continued to make them. Perhaps there wasn't much else to do.

Tied up alongside the wharf in the yacht club harbor, we were a popular attraction, especially on the weekend as people strolled along the waterfront. We were the only foreign yacht there, and one of probably only a half dozen that would call during the year. One of our visitors was Penko, who introduced himself as a "founding father" of the yacht club, and once the manager. He was now retired and spent most of the time on his tiny cruising yacht, a miniature of *Another Horizon.* He asked where we would go from Varna, and we told him Constanţa. "Oh dear," he said, "watch out for the gypsies. They'll rob you. The children will surround you and pick your pockets. Constanţa not good." *Okay, Okay ... we'll be careful!*

After several days of enjoying the Varna spirit, we hailed the friendly officials to come back and check us out. "Bon voyage. And please be careful of the gypsies in Constanţa," they declared. *We will, we will.*

Our friend Hristo helped us cast off our lines, and Penko blew his horn as we backed out of that tight little basin. The officials, the fishermen, and the sailors on other boats waved good-bye, smiling. They really seemed to care that we had come to visit.

We turned north and once again motored through the night without a whisper of a breeze. The next morning, at the small boat harbor of Constanţa (set apart, thankfully, from the commercial port), we were directed to tie alongside the wharf with a couple of fishing boats. At the end of this stone pier was a guard shack that housed two soldiers, on duty 24 hours a day. *Probably no gypsies here,* I mused.

The contrast of this place with Varna was immediately evident in the solemn faces of the Constanţa officials. They were kind enough, but grim as they issued us temporary visas. As they departed they warned us about the gypsies. "A difficult problem," they said, apologetically.

Statistically, there are more gypsies in Romania (close to two million) than anywhere else in the world (next in line is Bulgaria, with a half-million). These colorful nomadic people have been romanticized by Westerners, and have been hated as racial outcasts in the eastern European countries. With so much advance publicity, I actually looked forward to a gypsy encounter—heck, I was *scouting* for gypsies.

*   *   *   *   *

In all three of the countries we visited on the Black Sea, it had been less than 10 years since Communism fell. The day after the Berlin Wall came down,

Bulgaria ousted Todor Zhivkov, its leader for 35 years. Within days the Ceauşescus were executed, and Romania had been in economic despair ever since.

The mood of Constanţa matched that of the officials: glum. The town itself was not unlike Varna—at one time charming, but now just showing its wear and tear. Unlike Varna, however, there were no signs of rejuvenation. There did not seem to be any interest in tourists, at least in Constanţa, and we found it very difficult to make contact with locals. We smiled and said "salut" (hello), but they stared, with no acknowledgment. That disturbed us until we were reminded that under the long, bitterly repressive Ceauşescu regime, Romanians were forbidden to speak to foreigners. Old habits must be hard to break.

There was one friendly fellow, however, on the fishing boat tied ahead of us on the wharf. He came by one evening and offered us a bowl of freshly caught anchovies. The fisherman said they were popular in Romania, especially raw. "Ah," I said, doubtfully. He demonstrated by biting off the head of one, spitting it out, and tossing the rest, whole, into his mouth.

"Or cook them in oil and lemon juice," he said.

"Sounds, er, better," I said. But I was so touched, I accepted his offering with effusive thanks.

"Oh, you like," he decided, and he ran back to his boat for a bucketful more. We were overwhelmed—by his generosity and by the anchovy smell. I actually rather dislike anchovies, picking them out of Caesar salads and off pizzas, but I wasn't about to tell that to the nicest man we met in Constanţa.

During our stay in Constanţa we walked all over town, bought some groceries, had some meals in the restaurants, went to the locals' market—and we saw only one gypsy. We had seen more gypsies in Varna!

Leaving the phantom gypsies behind, we carried on to Odessa, in the Ukraine. That's about as far north as you can go in the Black Sea, and definitely as far north (46 degrees latitude) as we would go on this voyage.

In Varna we had learned that a new marina had opened in Odessa just a week before. After a bit of searching, we found it at the end of the ferry terminal in the heart of the old town—a lovely marina, completely empty except for a couple of local boats. We were, it turned out, the first yacht to call. This delighted the marina management, who took pictures, called the press, and kept giving us gifts. But it disconcerted the check-in officials, who were used to processing big ships. These perplexed gentlemen spent a considerable amount of time solemnly searching the boat, looking in cupboards and into the bilge. The Ukraine apparently had had a problem with illegal immigrants (partly because the country was doing so much better economically than its neighbors), and they were very cautious about any foreign vessel coming into their port. But really, we shrugged, even a gypsy wouldn't fit in our bilge.

And then the business of a deratting certificate came up. We must have a deratting certificate, they said. This certificate, declaring that there are no rats on board, is required of large ships entering the port. We were beginning to fail in the language department about this time. We were certain that we didn't need a deratting certificate, and we didn't feel like paying the $130 that they apparently felt we should. In desperation, I went in search of someone who could interpret for us, and found Anzor, the "chief engineer" for the marina.

It didn't take long to sort out the deratting business, but the immigration fellows were insisting that we could stay only three days—counting the day we arrived—and it was now late afternoon. "But we would have to leave the day after tomorrow, and when we leave, we must leave in the early morning. This means we would only have one day to see your beautiful city," I cried.

"They are insistent," Anzor said. "Three days only, including today." I was beginning to regret our offhand attitude about not having visas ahead of time. It might have been better to brave the bureaucracy in Istanbul than to lose out now, after spending so many days getting here.

Then I had an idea. "Tell them," I said to Anzor, "that I came all this way to spend my birthday in Odessa. I will be heartbroken if I do not see Odessa on my birthday." Anzor latched onto this sentiment, pleading for me. There was some mumbling between the two immigration officials, but it didn't sound like very sympathetic mumbling. Anzor's face was neutral, not giving anything away.

Finally they relented. I could have my birthday in Odessa, but we must leave immediately the next day. I smiled. If they hadn't looked so dour I might have attempted to kiss them on the cheek, but somehow I didn't think that would endear me to them. They might take back their largess. I hugged myself mentally instead, and repeated the only good Russian word I could remember: *spahseeba* (thank you). I must have appeared very self-absorbed and very selfish—so very American. But I didn't care. I had achieved our goal of four whole days in Odessa. Oh, and my birthday too. It really was my birthday on Sunday!

* * * * *

Odessa was the beauty of the three Black Sea cities we visited. The architecture was stunning and in better condition than in Varna or Constanța, and the major boulevards were lined with cooling trees. The gem of the city was the opera house. Recently restored to its original brilliance, it is a miniature of the Vienna opera house, and golden baroque inside. We saw two performances there, one ballet and one opera. It was not the New York Met or the City Ballet, but they were very, very good, and at only ten dollars a ticket for the best seats in the house, who could complain?

To see more of Odessa, we engaged a local travel agent, Ludmilla, to give us a tour. Ludmilla was a simply dressed middle-aged woman with white-flaxen hair. She seemed to reflect everything about Odessa that we liked: charming, lovely, upbeat, with a gentle sense of humor. Ludmilla told us that the people of Odessa enjoy humor and have an annual festival of humor, with performances of puppets, drama, musicales, opera, and ballets. "Everyone in Odessa is very optimistic," Ludmilla said, which was borne out by the smiling faces of the people.

On another day, we made a special trip across town to see the local market. We found hundreds of trucks and vans with the back doors open to display jars of oil, tins of caviar, packets of pasta, and cigarettes. Blankets were spread on the ground with shoes, toys, brooms, and soap neatly laid out. Ropes were strung between trees to hang clothing. There was an enormous barn for meat merchants, and another for milk products—buckets of cream, butter, yogurt, and cheese—with no refrigeration, of course, not even ice. It made me cringe to think of all the little amoeba creepies crawling around in this unprocessed, nonrefrigerated stuff. In one area there was enough clothing piled in *heaps* to clothe the whole city, I felt sure. And these goods came from where? I could not ask—language and courtesy made me keep my counsel. I wondered what this market had looked like ten years before.

Everyone in Odessa was an entrepreneur, it seemed. If you weren't a shopkeeper, you had a van stuffed with goods for the marketplaces. If you weren't a tourist guide, you sold wine in a tiny shop. If you weren't a taxi driver in a taxi, you were a taxi driver *in your own car*. Whenever we wanted to go somewhere in Odessa, we had only to stand on a street corner, wave a hand, and a private car would soon stop and take us anywhere in the city for one or two American dollars. U.S. currency was the key to this transaction. Hard currency was so difficult to acquire in these Eastern European countries, and so much more valuable than their own currency, that any negotiation in U.S. dollars was welcomed.

Because it was so, well, *cheap*, we ate out every night. Goulashes, grilled meats, pilafs, stewed vegetables, with everything slathered in sour cream—such delicious, creamy-fresh sour cream, probably bought in the market that morning. I ate it anyway, *and* I didn't get sick. As for beverages, we were surprised to discover that the most inexpensive wine on the menu was champagne, a local product of excellent quality. I was in heaven. On our last day we bought four cases. Storing the bottles in the bilge took over an hour.

When my birthday had passed and we were ready to check out, the officials—with a very Soviet look to them still (it was the hats)—again searched our vessel carefully. *No stowaways,* I murmured to myself. *No room in the bilge for them—too many bottles of champagne.*

After the officials stepped back onto the dock, Stephen and I continued our predeparture activities. We had a checklist to go down, just as airplane pilots do, to be sure we had done everything that needed to be done before we became "seaborne."

After a few minutes I noticed that the officials were still on the dock, by our bow. "Uh-oh," I said to Stephen. "I think we had better depart as soon as possible. These poor guys in hats are going to hang out here until we cast off our lines, and they are looking a little nervous that we are not getting under way."

Stephen looked out and agreed. We had overstayed our visit as it was. I danced onto the bow, waving and smiling, indicating that I was just about to collect our dock lines. Stephen started up the engine. With that whooshy engine sound, the officials made noises and shifted from their we're-waiting-and-getting-impatient posture to an it's-about-time, rigid, almost-ready-to-salute stance. It still took three or four minutes for us to secure the essentials before we could safely cast off. The officials held their station. They would not even bend to untie the lines for us. I had to skip up and down the dock, getting the lines untied while they solemnly watched. Not a nod, not a salute, not a smile. But I *liked* them! They were so Soviet, and for some reason I delighted in the fact that they maintained that rigidity, that solemnness, that you're-not-going-to-get-away-with-anything look about them. It was the Soviet attitude I had seen on television most of my life. They too were finding it hard to let go of the fact that we could wander around their country at will, drink their champagne in bistros, and *buy* champagne in large quantities to take away in our bilge. I suddenly wondered if they had noticed that. Had I camouflaged the wine sufficiently? Must have; they were letting us go.

*   *   *   *   *

With Odessa, we had come to the end of our quick Black Sea tour, and from there we turned south, still motoring with no wind for three days and three nights. One advantage of being so far north at midyear (this was June) was that the days were long and the nights *short*—barely six hours. This made night watches less dark, and me more happy.

During these nights, however, I was not only happy with the short night, I was ecstatic to be able, at long last, to listen to music during those dark hours. Stephen had surprised me on my birthday with something I'd wanted for some time, but did not think I would probably ever get—at least in time for it to do me any good: a Discman. Although Stephen could read during his night watches, I found it difficult to maintain my night vision while reading. If I read with the full light of a flashlight, it took me many minutes to adjust to the darkness again—that is, well enough to see into the night for any dangers. It helped if I added a piece of red cloth over the flashlight, but then the light was often too dim for me to read without straining my eyes. I bemoaned the fact that I could not listen to music during these watches. Music coming through the cockpit speakers would keep the off-watch awake, but a Discman would do the trick.

I was flabbergasted to open my birthday package and find just that. Stephen had found one in Odessa! It was probably from the black market, and he probably paid an exorbitant amount. But maybe not, and I didn't ask. I really didn't care; I had music to listen to. And on those calm nights as we chugged back down the Black Sea, I could even block out the noise of the engine with the headphones on, blasting Mahler into my ears.

Those windless, musical, Black Sea nights were marred by only one anxious moment, when early in my first midnight-to-four watch, a ship came up from behind. I could see a red light only; his port (left) side was exposed to us. At night it is really hard to discern a ship's movement in relation to your own. The radar helped, because the ship's blip moved in relation to our position, which was always the center of the radar screen.

On the radar, the blip of this ship—and it had the big blipness of a large ship—was rapidly heading at an angle toward us. I turned off-course to the left. The ship continued to bear down on us. If I turned to the right, I ran the risk of crossing his path, so I turned more to the left. But our speed was not going to be sufficient to pull away from him. Instead, I pulled back the throttle and came to a standstill, hoping he would pass us before hitting us. He was coming sooo fast. I called him on the radio. No answer. He probably didn't speak English, and didn't know that I was calling him. (The VHF radio usually has a horizon-to-horizon range, and so a caller on the radio could be as far as twenty miles away.)

When he was just a quarter of a mile away, he suddenly slowed to a dead stop in the water. He probably had not seen us until just then, and we must have scared him as much as he scared me. If he had been watching his radar, he should have seen us, but more likely he wasn't. At the last moment, when he was close enough, he must have seen our masthead light. In waters where there are not many sailboats, ships can be startled by our light, which is small and high. It has red, green, and white navigation lights together in one fixture—

typical for a small cruising yacht, but not like the lights on any other kind of craft.

For a minute or two, the two of us just lay there, like a cat and a dog, eyeing one another and trying to decide what to do. He was probably looking at his radar now, to see if we were moving. We stayed still, which I hoped would indicate that he could make the first maneuver. Eventually he began to advance slowly ... ahead of us ... gathering speed ... then taking off at a gallop again. I sighed. Would he be more watchful the rest of the night? I hoped so!

⋆   ⋆   ⋆   ⋆   ⋆

Three days later we zipped through the Bosporus again, this time with the current running fully with us. We flew by Istanbul, the minarets a blur in the haze of dusk.

Whitewashed

Greece

Our first Greek experience was in Cyprus, a rather large landmass sitting between Israel and Turkey. Cyprus is a divided country—the Islamic Turks on one side, the Christian Greeks on the other—and the usual hateful accusations are flung from one side to the other. There is a buffer zone between the two sides that is watched over by United Nations troops, trying to keep the peace. It had been some time since there was any real aggression on either side, but we heard the Cypriot Greeks "practicing" artillery often enough, just to remind the Turks they were not far away.

We made landfall at Larnaca—on the Greek side—on the southern coast.

We arrived just in time for their "flood" festival, so named in commemoration of Noah's flood. *Kataclyzmas* it was called, although there was little evidence of this origination in the celebrations we saw. It seemed to be mostly an excuse for a holiday, with some music and dance competitions, carnivals and magicians, food and fireworks. Walking the main street, we reveled in the jubilations, loved the people-watching, and ate at every food stall we came to.

About midway in the street we came across a large personage in a Ronald McDonald outfit. Yes. Ronald was here in Cyprus. He was here to advertise the opening of a McDonald's restaurant in central Larnaca. We laughed. Ronald McDonald speaking Greek.

The city of Nicosia is still the capital of Greek Cyprus, despite the fact that half of it lies in the Turkish-occupied lands. Although the Cyprus of the Greeks was at the time relatively prosperous (they had turned a 40 percent unemployment rate in 1974 into a 4 percent rate in the late 1990s), Nicosia had the feeling of a struggling town. The shops were empty, few people frequented the restaurants, and the streets were decidedly empty. But maybe it was the heat that day—over 100 degrees.

For five brief minutes we stood on the platform that marked the divide between Greek and Turkish Nicosia—between Greek and Turkish Cyprus. The U.N. soldier stood at our side, his weapon shouldered. The three of us looked out over the no-man's-land, an abandoned, weed-choked swath of barbed wire with flags flying defiantly on either side. People had been displaced on both sides; Greeks living north of the no-man's-land had to move south, and vice-versa for Turks in the south. Neither side was happy with what was lost in the partitioning. The no-man's-land looked as sad as the situation itself, for which there did not seem to be any solution.

*   *   *   *   *

Strung along the southwest coast of Turkey, at times only a few miles off that coast, are the Greek islands called the Dodecanese (meaning twelve islands, although there are quite a few more in the group now). This situation, with Greece so close, is not something that makes the Turks very happy, but that's the way it turned out after the Second World War.

Although only miles from the Turkish coast, the Dodecanese islands are quite unlike the Turkish mainland. Along that Turkish coast there is a narrow band of flat coastal plain, whereas the Dodecanese rise up out of the ocean into hilly terrain. The Greek towns and villages march up the hillsides in the form of small, square, white buildings, with fresh coats of whitewash on everything (walls, stones, paths, streets) and lots of plants and flowers everywhere. Everything appeared tidier, more colorful, and more cheerful-looking than the brown, brambly jumble of towns across the channel. The Greeks seemed more open, and jollier too—perhaps the difference between Islamic and Christian attitudes. And there were decidedly fewer "old rocks" (Roman ruins) in the islands than on the Turkish coast across the way. Instead, we found hundreds of churches.

The Greeks are similar to Southeast Asians in their religious consciousness, erecting shrines everywhere—backyards, streets, alleyways, fields, parking lots. The Greek shrines come in various sizes, from a tiny roadside "dollhouse" to a full-sized church, with many, many chapels in between. Families, even individuals, construct these chapels, dedicating them to their favorite patron saint (usually the one they are named after), as a way of gaining favor with that saint. The chapels are rarely used except on the saint's day, when an elaborate ceremony and feast take place. On one island with a population of about 600 we stood on the top of a hill and counted over a dozen of these chapels in view. It was hilly country, and as we walked along over a ridge, we could see a dozen more.

Each island must have been visited by a paint salesman with a different color scheme for the shrines. On one island they were all white with dark red roofs; on another, white with Mediterranean-blue roofs and trim; and on another, just all white, dazzling in the sun.

Monasteries are also widespread in these islands. On Patmos there is one dedicated to St. John the Evangelist, who was banned to that island in the first century AD. While in exile there, he heard from God regarding the Last Judgment, and while living in a cave he wrote the Apocalypse (the Book of Revelation). Sitting atop a mountain overlooking the harbor, St. John's monastery is surrounded by a *hora* (main town), a wonderful medieval town of narrow walled lanes with doors every so often. These "street doors" lead into interior courtyards, from which more doors lead to the apartments surrounding the courtyards. With the exception of the protecting wall around the monastery, the whole bit was whitewashed, and like a snow-capped mountain, the *hora* could be seen for miles and miles—at sea and from neighboring islands.

From the *hora* we hiked down a narrow stone path, following the medieval road that led to the monastery. Walking on these second-century stones, we could easily imagine the dark-cloaked monks plodding up the hill, leading a donkey or two laden with brush for their cooking fires or stones from the beaches to repair the walls. The antiquity of this place was like a cloak around us.

We sailed to Kalymnos, Lipso, Leros, Patmos, Arki, and Samos, each island bountiful with dolmades, feta, baklava, olives, figs, and goats. The latter were often heard at daybreak, heading out across the hills to the day's grazing spot. Most of the goats wore bells of different sizes and sounds about their necks, and the music of their walking was enchanting. For us to walk along their paths, often the best "roads" into the hills, was less than enchanting, however— even quite smelly at times.

* * * * *

For two summers in the Greek islands we shared the anchorages with bare-boat charters (sailboats hired for a week or two without a professional crew, hence the term *bare boat*). The skills of the crews aboard varied, to put it charitably, and we learned to be wary of them all. On one windy day, one of them came into our anchorage, put an anchor down right in front of us, saw that their boat was too close, and pulled their anchor back up—and our chain with it. That pulled our anchor loose and we were set adrift.

Another of these let's-have-a-great-summer-vacation wonders anchored ahead of us, but did not set the anchor well. Their boat came adrift and floated down on top of us in the middle of the night. Another came too close to a stern anchor we had set, and—even as we warned them—wrapped our anchor line around their propeller shaft. We spent most of the late afternoons (when the charter boats usually arrived) advising them where to anchor—as far from us as possible.

To alleviate our anxiety over *our* anchor dragging—from high winds, poor holding on the harbor bottom, or other boats pulling up our anchor—we often set an anchor alarm. A function of our depth sounder, the alarm alerted us if we drifted into shallower or deeper water. If we were on deck we could see the movement, of course, but at night—and often during the day—we were below and would not be aware of the danger. One day we were below when the alarm went off. We dashed on deck. Nothing seemed amiss, and we returned to the cabin a little puzzled. A few minutes later the alarm went off again. This time we were in time to see the captain of an Italian boat, anchored rather too close, answering his cell phone. The sound of the ringing phone was exactly the same as our anchor alarm.

*   *   *   *   *

The Aegean Sea is strewn with Greek islands, and we could not hope to see them all. We mainly visited the ones that got in the way as we passed through. Skyros was one such island, in the northeast Aegean. This is a small island with a tiny harbor, where we found room to tie up alongside the wharf right next to the ferry dock. We arrived midafternoon and were comfortably resting below, when all of a sudden the opening strains of Strauss's *Also Sprach Zarathustra* (theme music for the film *2001*) came blasting across the harbor. What on earth? We came topside to see the evening ferry pulling into view. The music was clearly for the arriving ferry. Were some royalty on board? Was it the Friday afternoon special? The music was very stirring, its grand sound exhilarating as it was broadcast on some powerful speakers. It just about brought tears to our eyes. But why this musical salute?

Apparently a café on the far side of this small harbor used it as an advertising device. *Every* ferry that arrived was greeted with *Also Sprach*. One local confided that she wished it were Greek music, but she couldn't really complain. "It's unique," she said. Indeed, but after a few days—three ferries a day—we would happily have heard *any* other tune.

In these small Greek fishing harbors we often heard mothers calling their children—well, really, the boy children. The girl children were rarely seen, except in the company of their mothers—at the market, for instance. But the boy kids roamed the wharves in small clumps of two to five, and mamas periodically called out to find them. Although we could not understand all the words, it was not hard to intuit what was being said.

Mama (loud, to reach across the water): "Christo, where are you?"

"Here, Mama."

"Come carry the water now."

"In a moment, Mama."

"*Now,* Christo."

"Coming, Mama."

The word "stah-see" was heard a half dozen times in this exchange. To our ears the word sounded like "taxi." But in Greek it means something like "stop," or "stop what you're doing," or "in a moment," or "stop, wait for me," (especially among children). Or from mothers, I think it means something like "get back over here immediately and give me a hand with the water."

The point of this observation is that Greek mothers and Greek little boys had voices that pierced the air like train whistles above these tiny harbors. There was no mistaking them. I was glad. Little boys need to be in touch with their mothers.

* * * * *

Although I do remember some delightful places among the Greek islands— such as Skyros, with its pretty hillside towns, churches perched on top of the hills, narrow winding lanes, whitewashed houses, and donkeys, goats, and olive trees—most of my memories of Greece are of crowds of tourists, charter boats in every harbor, and wind—far, far too much wind.

During the summer months there is often a strong northerly wind, called a *meltemi,* that blows down from Europe for days at a time, straight through the Aegean islands. One such time found us at the island of Serifos (one of the Cyclades). This harbor was not only crowded and windy, but the bottom of the harbor (a thin layer of sand over rock) was poor for holding an anchor, especially in heavy winds.

The *meltemi* hadn't actually started blowing when our anchor started to drag the first time. We reanchored, backing down on the anchor hard to dig it in. It felt secure. I hopped in the water and swam over it to make sure. Yup, looked good. But the next morning we dragged again. We moved to a different part of the harbor, hoping to find a better bottom. I swam on the anchor again. It was well dug in. I even poked around with my hand to be sure the flukes were lying correctly. By the next morning the *meltemi* was gaining momentum. We dragged again. (How fortunate we were that these dragging episodes happened in the morning, when we were on board and paying attention.)

We tried moving farther into the harbor, as close to shore as we could, in hopes of finding more shelter, if not a better bottom. Local fishing boats, piers, and shallow water all made it difficult to find a spot with enough room to swing with the gusts of wind that were now prevalent. I swam on the anchor again. Looked good … flukes buried well into the sand. But thrice burned, et cetera.

That afternoon the wind rose to a steady 40 to 42 knots, with higher gusts. Gale-force. By this time we dared not leave the boat unattended, and by sunset we instituted anchor watches. These are the same as watches under way, but the boat is at anchor. Normally, anchor watches are unnecessary. But if the anchor were to drag in gale conditions, instant reaction could be the difference between a badly damaged boat and one that's preserved.

By the time of my midnight watch I had had no sleep. I had been listening to the wind and nervously glancing out the ports, looking for any movement. Even though I knew Stephen was outside watching, I had to keep checking for myself. I started out the midnight watch with my teeth grinding and every muscle tied in a knot. I remembered the Bali night and decided to try to do something about my jaw this time. I hauled out my little Discman and put on the Bach Mass in B minor. You may think this an odd piece of music to play in the middle of a gale, but you see, I could sing all the parts—no one could hear me in the wind, not even the off-watch—and it kept my mind on something else besides the howling in the rigging. It was especially pleasing to spit out the Ks in the opening *Kyrie*. I felt better.

The next morning, Stephen went ashore to see if he could find a place for us behind the town quay. Although the dock had been packed before, and we thought it was unavailable to us, boats were beginning to find space behind the first row.

We were nervous about asking the yachts already secured to the quay if we could come up behind them. This was an invasion of their security, and we were embarrassed to ask the favor. Our queries about tying up brought Stephen to a British boat with a young family on board. He made our plea.

Adrian looked at him. "American?"

"Yes."

"What's the name of your boat?"

"*Another Horizon.*"

"Oh, you're the weatherman. Oh, my, we must take care of the weatherman." It turned out that *Dawn* was one of our ghost listeners. They could listen but not transmit, so we were unaware of their presence on the radio.

The issue was, I realized later, how the crew of *Dawn* happened to have had the foresight to be behind the quay *before* the *meltemi* came down on us. "I listened to our weatherman," Adrian said. "Didn't you?"

By the end of that day, boats were packed four-deep behind the quay, nestled in, bows to sterns, like a bunch of puppies pushing into their mother's teats. Even in the relative protection of the quay, wind waves blew over the top of the stone walkway, spraying us on the other side. The air was tinged brown with the dust that the wind blew off the land.

Even when we were "secure" behind the quay, we could not ease our vigilance. One afternoon when we were below decks, we heard yelling. Out in the cockpit, looking aft, we saw a sailboat whose crew had decided to move, for whatever reason. They had released their lines to the quay, and had raised the stern anchor that was holding their boat perpendicular to the quay. But they hadn't raised it all the way, and they hadn't moved far enough away from the yachts still tied and anchored. As they motored out of the area, their dangling anchor was catching the anchor lines of others, us included. More chaos.

Why didn't everyone just stay put! I raged silently. But so many of them had chartered their boats, and gale-force winds be damned, they had to finish their vacation. We came across this phenomenon a number of times in the Med. And who were we to criticize? We had the leisure to stay in harbor with bad weather. Charterers had a week, maybe two, to have fun, relax, and enjoy the good life. Well, not here in Serifos, where the *meltemi* raged for twelve days.

When at last we escaped Serifos, we headed for Piraeus, the port for Athens. Midsummer is not the time to be on mainland Greece any year, but this year was especially bad: days and days of temperatures hovering around 100 degrees. It was both hot and dry; our sweat evaporated immediately. We had to be careful of dehydration most of the time. In the tropics we usually had some moisture in the air, with cooling trade winds across large expanses of water. We could swim most of the time too. But here in Piraeus the water was too dirty to swim in, and the harbor was small and surrounded by large buildings, so no breeze could reach us. Even though we drank water by the gallon, we felt debilitated, and our urine was dark yellow—a sure sign we were dehydrated. We drank water until we were bloated.

Despite the heat, we went into Athens proper to see the things one must see in Athens. We arrived at the Acropolis at opening time, the coolest time, and trudged up the stone paths worn slick by the passing of millions over the centuries. Even in our "nonskid" boat shoes we slipped and slid. At the top of the hill we stood in awe before the Parthenon, reputably the most important monument in the Western world. Although we had seen a lot of ancient monuments and "important" ruins in the last two or three years, we were not disappointed by this enormous temple and the surrounding buildings that make up the Acropolis complex.

Just west of Athens and Piraeus is a narrow strip of land connecting mainland Greece with the Peloponnesus peninsula. Ages ago, Nero said, "Let's dig a ditch here and we'll save loads of time bringing our boats from the Aegean to the Ionian Seas." But neither he nor other clever people through the years got very far with the idea. It took the French to finish the Corinth Canal in 1893. The Canal is a ditch about 3 miles long, lined with sheer, vertical cliffs up to 250 feet high. It is 80 feet wide, just two times our boat length. Only small cargo ships can transit, and to judge by the amount of paint left on the rocky sides, some were not quite small enough. On our transit we followed one of these small freighters through the ditch, watching his topsides come within inches of the walls.

A few days after our passage through the Canal, we came to the town of Itea, near Delphi. One evening, as we were finishing some souvlaki and salad at a seaside café, we heard a band coming up the street. And behind the band were a dozen or so priests and acolytes, with banners, icons, and incense. They were wearing the hottest-looking robes imaginable—heavy and dark, neck to ankle. And behind the priests came a huge crowd of people, many carrying lighted candles. "What is this?" we asked our neighbor. It was the local church's name day, we were told.

Every church in Greece is named for a saint, and every Greek Orthodox person is also named for a saint. Your saint's name day is actually more important than your birthday, and when a local church celebrates its name day, and it happens to be *your* name day, you must be sure to be there. People travel miles to be present at a name day celebration.

The band stopped in the middle of the main intersection of Itea, the priests sang a long chant, and then the procession moved on. In the streets later that night there was dancing and singing of a more secular sort.

The trouble with Greek fun and games—singing, dancing, or even just eating dinner—is that everything starts after 10 PM and often continues into the wee hours. Since we were usually up at 6 AM to collect weather information, to start a long passage, or to keep a radio schedule, we started nodding off at 10 PM. It was difficult for us to appreciate the Greek evening culture. At 4 AM I awoke and heard them singing, and I knew they were dancing in the streets. I wanted to get up, but fatigue defeated me. I had to just imagine the scene.

From Itea we turned the corner into the Ionian Sea and entered a different world. The winds were lighter, and the islands were greener and less dry. The humidity was often high, in fact, making it hot and sticky instead of hot and prickly. The harbors were picturesque, lined with pine trees, backed by high mountains, and scored with long switchback roads that zigzagged to tiny mountain villages.

We headed for an anchorage called Nisos Petala. We were just about to take the sails down when Stephen said, in his do-it-now-ask-questions-later voice, "Go to the left, quickly." By a piece of luck he had happened to glance at the depth sounder and saw that we were in just ten feet of water. According to our location on the chart, it should have been sixty feet. We could see the rocky shoal through the clear water, and it extended for two miles toward shore. We were clearly not where we thought we were.

We headed out into deeper water and looked carefully at the chart. Where could we have gone wrong? After close examination, Stephen found a teeny-weeny note at the bottom of the chart that said, "Later data indicate that longitudes should be reduced by one minute." In other words, our course was one mile too far to the east (toward shore) *and,* as we could now see, we were heading for the wrong harbor! We had become used to this sort of discrepancy in the South Pacific, where many charts have not been updated since the eighteenth or nineteenth centuries. But here in the Med the chart data was supposed to be modern and accurate, and yet we were caught out with this singular old chart.

* * * * *

When we were in a place with TV reception, we clicked through the channels to see what was available. We had a small-screen TV that we could hook up when we were at a dock, and we had installed a TV antenna on our stern a few years back. It was always interesting to see what was on the TV, even if we couldn't understand a thing being said. The advertisements, for instance, often gave us some insight into the culture.

While watching TV in Greece, we saw a number of "infomercials" for something that appeared to be an agency for abused women and children. "What is this?" we asked a Greek acquaintance, discreetly.

Exactly as you observe, it was suggested.

"So, if there are ads on local TV for an agency for abused women and children, we assume that this is a condition that exists?"

Long pause … "Yes."

This seemed so contrary to what we saw around us: happy people, smiling children. The men were on their fishing boats; the women brought food, saw them off, and welcomed them back. Moms called to young sons across harbors. We didn't understand the complexities of family relationships here, but we couldn't help but be disturbed by the TV ads.

"The worst part … the church does not condemn this," we were told.

"You mean they do nothing to stop it—this abuse?"

"They … support such … what is the word … *behavior.*" Well, that explains a little. There was a group of concerned citizens, it appeared, to help these helpless ones. There was little to suggest an alternative. But TV, available in every living room, offered a signal of awareness, if nothing else.

What can we say about this experience? That there is something else in the "whitewash" of this country? Like the begging in India, physical abuse is not an unfamiliar phenomenon at home. And like the begging, the context of the abuse was so out of sync with what we saw in the natural course of our day. But *unlike* the begging, the physical abuse in Greece—as it is anywhere—is hidden.

*   *   *   *   *

For all its beauty and history, Greece was a surprisingly difficult country to traverse. Its geography, people, and weather confounded us at every corner.

To the Bride of the Adriatic

To Venice

We left Corfu, at the north end of the Ionian, bound for Dubrovnik in the Adriatic. It would be a passage of about 40 hours, including two nights. By now it must be a well-known fact that nights are not my favorite passage times, and in smaller bodies of water like the Adriatic, where more ship traffic could be expected, I was especially anxious. And at this time, we had had a bit of bad luck: our radar had given up the ghost. We had not been able to fix it ourselves, or find anyone on shore who could help. We would be without my "periscope into the night." My anxieties doubled.

Never mind ... there was enough to worry about in the *daylight* hours of the first day. Leaving Corfu, we sailed along the channel between Corfu and Albania. This channel at its narrowest point is less than a mile wide. The beaches of Albania looked alarmingly close. On a hill overlooking the strait I saw a watchtower. I could not tell if we were being watched.

The contrast between Corfu on the left and the Albanian coast on the right was marked. Corfu was green with pine forests and olive orchards; Albania was dull brown, with few trees. Most of Corfu was developed, with homes along the coastline; Albania was nearly barren. We did pass one Albanian town close enough to inspect it through the binoculars—drab, blockish buildings with no green spaces. The buildings blended into the gray-brown hills behind—a desolate, dreary-looking place.

We had been alerted to monitor Channel 11 on our VHF radio while we transited this channel, in case the Albanian Coast Guard should hail us. And once out of the Corfu/Albanian channel, we maintained an offshore distance of at least twelve miles, the international limit of territorial waters for any country. But given our Eritrea/Sudan border experience, we knew that that limit wasn't always acknowledged by all of the world's countries. Some countries consider vessels within rocket range of their shore a threat—never mind that we were too small to have such a rocket. We were still inching away from the Albanian coast when night fell.

As usual, the worst of the ship traffic appeared on my watch—midnight to 4 AM. I was by this time in the voyage a little better at gauging a ship's movements and usually less panicky when they appeared to be coming straight at us. But this night, at 2 AM, I was confronted with an armada of ferries making their nightly Brindisi (Italy) to Corfu run, and I got sweaty palms. It was truly a frontal attack; at least a half dozen of them were lined up across the horizon, heading straight for us. In the manner of a proper seaman, I made a sharp right turn to let them pass "port to port." The ferries began to pass without incident, but there was one I couldn't seem to shake. Through the binoculars I could see that it had a small strobe light on its highest mast. The strobe indicated that this was a high-speed ferry—one of those hyper-hydroplaning types—that was running at least twice as fast as the others, and indeed was approaching at an alarming speed.

Although we expected that with our radar reflector and our navigation lights we should be visible at night, we already knew that not all ships keep a good lookout, and that our particular navigation light is not easily sighted or identified. Contrary to the situation in the Black Sea, however, the stretch of water between Italy and Corfu is well-traveled, and I had to believe the captains of these ferries were keeping careful watch. But it was not hard to imagine that this high-speed ferry with its little strobe light would expect everyone else to get out of its way. *Well, I* **would**, *if I could just figure out its "way,"* I mumbled to myself. At not quite the last minute I realized that the charging bull was *not* bound for Corfu, like the others, but for some other point farther north. I quickly turned *left*, out of its path.

That was the first night. The second night (on my watch, of course) I saw a large cargo-type ship approaching from the north, but far enough to the right that I thought it would pass us safely without any change of course on our part. Scanning the horizon, I saw some small white lights flashing and small red lights blinking—not ships, I was sure, but what? Then a large, bright orange light appeared dead ahead. The orange light looked like a fishing trawler, and I began to think the flashing lights might be buoys on fishing nets that this boat was tending. We had seen this before. Our practice was to go around (outside) all such buoys or lights because the nets are sometimes strung between the buoys, and we could easily get fouled in them. But this night the flashing lights, especially the red ones, did not seem stationary, and they seemed to multiply and move as we moved. I couldn't figure out how to get around them. And then I suddenly realized that the cargo ship that had been coming toward us on the right had disappeared. His lights were gone. Without the radar I had no way of checking for its blip, or to see if the trawler was moving, either. There were way too many lights, and way too little time to figure this out.

Time to wake Stephen; I needed help.

With a second pair of eyes scanning the horizon, we determined that we could not get around the erratically flashing lights, so we headed for the fishing vessel, *through* the blinking and flashing lights, keeping a keen eye for any net buoys. Fortunately, we were motoring in light winds, which gave us more maneuverability. We came within a quarter mile of the "trawler," which was like no other fishing vessel we had ever seen: huge, long, flat on top, weird lights on deck, and we could see no fishing apparatus on it.

Suddenly it dawned on me. The flashing red lights were *helicopters,* the noise of them blanketed by the noise of our engine. They were flying low to the water and around the "fishing boat," which we now realized was a helicopter carrier. We were still mystified by the flashing, but stationary, white lights, but by this time we were pulling away from the whole mess. Astonished, I said to Stephen, "We must have just blundered through some major military operation."

"Hmmmm, but *whose* military?" Stephen asked. We were then just off the border between Albania and Yugoslavia, with Italy on our left not that far away.

We learned later that NATO had ships all over the Adriatic during that period, and what we saw must have been one of their exercises. But what got me was that we were *allowed* to waltz right through it! Weeks later, on our passage south through the same area, we came across a small white float that had "target" written on it. One of our blinking white lights?

We arrived off Dubrovnik at first light the next morning with no further incident. We found our way to the commercial port, where we checked into Croatia. Dubrovnik is the southernmost entry port for Croatia, one of several ex-Yugoslavian countries in this area. As we drove into the port we were startled to see that the hills all around had been burned off. The fires must have been severe; all of the brush, fields, and trees were burned, right down to the homes along the shoreline. Hillside buildings had been gutted. While I was waiting for Stephen to complete the check-in formalities, I asked the dockmaster about the fires.

"A month ago," he said.

"Intentional?" I asked.

"Eight fires, all at once. What do you think?"

"Sad," I said. After checking in, we proceeded three miles up the Dubrovnik River to a marina amid the burned mountains, in an otherwise idyllic, fiord-like setting. I asked the woman at the marina reception about the fires. They had obviously come very close to the marina. "Yes, very scary," she said.

"Intentional?"

She shrugged. "Up north, yes. Here, we don't know. It might have been lightning."

A few days later, in a taxi, we asked the driver about the fires. "Croatian military did it, I think; just in case there were Serbs in the hills."

"That is where the Serbs hid during the war?" I wanted to know.

"Yes."

"They shelled Dubrovnik from there?"

"Yes, guns, there," the taxi driver pointed. So everyone had his or her own theory about the fires. None of them denied that it was frightening to watch the burning for two days.

Croatia was subject to ethnic conflicts from 1991 to 1995, and the old city of Dubrovnik in particular was a target for Serbian guns. In the last few years, however, thanks to some funds from the United Nations, the old town had been lovingly restored to near-pristine condition. Walking along the ramparts of the city walls, we could see how much damage there had been. All the roofs in the old town were red tile, and about half of them were covered with bright new tile, making clear the effect of the war.

There was more evidence of the conflict in outlying areas: shell-pocked walls of buildings, boats full of holes in our marina, and fire-gutted homes. Despite these reminders, there was little talk about the war years. Croatia was looking to the future, not to the past.

The islands off the Croatia mainland saw little activity during the war, so there was no damage to their buildings. Korčula, north of Dubrovnik, was one of these islands. We pulled up to a stone pier, just below the main gate to what must be one of the most perfectly preserved medieval towns in the world. Built around a small hill, the town was nearly all blond stone. Narrow streets were covered with stone arches, and the streets led down to the gates through the surrounding walls, to the rocky shore. It took only an hour to circumnavigate the whole town.

One morning during our visit, a pleasant middle-aged chap came to our boat with some flyers about a dance performance that evening. "The Moreska," he said, "a sword dance. It is danced only on Korčula, and only by men born in Korčula."

"There are no women?" I asked.

"Only one, and she is from Korčula too. It is a very exciting dance. You must come." We love native dancing, so there was no question that we would attend.

The dance took place in an old stone courtyard. Tiers of benches had been placed in a semicircle around the edges of the yard. We arrived early and had our choice of seats. We headed for what we thought would be the best seats in the house: front row and center.

Our friend from the morning popped up just then. "Don't sit in the front row," he advised.

"No?"

"People have been hurt there."

"Hurt?"

"The swords, you see." Well, we didn't see at the time, but we certainly did later, during the performance. We sat in the fourth row, to be safe.

The origins of the dance reach back into the centuries. It tells the old story of a maiden kidnapped by an evil king and his cohorts (in black), then rescued by the handsome knight and his entourage (in white). The battle to secure the freedom of the maiden was danced in two concentric circles of men: black inside, white outside. They moved in opposing directions and made constant contact with their swords as they danced—a bit like fencing with twenty opponents. We noticed two young boys at opposite sides of the arena, outside the circles, holding a number of swords. As the dance progressed, various dancers tossed damaged swords to one of the boys and received a fresh one in exchange. The dance was very physical—the dancers were all sweating and panting at its end—and more and more swords were tossed out of the ring. Fortunately, before all the swords wore out, the maiden was rescued.

*   *   *   *   *

In the Adriatic we discovered some more of the "named" winds of the Mediterranean, like the *meltemi* in the Aegean. The Adriatic has the *bora,* a northerly wind, and the *sirocco,* a southerly wind, both of which can build to a gale in no time. At the island of Hvar, we were caught by a *sirocco.* In the middle of the night a heavy swell came into the harbor, dangerously rocking the boats at our wharf from side to side. We had neighbors lying closely on both sides of us, and as the boats rocked left to right, we worried about our rig getting caught in the rig of our neighbors, causing damage to both boats. We stood watches through the night again, adjusting our lines when we could, to minimize the danger.

At first light, we left Hvar in a hurry and made a rough channel crossing to the town of Trogir on the mainland. There we found a small marina inside a river mouth, right in the middle of town. We tied up there, thinking it would be more sheltered. Unfortunately, there was no breakwater for southerly winds, and the waves came crashing into the marina with such force that the docks were nearly ripped apart.

"Why is the marina unprotected like this?" we asked.

"It isn't usually this bad," they said. Just our luck.

On another day we tucked into a small cove that had been recommended to us by friends. Excellent protection, they said, and just lovely surroundings. The cove *was* lovely, with pine trees coming down to the rocky shores that surrounded a very small body of water. Three boats were already anchored there. We moseyed around, but I finally admitted to Stephen that I didn't much like the cramped feeling of the place. Without a word, he turned around and motored out.

An hour later we tied to a wharf opposite the small town of Pasman. At sunset the wind died and the evening was blissfully peaceful.

"Must be 'lovely' at that little anchorage," Stephen remarked.

"I'm quite happy here," I retorted.

Around midnight I awoke to an eerie feeling. I couldn't tell what was wrong. The air was absolutely still—too still. Then I heard a peculiar roar. I got up and went out on deck. The noise came from across the river. It sounded like wind and rain—gale-force wind and torrential rain—coming closer. In a moment, in the ambient light of the wharf, I could see a line on the water. On our side the water was still calm, but on the other side, the water was jumping with wind and rain. The line came steadily toward us. Bam! It hit. The wind went to 40 knots, and the rain fell in sheets. "How lovely do you think that anchorage is now?" I shouted above the noise, as I ducked below.

These stories may make Croatia sound as if it were constantly blasted with terrible weather. Not constantly … I tell these stories just to demonstrate how volatile the weather is in almost any area of the world. The South Pacific, with its "predictable" trade winds, has fronts, line squalls, and thunderstorms. Southeast Asia has its monsoons. The Mideast has a two-month weather window, and we were through the area in two months, so no really bad weather caught us. We were lucky in the Black Sea. The eastern Mediterranean has *meltemis,* lots of them. Why shouldn't the Adriatic have dreadful weather all its own? There didn't seem to be any season when we could sail anywhere, even in the beautiful Mediterranean Sea, without worrying about storms.

From our last Croatian port, we made an overnight passage across the top of the Adriatic to "the Bride"—Venice. At daybreak we were again in the path of large ships—cruise ships this time. They were making an early-morning arrival to give their passengers the benefit of the day in port. We wallowed in their wake.

Sailing into Venice was exactly as we had dreamed for so long—St. Mark's Square looming ahead, the ferries and vaporettos crisscrossing our bow, the Lido falling to our stern—a very romantic picture. And it was a very romantic occasion that we had planned for this visit: our 25th wedding anniversary.

We pulled into a marina at the eastern end of Venice, a district and island called St. Elena. Although it was an island, it was possible to walk over bridges from there to St. Mark's Square. At a large park on one side of the island, joggers loped in the morning, young mothers pushed their baby prams in the midday, elders sat on the bright red benches in the late afternoon sun, and young (and old) lovers wandered under the trees in the evening.

Our stay in Venice exemplified the independence voyaging afforded us. Here we were in a local setting, but only minutes from some of the best sights of our world. I loved the "local" part of it as much as I did the beauty and grandeur of St. Mark's Square. We stayed long enough for the merchants to recognize us as we bought coffee, tomatoes, and pasta. Their greetings were always warm, even though they knew my responses would be in dreadful Italian. The trattoria a block from the marina welcomed us many evenings; we were nearly as regular as the locals who came for their "plates" to take home. We enjoyed walking in "our" park too, wandering under the trees, watching the children, the dogs, the lovers....

* * * * *

Directly across the top of the Adriatic from Venice is another ex-Yugoslavian country, Slovenia. This tiny country of barely two million people has only a few harbors on its short coastline of 25 miles, but we decided it might be worth a look. Because the town of Piran was the closest—only 50 miles from Venice—it became our destination. Piran is a charming, old-world town, and the birthplace of Giuseppe Tartini. Unless you are a violinist or an aficionado of baroque music, you would never have heard of Tartini. But everyone in Piran certainly has, because there isn't a street corner that doesn't have something on it named for him. I was interested in this attraction because when I was a young student of the violin, I sawed through a number of Tartini sonatas. Of course I had no idea then that he was born in Piran, but now I was enchanted.

While we were with the Piran officials, checking into Slovenia, I chatted with one of the port police and asked if they had many American yachts call at Piran. "Rare," he said. I felt as if we had made a voyaging discovery: Americans in Slovenia! Later in the afternoon, however, as we took pictures of the harbor, we noticed another sailboat coming into the tiny marina—a boat we did not recognize, with an American flag flying. We quickly helped them come alongside and took their lines to secure them to the dock. The transom said they were from Florida, but their voices were distinctly accented, suggesting not Florida or anywhere else in the States. Luk explained that they were from

Slovenia originally, but had left Tito's Yugoslavia some thirty-five years earlier to resettle in Florida. They had recently retired and decided to return to their homeland—on a sailboat they had built themselves. Nada suddenly burst into tears. We offered our hands to bring them ashore. I was a little misty-eyed myself. What an extraordinary story, and wasn't this a little bit peculiar? Americans welcoming them back to Slovenia, their homeland.

I saw my friend from the port police the next day. "So, another American yacht," I said, "two in one day!"

"Ah, but the other one is really one of us," he replied, grinning proudly.

*   *   *   *   *

From Slovenia, we began our trek back down the Adriatic. We had originally planned to go down the west side and call at several Italian ports, but we were discouraged from this plan by *Italian* sailors. They explained that the western Adriatic is very shallow, and the entrances to the ports are often silted and too shallow to enter. And the harbors are few and far between, so that in bad weather it is more difficult to find shelter. It was now October, and the summer weather had definitely ended. The weather coming up the sea in that month was just a taste of the more frequent changes we could expect. It didn't take much to convince us that it would be better to travel back south through Croatia to Dubrovnik, and to cross to the west side from there.

As we came back up the river to the Dubrovnik marina, we were pleased to see that the charred hills had acquired a green fuzz in our absence. The burned trees appeared a deep bronze in the late afternoon sunlight, turning the rather desolate-looking landscape into a thing of some beauty.

The morning we departed Dubrovnik, we motored down to the commercial port to check out. On the radio, Stephen announced our intentions to the port captain, who in turn sent the officials to us at the wharf. They were two young, fresh-faced lads, tall and blond, from Immigration and Customs. As they stamped our passports and ship's papers, they asked where we were from and how long we had been sailing. We explained that we had left San Francisco five years ago and had come across the Pacific and Indian Oceans, and up the Red Sea to the Mediterranean. They stared at us, eyes wide. Everyone in this part of the world assumes that an American yacht in the Med has come across the Atlantic, which isn't that far, after all. But our route was "off the globe" to them; the Pacific might as well be Mars.

"Just the two of you?"

"Yes."

"Any storms?"

"Not really."

"How long before you are home?"

"Oh, a few more years." They laughed. Such a life must have been beyond their dreams.

From Dubrovnik we were heading southwest for some place on the coast of Italy, as far south as we could manage in a day, a night, and another day. Angling across the bottom of the Adriatic, we would again pass the present-day Yugoslavia and Albania, but our distance from their shores would be increasing steadily. Mindful of our experience approaching Dubrovnik from the south, we were only slightly disconcerted when a small, high-speed jet buzzed us, in the middle of the day (for once). I mean, right over our mast. And then a helicopter whopped by, and then a few more planes of various sizes, all with a very military look about them. Some of them dipped down to get a closer look at us. When a second jet screamed over our mast, I said to Stephen, "And just where is Kosovo from here?" A quick check of the atlas and the charts confirmed that Kosovo was right "over there," in the direction these aircraft were coming from and going to.

The BBC radio broadcasts had kept us abreast of world events, as always. We surmised, therefore, that this plane activity was the result of the first peace accord in Kosovo, signed just the day before. The planes were on reconnaissance missions to check for the removal of troops—which, as we now know, never happened, as that sad chapter of ethnic conflict continued for so many more months.

At the end of the day we were still off the Albanian coast, but out toward the middle of the Adriatic. At sunset we noticed a couple of fishing boats coming off the coast, chugging along, nothing out of the ordinary. But a few minutes later a couple of rigid-bottom inflatables (RBIs) came whizzing into view. They were about 25 feet long—fancy boats for the coast of Albania, I thought. We had seen boats like these, in expensive tourist areas, used for dive expeditions, or as ship-to-shore vessels for large, fancy yachts. They have open cockpits; large, high-horsepower outboard engines, most often two; and sometimes a small awning to provide sun protection for the helmsman at the midcockpit steering station. The two RBIs we saw were heading due west. Unlike the fishing boats, they did not slow down when they reached mid-sea, nor did they alter course. They had a serious goal to the west.

"This must mean," I said to Stephen, "that they are crossing to Italy, and that they intend to land on the Italian shore in the middle of the night. Can you think of any reason why an Albanian craft would be streaking across the Adriatic through the night to reach Italy in the dark?"

"Whatever it is, it can't be legal," Stephen replied. We steered a careful course to stay away from them, although that wasn't difficult, since they were traveling at a relatively high speed.

Several days later, coincidentally, we saw an article in the *International Herald Tribune* reporting on the illegal smuggling of people from Albania to the Italian coast. The article described the RBIs, the nighttime flight, and the relatively huge sums of money that the Albanians were raking in for this activity. The illegals of the week were Sri Lankans.

*   *   *   *   *

Our passages in the past few months had been made more anxious by the weather, the lack of radar, erratic and weird ship traffic, military actions, and illegal RBIs—and also by our "wonky" engine (as the Aussies would say). We seemed to end up motoring a lot in the Mediterranean. We often had head winds, or no wind at all, and we are not sailing purists when it comes to keeping the passages as short and as efficient as possible. If motoring would get us there before dark, or in one day instead of two, we did not keep sailing "just because." We turned on the motor.

With all this nonpurist motoring, we had become acutely aware of several problems with the engine. We had had an oil leak for months, but by this time in the Adriatic it was so bad that we had to stop the engine every six to eight hours to add more oil. And then the engine wouldn't restart. This appeared to be an electrical problem, but Stephen's probing of all the electrical items seemed to indicate otherwise. We would sit in the cockpit glaring at the ignition, willing it to get with it and start, while we slopped around in the inevitable swell. After about an hour and many attempts, the engine would mysteriously restart.

As if that weren't enough, there seemed to be something the matter with the freshwater cooling system. The water reservoir would suddenly, inexplicably, go dry, and we'd have to refill it. And then it would boil over. And then go dry. Consequently, we had to check the reservoir every hour to be sure the engine wouldn't overheat. If it overheated, we should have been able to tell that from the temperature gauge—but it wasn't working either!

Every hour as we checked the water, we'd pat the engine and tell it what a good job it was doing and to keep up the good work, because we had to get to Malta to find a proper engine mechanic. I had just read a story about a yacht like ours with engine problems that the captain knew he should be attending to, but wasn't in the right place to do so. He was in the South Pacific, motoring through the pass of a coral atoll. The engine stalled, and in a flash, the boat was on the reef. The boat and everything in it was lost on that reef, as the sea pounded it to death. And all because of a wonky engine. We may have been a sailboat, but we needed a dependable engine to be safe.

In the first week of November we sailed around the heel of Italy and pointed our bow to the tiny, beige island just below Sicily. The engine started one last time as we entered the channel of Valletta, Malta's large and intricate harbor. We hoped that in Malta we could solve the engine problems once and for all.

Leaving the Adriatic, it was a marvel to realize that inside of six months we had "conquered" two of the most influential cities of the world's history: Constantinople (now Istanbul) and Venice. If pride were not a sin, I'd be proud.

∗ ∗ ∗ ∗ ∗

And a final note: how many readers have rushed to their reference books to discover why the chapter title doesn't sound right? I had it in my mind that Venice was the "Bride of the Adriatic," a filmy, lacy, misty vision that can certainly be Venice in the early morning fog. But in fact there are two allusions here—"Bride of the Sea" and "Queen of the Adriatic"—and I'd gotten them mixed. The latter refers to the historic beauty of the city, but "Bride of the Sea" refers to an ancient "wedding" ceremony performed by the Venetian doge. He threw a ring into the Adriatic, saying, "We wed thee, O Sea, in token of perpetual domination." The mix-up still seems to be an appropriate chapter heading. We had celebrated our wedding anniversary in Venice, after all. And that doge quote could have provided the title for this book. "Perpetual domination" definitely described the sea's hold on us.

Temples and Ta'xbiex

Malta

Tiny and beige, the island of Malta has an extraordinary history. Because of its strategic location in the Mediterranean, just south of Sicily, it was a target in any conflict that swept the area. Phoenicians, Romans, North African Arabs, Normans, Castilians, Turks, French, and the Knights of the Order of St. John have all left their mark on this small isle. Today the island is invaded mainly by British retirees, known to the Maltese as "wrinklies."

The most fascinating remnant of the island's past is the megalithic temples, proclaimed to be "the oldest surviving free-standing structures in the world." Five thousand years old, give or take a few hundred, these temples are constructed of huge Stonehenge-like stones. Unlike Stonehenge, however, the tall, erect stones of the Malta temples were placed shoulder-to-shoulder to form walls, corridors, and rooms. There are a few horizontal stones, thought to be altars or lintels.

Only a few days after our arrival, we had occasion to take a look at the temples. We bounced across the island in one of Malta's fine old buses. Colorfully decorated in yellows, reds, and oranges, the old bodies of the buses are fitted out with engines that either purr or cough. The bus interiors also vary in degree of comfort. The inside decorations are the whim of the driver and are usually religious in nature, a statue of Mary or Jesus at the very least.

We found the temples near the town of Qrendi. The temples themselves— the two principal structures—are called Haga Qim and Mnajdra. (I never tired of *looking* at Maltese names. Pronouncing them, however, was a lot of work.) We walked among the stones and marveled at their size and age.

The next week we were in the car of our sail-repair person, who was asking polite questions: How did we like Malta? Had we seen much of the island?

"Oh, my, yes. We were so impressed with the Haga Qim temples—"

"You saw them?" he cried. "It's a good thing! They fell down last week."

Fell down? A storm had passed over the island with strong winds, and the stones had fallen like dominoes, one on top of the other. We were aghast. They had stood for 5,000 years, and after we looked at them, they fell down! "Oh, we'll put them back up," Tony said. "Don't worry."

Indeed, we had no time to worry about stone monuments. We were now frantic to prepare *Another Horizon* for the winter, for it was getting late in the year. We needed to get locals working on our various projects before the winter winds started to blow in earnest. But first we had to get the boat hauled out of the water and settled into a boatyard, where the work could be more efficiently executed.

This was a new experience for us—the Maltese haulout. We were already in position, Joseph told us, by being tied up at a stone quay, one of many that line the large harbor. From our berth, the yard in which we planned to spend the winter was just across the road and behind a fence—only 50 feet away. But how we covered those 50 feet was the most heart-stopping experience of this kind that I can remember.

Haulouts are often accomplished by a cradle on a railway track that starts in deep water. The boat enters the cradle in deep water, and a tractor pulls the cradle out along the rails to some spot in the boatyard. More modern yards have a Travelift, which moves out over a small slip that contains the boat and then lowers straps into the water, positioning them under the hull. The boat is lifted out, cradled in the straps, moved to a spot in the yard, and put into a cradle there. But not in Malta.

At the appointed time, a large crane was maneuvered onto the road between *Another Horizon* and the empty slot on the other side of the fence. The crane arm swung out above our deck. Straps were lowered into the water and under the hull. With a loud creak and groan, the crane lifted all 30,000 pounds of *Another Horizon* out of the water and swung her across the road, over the fence, and into the yard, where the yard workers propped her up with wooden two-by-fours.

Once well-braced in the yard, we were thankful for our position on land. The winter winds began to blow, and we could see that many parts of the Valletta harbor were not winter-worthy. With a northeast wind, what the locals called a *gregale*, a swell swept into the harbor and set the Med-moored boats rocking and pitching. From our boatyard position we could look out over the harbor and watch the moored boats dive and plunge. There was no doubt in my mind that we could not have tolerated living aboard under such conditions. As inconvenient as it was to be "on the hard," I was thankful for once to be rock-solid on land.

But inconvenient it was. For instance, liquids from the interior of the boat normally are passed through the hull by pumps and swished out to the sea. With the boat sitting up in the air, it is not possible to swish any liquids. To take care of one's body excretions, for instance, one had to get on a ladder alongside the hull, climb down from deck height to the ground (around ten feet), then walk along a muddy path to the yard's toilet. Depending on the day, this could be a wet, cold, smelly, and definitely inconvenient way to go to the bathroom.

Showers too had to be taken in this manner. Juggling shampoo, towels, and clean clothes, I would try to keep my shoes dry while I showered (hoping that my clean clothes would not fall off the hook onto the wet floor), wiping the shower grit from my feet before putting my shoes back on. This to-ing and fro-ing from the outhouse and shower got old very rapidly. I like it when my home is self-contained. I'm less enamored of the "camping" aspects of living on the hard—going to an outhouse even to brush my teeth. Although I could cook on the onboard galley stove, I had to load up the dirty dishes in a bucket, haul them down the ladder, and then take them along the possibly wet, cold, smelly, muddy, and definitely inconvenient road to the washroom.

We would soon be heading for the States for the holiday period to get our stateside lives in order, however, and it was reassuring to know that our home would be safe on land while we were away.

Before leaving we had to be sure that our local workpersons were signed up and ready to take care of our needs. The engine, as we have noted, needed attention yet again.

We called in three mechanics, all of whom said the engine would have to be removed from the boat to be overhauled. It had hundreds of hours of use, they said. It was clear there were multiple problems, they said. It had to come out. Yeah, yeah, we said. I think we've heard all of this before, and we don't care for your analysis. But when the fourth guy came along and said the engine had to come out, we relented. How, we queried Chris, could they accomplish that heavy task with the boat sitting ten feet up in the air?

Back on stage came the crane, still on the other side of the fence. The crane operator swung its long arm over the fence, the tip hovering over our cockpit. A one-inch-thick cable with a giant hook on the end was lowered through the companionway into the innards of the engine room. With incredible delicacy, the crane operator plucked out the engine. Not a single human hand touched the engine, and not a single piece of nonhuman material surrounding it was kissed. With the same precision, the engine was lowered onto Chris's truckbed. And Chris drove away with the whole engine, every bit of it. Nothing *strewn* this time—it was gone, kit and kaboodle.

And we drove off for the airport and home.

*   *   *   *   *

We came to Malta for the winter season because we understood they spoke English. Since we anticipated doing a lot of work on the boat, we thought it would be easier if we could explain the problems in English to people who also spoke English.

But it turns out that the Maltese generally do not speak English unless English is spoken to them. Otherwise, they speak the mysterious and complicated Maltese language that reflects their long history of occupation. Depending on which linguist you talk to, the roots of the language are Phoenician or Arabic; the grammar has a Semitic base; and the vocabulary is strewn with Sicilian, Italian, French, Spanish, and English words. The alphabet is written in Roman characters, but it is actually a transliteration of Semitic sounds. How else would you get the name of the town we lived in for six months? Ta'xbiex is pronounced something like "Tashbeesh."

I tried to get my mouth around the *x*'s, *md*'s, and apostrophes. The nearby town of Mdina wasn't so difficult, but the fishing boats called "dghajsa" looked like a bit of a tongue twister. I managed the usual "hello" (*bongu*) and "thanks" (*grazzi*—there's the Italian influence), and with much difficulty, "please" (*jekk joghogbok*), for which I usually got a slight smile and a merry twinkle in the eyes.

* * * * *

Language was always something with which to struggle as we went around. We were adequate in French, which carried us through the Pacific well enough. But our only other language was German. Since the Germans didn't get into colonization much in centuries past, there is little of that language other than in Europe.

We found, however, that we were rarely without someone in our vicinity who could speak some English. Although the English was, at times, rather rudimentary, more often than not it was adequate for our purposes—directions, costs, basic items in a market. It was when we had to *explain* something that we often had difficulty, resorting to flapping hands, drawings, and phrase-book translations.

We always had a phrase book with us for the language of the country we were visiting. Learning a few simple words—even if they were learned phonetically—was usually a good icebreaker. Thais, Yemenis, and Turks didn't expect us to know their language, and so when we made an effort to go beyond "hello" and "how much," they were pleased. Thai and Arabic were certainly the most difficult languages we faced, with their non-Roman alphabets.

Occasionally some sound effects were effective. Stephen is lactose-intolerant, so he is unable to eat any dairy products made with cow's milk. Goat and sheep milk, however, are fine. In the eastern Mediterranean in particular, it was possible to find goat or sheep's cheese and yogurt, which delighted us both. Inevitably I would forget the words for goat or sheep, and without a dictionary, the Greek or Turkish words, for instance, were beyond me. I was not shy, however, about "moo-ing" or "baa-ing" while pointing to various products in the markets.

I was frustrated in Italy and throughout the Caribbean by our lack of Italian, and especially Spanish. It was our experience, in fact, that the stranger the land (Oman and Turkey, for instance), the more likely it was that English could be found. But in the small towns of Europe and Central America, English was not prevalent.

I am envious of people who have done well with languages, and I'm sorry to say that they are not usually Americans. We marveled at a German friend who was with us in Turkey. When we celebrated the American Thanksgiving at our marina, one American told the story of our holiday (in English, of course) while our German friend simultaneously translated it into French and German. About this time, someone told us this joke: What do you call a person who speaks two languages? *Bilingual.* What do you call a person who speaks three languages? *Trilingual.* What do you call a person who speaks only one language? *American.* Although I can manage in French, count in German, and stumble around in Spanish and Italian, I reckon I am an American in this case. I have never really gone after a language long enough to become fluent.

One of the disconcerting things about my lack of language facility is that there were many times when I knew that the locals were talking about me. Indonesians would giggle as I passed. Samoans called out their three English words and then chattered among themselves as we passed in the market. The Turkish women frowned and turned toward one another as I walked by with a cheerful *merhaba* (hello). What were they talking about? What were they saying about me? It was so frustrating not to know. But perhaps that was only fair. If I couldn't understand what they were saying, why shouldn't they say whatever they wished? And so it was in Malta. The old neighbors in our corner grocery glowered at my *skuzani* (excuse me). When I switched to English, there was a flurry of *x*'s and *q*'s without *u*'s. What were they saying about me? I was just insecure enough to want to know.

*   *   *   *   *

We were justified in coming to Malta, however, when it came to describing the engine's ills. Chris understood, and he could talk engine language that we understood. Tony knew what had to be done to the portholes. Nick said he would get the bottom painted before we returned. They all spoke excellent English, and we were sure they understood that all the work had to be done by the time we returned from the States.

We returned after the holidays to discover that *nothing* had been done while we were gone. And we were very sure this had nothing to do with language difficulties. So we would have to remain in camping mode until the engine was reinstalled and we could be launched into the water again.

In the meantime, we looked for some off-the-boat amusement to pass the time. One Sunday we followed some Maltese friends to a restaurant on the north coast for a rabbit dinner. Rabbits are raised on Malta for food, the way we raise cattle for meat. The restaurant we visited served a rabbit dinner, especially on Sunday. Since your dinner must be freshly, ah, slaughtered, it was served only on that day. Rabbit is like lamb, kangaroo, or Bambi for me; I just had to put the image of the little hippity-hoppity out of my mind and eat. It was delicious.

Malta was on the edge of spring, and some wildflowers had begun to appear. The fields near the restaurant held some photographic promise, I thought, so I wandered down the road toward a headland. There was a tall curbstone at the side of the road. I stepped up and began to walk along it for a better visual advantage. I wasn't paying attention to my feet. I was looking out over the fields—and I accidentally stepped off the edge. I went headlong onto the road, a newly "paved" road of large, rough-cut stone. For some reason I could not get my hands up in front of me to brace the fall, and I fell flat on my face, quite literally.

The area from the bridge of my nose to the tip of my chin looked like raw hamburger. The cuts appeared to be mostly superficial, but after some poking and prodding in front of a mirror, I could see that I would not be able to repair all the damage myself. A jagged piece of upper lip just wouldn't stay in place.

Our Maltese friends were immediately on the case. They would take us to a local 24-hour emergency clinic, the equivalent of our hospital emergency rooms. The clinic personnel took one look at my face and rushed me into the treatment room. The cuts and abrasions were cleaned; I was sewn up and sent on my way.

"What do I owe?"

"Nothing."

"I need to sign a form?"

"No."

"There is nothing else for me to do?"

"No." I was finding it hard to leave without having signed forty forms and paying large sums.

"Come back in a few days so we can check the stitches," they said.

I went to the clinic three times in all—with no appointment, no waiting, no charge, and no forms. Here was socialized medicine at its best. If not shiny new, the clinic was clean and the staff very able. I was impressed. My face healed nicely, the scars blending well with the rest of my age-related imperfections in that area.

About the time my face started to return to normal, Stephen began to complain of an intermittent sore throat. After a week of complaints, I decided it was time to seek advice. In Malta, every neighborhood has a pharmacy—a real drug dispensary, not one of the super drugstores that we have at home. And in these Maltese pharmacies a doctor presided at a clinic for a few hours each day. These were not free clinics like the one that fixed my face. In the pharmacies, one visit cost all of five dollars. But again, no appointment was necessary, and there was no paperwork. We went to our neighborhood pharmacy doctor and he diagnosed Stephen's problem as a form of angina.

We were astonished. Stephen had just had his annual physical! Dr. Borg said that this "presentation" of angina (the sore throat) was rare, and hard to detect. He himself had never seen it before. Not only were we astounded at Borg's diagnosis, but we were truly amazed at his diagnostic talent.

He sent Stephen down the street to a heart clinic, where they worked him in at the *end* of their regular clinic hours that day—*at 9:30 PM*. They did tests and said it looked like heart spasms. He needed an angiogram.

"Okay," said Stephen, "where do I do that?"

At the state hospital up the hill, it turned out, but there was a problem. There was a two-month waiting list for this test. Yes, you could easily have a heart attack and die while waiting for the test.

"And this is the worst of socialized medicine," said our Maltese friends.

Stephen was on a plane back to Berkeley the next day, and within 48 hours of his arrival he had had the angiogram and an angioplasty was performed on the spot. I will never again complain about U.S. health services, but we were very grateful for the Maltese services too. And weren't we glad Stephen's heart spasms happened, and were diagnosed, while we were on land with an accessible airport.

*   *   *   *   *

As April approached, the engine still had not been completely overhauled. Chris was trying to order parts from Italy, since Malta was too small to have a handy inventory. And the Italians ... "Well, they're Italians," said Chris. They sent the wrong parts, they said they couldn't get some of the parts at all, and, by the way, did we know this engine wasn't manufactured any more? *Yes, we did!* And, therefore, parts were hard to find. The Italians were faxing Estonia, and hoped to be back to us in the near future.

The Easter holidays came into view. Malta is about 98 percent Catholic, and the church is central to their lives. Surprisingly, Good Friday is more significant to Maltese than Easter Sunday, and it is celebrated with elaborate processions from the churches through the streets of the towns. Although each church had its own variations of this event, in general they consisted of carrying large, heavy platforms with representations of the twelve Stations of the Cross on them. Six to eight men hoisted these heavy platforms to their shoulders as they walked through the streets. The physical strain of carrying the platforms was visible in their faces. In between the platforms were costumed characters from the time of Jesus' crucifixion (Judas and the disciples, for instance).

The Maltese love pageantry of this sort, and they will take any excuse for a parade. During our months on the island we saw a number of reenactments of Maltese historical events, with elaborate and colorful costumes, musical bands of varying talents, knights on horses, and cannon and muskets fired. At one such event we were ambling down an old cobbled street in central Valetta, the capital of Malta. Suddenly there was an eighteenth-century carriage with two brace of horses galloping up the street, a fairly narrow road with tall stone buildings on both sides. The sound of hooves and carriage wheels on the cobbles echoed, exaggerating the hurried sound of the vehicle charging toward the town gate. There was a Grand Master in that carriage, and we peasants stepped hastily aside to let him pass. It was a thrilling sight, and one of those times when the sight and sound of the moment surrounds and encompasses you so completely that you almost believe you are in a time warp.

*   *   *   *   *

As April and Easter passed, we were getting impatient with our engine mechanic, the Italians, and the Estonians. The weather was warm, the winds were blowing favorably, and other yachts were heading out. And we had no engine. The days dragged on into May, but finally the engine was reinstalled and we were relaunched. It was time for us to depart Malta.

We checked out with the officials one afternoon, announcing our intent to leave early the next morning. Returning to the boat, we turned on the engine for a last check and discovered that the alternator (the part of the engine that charges the batteries) had quit! *This is ridiculous,* I screamed inwardly—months out of the water, months of ladders, months of outhouses. Stephen pleaded with the mechanic to please come immediately and get things in order, while I fumed. Chris did come straight away and took the alternator, promising to return in the morning. By early afternoon the next day he hadn't come back. Since there was smoke still coming out of my ears, Stephen called. Chris said that the alternator had burned up during our test run, just after we had been relaunched. He was very sorry, and he was trying to get it ready for us "in a few hours." But we didn't have a few hours. Since we had checked out of Malta the previous day, we were already supposed to be gone.

International Maritime Law says that any vessel has 24 hours of free time, if required, to stay in any country without formalities. That is, if you have engine problems, you can stop in any country for 24 hours to fix said engine and then depart again, without going through the extensive, tedious formalities of checking in and out.

Desperate to forestall any more delays, we hurried to the Maltese officials and asked what we could do. Our 24 hours would be up at 3 PM. If we could depart by sundown, they said, we would not have to check back into the country. At five o'clock, Chris came with the alternator. It was installed, it worked, and just as the sun touched the horizon we called the Malta Port Authority on the radio to announce our departure.

We now faced a nighttime passage to Sicily, something we had wanted to avoid on our first passage after so many months. Getting back into the sailing routine, and finding our sea legs, is far more difficult in the dark. However, this passage gave us an opportunity to try out a new piece of equipment we had brought from the States. It was a Christmas present to each other: a night-vision scope.

The technology of this equipment came to public notice during the first Persian Gulf War. News programs showed shots of Tehran at night, the eerie yellow-green picture of trees and desolate streets illuminated with one of these night-vision instruments. Ours was small and designed to be held to one eye, like a spyglass. This equipment had been available when we started the voyage, but it was very expensive, and with our radar we thought it redundant. But early in our stay in Malta a friend showed us one, and we were astonished. We stood on the balcony of his apartment, looking out into a dark bay. With the naked eye we saw a single light on the water, and nothing more. Through the night-vision scope we could see that the light was a sailboat; we could see what direction it was sailing, and even the people on board. Even more incredible were the two fishing boats we could see through the scope—two fishing boats that had no lights, and therefore were *not* visible to the naked eye.

At this moment, standing on our friend's balcony and staring through this phenomenal instrument, I thought of our incident in the Adriatic, when we went through the NATO exercise off the coast of Albania. I realized instantly that we were allowed to wander through that exercise because they, of course, *had night-vision scopes.* They could see what we were, could read the name of the boat, could see the American flag, and could see us on deck frowning, trying to figure out what was going on. They probably had a good laugh.

It was also immediately evident, standing there on our friend's balcony, that if *we* had had one of these little jobbies, we would have known instantly that the odd, blinking red lights were helicopters, saving ourselves hours of anxiety.

I used to think of the radar as my periscope into the night, but with the night-vision scope it was now as if the *lights were turned back on.*

We crossed Malta Channel, sailing to the bottom of Sicily in a brilliance of night-vision scope light—watching the waves heave, watching the terns flutter over the crests, watching the fishing boats pass in luminous detail—watching every aspect of our passage as if it were daylight. Incredible.

Marking Time

Western Mediterranean

Leaving Malta we were a long way from home, but we had already started thinking "home." I don't know why, but ever since Stephen returned from the States with the tiny wire stent sitting quietly alongside his heart, we were both silently thinking ahead—much farther ahead than usual. According to the voyage plan, we still had two years and thousands of miles to go. Still, the word "home" kept creeping into our conversations: "when we're back home …" "if we were home …" "in our new home …" But of course we couldn't just charge on, willy-nilly. There was the weather to consider. It was May now, and we couldn't prudently cross the Atlantic until after the hurricane season was over, which meant late November at the earliest.

I was momentarily conflicted, wishing we could be making miles toward the finish. But once the anchor was down along the shores of Sicily, we couldn't resist the lure of the narrow streets of Syracusa. Or the taste of the *cassata,* and the sweet, twenty-five-cents-a-pound mussels in the markets. Thoughts of home slithered away. We had seven months to kill before crossing the Atlantic, and we'd probably never have a chance to be here again. *Pay attention to this day, and leave tomorrow for tomorrow.*

We sailed past Mount Etna, which was smoking but not erupting, then hesitated briefly at the bottom of the Messina Strait, trying to figure out how to get through it. We would be passing between Scilla and Charybdis, you see.

Messina Strait is that very narrow piece of water between the northeast corner of Sicily (near where Charybdis is said to whirl) and the toe of the mainland (where Scilla is said to dangle her heads and feet). The line between the landmasses marks the division of the Tyrrhenian and the Ionian Seas, and because the density of the water is greater in one sea than in the other, there is a constant current *under* the surface of the water, going south. The usual tidal current goes both ways on top, however, and by forcing itself through such a narrow space, it can become very strong. The confluence of these two currents—underwater and surface—creates enormous whirlpools that are a force to reckon with. The passage between the most famous of the whirlpools, Charybdis, and the still-thriving cliff town of Scilla challenged us, as it has thousands of mariners from the time of Odysseus and before.

Because of some rearranging of the land by earthquakes over the centuries, the strait is not nearly as frightening as it might have been for Odysseus. Still, we were surprised by the currents—especially because they were not flowing the way they were supposed to, according to the tidal charts—and by the size and strength of the whirlpools. Near Charybdis ("the sucker-down") we had to veer off our course to avoid the turbulent water.

The ancients also talked about strong winds blasting down the steep slopes of Sicily and off the high cliffs of Calabria—that would be Scilla ("the render") blowing her head off (sorry, it's six heads, isn't it). The combination of wind and currents, especially when they're in conflict, is enough to daunt any mariner.

The most amazing event during our passage, however, was not the wind, the current, the incredibly choppy water, or the whirlpools. It was the sight ahead of us, just opposite Scilla. Stephen pointed it out to me. The look of the water completely changed. Instead of jumping dark blue with white all over, the water had a flat, dull-gray sheen to it.

We watched this area curiously, not quite aware that we were approaching the Scilla headland. We had dodged Charybdis, but Scilla's twelve feet were still "dangling" off to starboard, ready to pluck us away or squash us into the sea. But really, this dull-gray area looked like calm water, absolutely flat, with not even a little burbling. "Oh, this is weird," I said to Stephen. He agreed.

Our bow crossed the invisible line into the gray water—flat, dead gray, but *not* calm. The wind continued to blow at nearly 30 knots. "This is weird, really weird." We speculated that the currents were canceling each other out so that the water lay flat, even though the wind continued to blow. But there wasn't even a wind *ripple,* let alone what should have been (at nearly 30 knots) a wind *wave.* Really, really weird.

We were relieved to pass Scilla at last and plow fully into the Tyrrhenian Sea. We were all the more relieved to see that not only was the water calm now, it was also blue again. And the wind had stopped blowing—completely, just like that.

The southwest coast of Italy was unexpectedly charming and lovely. Unexpected? Yes, for me. I had traveled lots in Italy over the years, but only to major tourist cities—Rome, Venice, Florence, Naples, Milan. I had done some of it on my own, in my twenties, and some of it with Stephen, in my forties. I had tramped through all the museums and gazed at all the architecture, reading my history as I went. And I loved it all. Italy was and is one of my favorite places in the world.

But this southwest coast was a more intimate and personal Italy. The harbors were tiny, and the towns were nestled into clefts of the high cliffs that dropped precipitously into the ocean. There were only one or two streets in each town. Otherwise, you moved from one place to another up stairways, or along dusty switchback paths. There were gardens of fig and loquat trees, rose bushes already blooming, and grape vines and vegetables interspersed with daisies and poppies. The proverbial red and white geraniums filled window boxes and pots at doorways. Farther up the hills the buildings soon stopped, the cliffs being too sheer to build on—but not so sheer that lemon trees couldn't be carefully planted in terraced ledges. The villages were perfumed by lemons.

There was no great art in the churches there, and no famous architecture— just good fresh food and crisp local wine, clean-scented air, and plain, open people. They came down to the stone wharves to ogle our yacht, gesturing among themselves about our tall mast and strange pieces of equipment, and probably talking about us, what strange people we were—Americans, you know. And they smiled. I love Italians.

* * * * *

As we sailed on to Punta Campanella and Capri, to Napoli, and across the Golfo di Gaeta, we argued about whether we should take the time to "do" Rome. Rome was part of my twenties, but Stephen had seen only the airport. I balked at the time we'd waste finding a secure berth, a way to get into the city, and hotels. It would take at least a week, and what with waiting for weather, probably two weeks before we could continue.

"But how could we be wasting the time?" Stephen argued. "We have months to go before we need to be in Gibraltar, ready to cross the Atlantic. We have time … we have time." Stephen argues well, and he was right. We sailed on to Rome.

Theoretically it is possible to sail up the Tiber all the way to Rome, but as a practical matter it's not possible for a vessel of our size and depth. We could, however, enter the river, move up a few miles through a couple of bridges, and tie alongside the concrete walls that line the waterway. That put us in the airport suburb of Fiumicino, a short train ride from Rome. The nontourist town of Fiumicino was a sharp contrast to the hub of Rome, where lines to see the Sistine Chapel were over a mile long. A busy town, but not bustling, Fiumicino did not suffer the touristic scourge of Rome. Although you could walk to the airport from town, and we did, few foreign arrivals ever saw the town. They were into buses and taxis heading for the city the moment they left their planes. At most, a few tourists found their way to the train station, only two blocks from the Tiber. Did they even know that?

As soon as we could, we hopped the local train into Rome. Unfortunately, nearly all the sights in Rome were wrapped in scaffolding and shrouds for cleaning, polishing, refurbishing, and restoring, in preparation for "Roma 2000." A huge billboard digital clock across from the Forum ticked away the seconds to the new year, new decade, and new millennium. Watching the clock was both mesmerizing and preposterous. With eighteen million (plus or minus) seconds left, the clock was working its way down before our eyes.

There are lots of ways to mark time, but this clock was crazy—as if every second counted for something, if we only knew what. I wondered what was going to happen when the clock reached zero, and did they have it calibrated well enough that it would reach zero at the right time? "Let's get out of here," I said to Stephen. "That clock is driving me nuts."

It seemed ironic that with all the millions of dollars Italy was pouring into the restoration work, there was little apparent change in the *causes* of the deterioration. Cleaning façades doesn't stop the automobile emissions from blackening them again. Inside the churches, things were no more subtle. We attended a High Mass in one of the four Patriarchal Basilicas, where they were cleaning fourth-century mosaics above the altar. But during the service, the incense floating above the altar was at times so thick you couldn't see those mosaics, clean or unclean!

I put my foot in my mouth with Giuseppe, our Italian neighbor in Fiumicino, when I said something about the polluting traffic around the city center. "Ha," he said, "you know the cause of this pollution?"

"Well, there seem to be an inordinate number of vehicles whizzing around," I suggested.

"No! It's the tourists!"

"Ah," I replied—noncommittally, I hoped. A lecture on Italian politics was forthcoming, I could tell.

"Not what you think," he said. "The Pope's the problem." Giuseppe's English was good (compared to my Italian), but this conversation was still a little elliptical.

"So, tourists and the Pope," I ventured, "two things you can't do too much about, I guess."

"Italians, a proud, industrious people," [true] he countered, "they don't need the tourists. But the Pope ... well, *him* you have to pay attention to."

"What is it about the Pope?" I asked.

"He rules Rome; he says what happens, what doesn't." Giuseppe prattled on, and I smiled and nodded. A guest in his country, as close as I was to being one of those "tourists," I dared not challenge his view of Rome's difficulties.

*　*　*　*　*

Leaving the mainland, we sailed a short distance west to Sardinia, and then to Corsica. Although Corsica is French, its history is largely Italian. Except for the francs we were using, at times we wouldn't have known we had left Italy. The official language is French, but the locals speak Corsican, a curious blend of French and Italian. The food is also a blend of French and Italian, and since those nationalities were rivals for my favorite cuisine at the time, I was in food heaven.

We had fish soup with garlic croutons (French), swordfish in a tomato-onion sauce (Italian), stuffed eggplant with a peppery, perky, peppy stuffing (a Corsican specialty), and a floating-island dessert (liquid custard and caramel with meringue puffs floating on it) whose taste defies description. The bread was French, with that crispy crust and melt-in-the-mouth insides that go stale in an hour. And the wines! The Corsicans make their own, and like Italian wine, there doesn't seem to be a bad one in the lot.

We stayed rather longer than we had planned in Bonifacio, because another strong weather system came sweeping down from the continent and set up gale-force winds over the area.

In the midst of the gale, a couple of charter boats came into Bonifacio with the wind whistling straight down the narrow harbor, which made it very difficult to get into the marina. In order to slow his boat down, one poor chap's strategy seemed to be to hit something. After he crashed into three boats and two docks, another charter skipper hopped aboard and helped him out. A second fellow came swooping down and tried to use his engine to control his course. There were huge blasts of forward and backward—which might have been the right idea, if only he had turned the wheel at the same time. Most of the afternoon we were alternately out on the quay helping with lines, and on *Another Horizon* fending off other boats.

That evening we climbed to the *haute ville*—the high town above the harbor, atop an astonishingly vertical cliff. Looking out over the open water, we saw more white than blue as the wind tore the tops of the waves into furious whitecaps. I mentioned this to one of our charter boat neighbors later.

"Yes," she said, "in French we call it *les moutons-de-la-mer.*" Sheep of the sea—a rather apt description.

We waited five days in Bonifacio for the winds to abate.

* * * * *

Many of us have dreams in which we arrive at some significant destination, full of pride and joy at having arrived. For Stephen this dream destination was Villefranche-sur-mer, on the south coast of France between Nice and Monaco. Years before, he had driven from Cannes along this coast and had gazed out over the harbor, watching yachts bob at anchor. It was an idyllic harbor, he reported to me, and he wanted more than anything to sail there, walk to the road, and look down on *his* yacht, bobbing at anchor. And so we did.

Villefranche-de-mer was indeed a pretty harbor, and a quaint town. The gardens were dazzling. Fuchsia pink bougainvillaea in massive banks, covered high walls in long expanses, blindingly brilliant in the sun. Jacaranda trees, with their purple blossoms, clashed with the bougainvillea. There was a vast array of fattening foodstuffs to be had—breads, cheeses, pastries. Fortunately, the fruit and vegetables from Provence were everywhere, and not too expensive: zucchini with blossoms, broccoli, raspberries, tiny juicy strawberries. So much fresh food is anyone's paradise, but it's a sailor's Eden. It was a struggle to decide between eating out, to taste the local specialties, and eating in, with foods from the markets.

* * * * *

The Riviera turned into the Costa Brava with hardly a comment. We moved from French to Spanish and from brie to burgos, barely noticing the difference—until we came to Barcelona. Sailing into Barcelona was a minor thrill—not quite like Istanbul or Venice, but stirring enough.

Barcelona is architecture. There is the usual Gothic this and Roman that—castles, fortifications, and churches. But Barcelona is best known, architecturally, for the *modernistas,* especially Antoni Gaudi (1852–1926). His "cathedral" (La Sagrada Familia) has been a work in progress for 120 years now, and still the exterior has not been completed.

Walking in Barcelona was a treat, especially ambling along La Rambla. On this wide pedestrian boulevard in the heart of town, we found, among other entertainments, a multitude of industrious actors ingeniously costumed to appear like statues—dancers, historical figures, soldiers, Indians. They stood stock-still until someone dropped a coin in their bucket. At the clink of coins they came alive with a little mime routine—throwing a kiss, drawing a sword, bowing and scraping—before returning to the statue pose. We dropped coins in all the buckets—as many as two dozen on a fine afternoon—just to see the routines; they were all delightful. One day we came across a specter of death, a "statue" holding a sickle and standing on a tombstone, looking down at the epitaph. I put some pesetas in the bucket, but nothing happened. Puzzled, I put in some more pesetas. Still nothing. After several minutes of waiting, watching, and muted discussions, we finally realized that this actually *was* a statue. Joke's on us.

We had fun standing around watching others do what we had done. Some, in disbelief, looked up under the cowl that was pulled down so you couldn't see that there was no face. One guy even stuck his digital video camera underneath the cowl to record an image, then checked the camera further, only to see that no face had been captured. We tried to figure out which of the people standing around this minispectacle had constructed the joke. He or she *had* to be there, watching too.

Barcelona is a big city with big-city problems: pollution of the sound, sight, and smell varieties, for instance. And there is crime, mostly petty theft, especially by pickpockets. We had been repeatedly warned about the pickpockets and had heard of many methods they employ, so we were prepared, and (we thought) very, very careful.

One afternoon we were walking around the cathedral in the Gothic Quarter and were suddenly accosted by two young women. One of them waved a piece of cardboard in my face, with something written on it. While she distracted us, the other one moved behind Stephen to pick his pocket. We had heard of this ploy and immediately pushed them away with strong arm movements, loud vocal rejections, and clear indications of our distaste. Well, they saw we were onto them and quickly left us.

A while later Stephen discovered that some printed material about the walk we were taking was missing. He had had these pages in the pockets of his pants, and thought he must have dropped them while juggling the video camera and the papers as we walked. We began to retrace our steps to look for the missing pages. We came to the little street where the women had approached us, and incredibly, there were our pages, crumpled into a ball and thrown into the gutter. How had they done that? We were certain they had not come within reach of Stephen's pockets. We saw our women walking on the streets some time later. One of them had the piece of cardboard folded and tucked under her arm. They looked just like any other people on the street. Joke's on us again.

We made a one-day trip outside the city to Monserrat, a monastery on a singular mountain that rises up from the coastal plain like a monument. In the church we heard a magnificent boys' choir give a brief (twelve minutes) concert—one religious tune and the Catalan anthem.

Catalonia has been a semiautonomous region of Spain for centuries, even after marriage forged the union of Castilla and Catalunya in 1479. More recently, at the beginning of the twentieth century, the Catalan Nationalist movement was so strong that the province was actually autonomous for a brief period. But infighting and rampant violence ruined the independence effort, and the area returned to the Spanish Nationalists in 1939. Nevertheless, the community is still known for its independent spirit. The Catalans speak a separate language almost exclusively. They have an almost-separate government, a unique history, a different cuisine—and their own anthem.

When the Monserrat choir began to sing the anthem, we were surprised how many of our fellow listeners jumped immediately to their feet to sing along. We thought everyone visiting the monastery was a foreign tourist, as we were. But this was August, when most Europeans take their vacations. We were moved by the stirring song, soaring to the rafters of this very Baroque church.

Barcelona will stand out in our travels. It is a vibrant city, appealing for its sights, its food, the art and architecture, and for the feeling of pride and (can I say) assertiveness of its people—including pickpockets and mimes.

From Barcelona we harbor-hopped along the southern coast of Spain, heading for Gibraltar. Gibraltar was one of those "marks" of the voyage. World voyagers heading west nearly always stop here to stage their Atlantic siege.

Prudential Insurance still says the company is "solid as the Rock of Gibraltar," but high above our marina, on the west side, we discovered caves, tunnels, and warrens that had been excavated over the centuries to provide armed positions and shelter from the succession of enemies that sailed by. Like Malta, the Rock stood in a strategic position, ever important in whatever conflict advanced through the area. During the Second World War, in particular, the British removed large portions of the rock, depositing them to the north of the isthmus to create a landing strip that is still used today for Gibraltar's airport.

* * * * *

Straight across the water from Gibraltar is Morocco. We had intended to sail across the narrow strait from Gibraltar to Morocco, but watching the ferries running daily—and quickly—across this busy and sometimes turbulent body of water, we decided it would be easier to take the ferry.

Our visit to Morocco was capped by a visit to a rug shop. The very thought of going into one of those shops gave me the willies. I knew what it would mean—hassle, hassle, hassle—but I really was interested in buying a couple of small *kilems* (the woven rugs without any pile). The problem with buying things in Morocco (and so many other parts of the world) is that you don't just buy something, you must bargain for it. And you *must* bargain. In the Arab world it would be insulting not to. Now, the problem with bargaining is that you need to know what the starting price is, so that you have some idea of where you might end up. If the starting price is $3,000, say, that's one thing; if it's $500, that's another. But there's no way to find out the starting price without asking, and once you've asked you are committed to the hassle, even if—now that you know the starting price—you know you don't want to buy it. There were days when I was in the mood, and I was good at it. On other days the hassle made me furious, and I missed out on a lot of beautiful native crafts as a result.

On this particular day, after entering the shop, I stood to the side to watch another customer work through the complexities of a purchase. I saw one or two rugs that fit my needs, and I indicated my interest.

The first step of the process is to look at dozens of rugs, indicating how "hot" or "cold" they were getting toward your desired purchase. After I had said "no" to a dozen room-size beauties, I got it across that I wanted a *small* kilem. The medium-sized kilems came out, and after some minutes, they finally got down to something close to my size. They flipped one at my feet that really was beautiful. I sucked in a breath and ventured forth. "How much?"

"Fifteen hundred dollars."

I hoped my gasp wasn't too audible. That was about thirty times what I was interested in paying, so I shrugged and started to walk away. "No, madam, do not walk away. This is your rug. We will find a good price for you. How much will you pay?"

"This rug is more than I can afford," I said.

"Just tell me what you can offer me for it," he said.

"I don't want to insult you with my price," I tried; "it is not enough."

"You can't insult me," he countered, "just offer me your price."

"I can't, this isn't a rug for me."

"Here (giving me a pen and paper). Just write down what you offer." Well, if he was going to be that persistent … I wrote down $50. He crumbled the paper in mock disgust and walked away. I did likewise—that is, I walked away.

But in a jiffy he was beside me again. "Four hundred and fifty dollars." (What a price break!)

"No, this rug is too valuable, and I can't afford it."

"Four hundred dollars."

"Fifty dollars is all I have to spend," I countered, trying not to raise my voice.

A haughty look passed over his face, and I got the lecture about how it had taken the Berber woman who made this rug ten years, *ten years* (this was a two-by three-foot rug), and how she had gone blind in the process!

"I know," I said. "I am not worthy of this rug. You must find someone who can pay an adequate price."

"Three hundred dollars is my bottom price," he said. "This rug would cost a thousand dollars in Tangier, and twice that in your country."

"I know, I know, but fifty dollars is all I have."

"You can pay with credit card, with installments, with personal check, any way you wish."

"Thank you for your kindness, but I will not buy it today," and I walked away again. I had just reached the door when he was at my side one more time.

"One hundred and fifty dollars. I give it away for one hundred and fifty dollars." (One-tenth of his asking price!) But I had now made a stand I did not wish to back away from, and besides, I really didn't want to spend that much on one rug. I walked away, and he did not appear again, a clear sign that he had indeed reached his bottom price.

The next day, in Tangier, I purchased three rugs of better quality for one hundred and sixty dollars. They were all "discounted" because of my "bulk" purchase—which included, in addition to the rugs, two leather hassocks, some dolls, and a silly leather camel, six inches high. I paid for this purchase with some crisp, new twenty-dollar bills, the ones with the huge face of A. Jackson. These bills were a bit of a novelty then, and as it turned out they were coveted by the carpet dealer. If only I had known. *If I pay with these new American dollars, which are so hard to come by in your country, I think ...* I was just getting back into my bargaining stride when it was time to leave Morocco and return to Gibraltar.

Back at our marina we found that the seven months of waiting had passed. We could begin the journey home.

Across the Pond

The Atlantic

Escaping the Mediterranean Sea to begin what was clearly now a journey home would not be easy. The Strait of Gibraltar is, at its narrowest, eight miles across, yet that is a very narrow opening compared to the broad sea to the east and the open Atlantic to the west. Water moving from large areas through narrow openings always poses problems. In the Strait of Gibraltar, strong tidal currents do the usual run back and forth. But on *top* of these currents there is an even stronger overriding current flowing *into* the Mediterranean Sea at the surface, replacing evaporated water and the more saline and colder water that flows *out* of the Med along the seabed. Currents can run in opposite directions *at the same time* in different parts of the strait! Could this be more confusing?

The winds blow only east or west—that is, with you or against you. So getting both the current and the wind going *with* us was the challenge for our escape. These conditions occur only about one-quarter of the time—perhaps seven days out of a month. And that, of course, is only an average. We could wait for weeks until everything was going in the right direction.

We read all the literature we could find about the complexities of the area; we examined the charts closely to see if we could figure out where those "seabeds" were; and we clung to the weather forecasts.

Finally, in late September, it all came together in a favorable configuration, and we set sail for the islands of Madeira, 575 miles west of the strait. We started in the early morning, and it took most of the day to sail out of the Mediterranean. At sunset we faced the open Atlantic at last, between Capo Trafalgar of Spain on our right and the headland of Cap Spartel, on the corner of Morocco, on our left.

As the afternoon dragged on I began to see fishing boats in front of us, laying nets. At first they were north of our course, and we were far enough away that I did not worry about them. But as the sun was heading for the horizon, I spotted one of the boats almost dead ahead, laying a net going south. I surmised that if I tried to go around his southern end, we couldn't get around him before sunset. Instead I decided to go north, where I assumed I would find the beginning of his net, and we could scoot around it that way.

Turning right and easing the sails, I soon saw a black flag that appeared to mark the beginning of the net. I looked south and saw the fishing boat at least three miles away, continuing to lay his net—an incredibly long, and lengthening, drift net. *Well, all right,* I thought, *I've found the northern end, and I can turn back on course.* I turned to the left.

Back on course, we were heading almost due west, directly into the setting sun. The glare on the water was terrible. Suddenly I saw a line with tiny floats on it, inches from the bow. What I hadn't seen in the blinding light of the sun was that this guy's net continued to extend *north* of the flag for another *two miles.*

These nets were the notorious drift nets in which dolphins are inadvertently caught, because both the nets and the dolphins move right on the surface of the water, as do sailing yachts. We ran straight onto the net. Very quickly it scraped along the front edge of the keel, then fully under the boat, and finally lodged itself between the keel and the rudder, stopping us dead—just dead in the water.

I yelled at Stephen, dozing below, and I began my flapping routine. This is behavior that drives Stephen nuts, but it's part of my way of dealing with the jeez-I-hate-this situations. I was in constant motion, with my mouth running full steam: we should do this, try that, pull on that; look out, it's not working; what are we going to do? We lowered the sails, we made numerous attempts with the boat hook to push ourselves free, we tilted the boat on its side—all to no avail. As we eliminated one option after another for getting ourselves free, I began to realize we were nearing a solution I didn't want to think about: jumping in the water and doing whatever was necessary *under* the boat to free us from the net. On *Another Horizon,* free-diving under the boat (cleaning the bottom, picking up stuff that fell overboard in an anchorage, checking the anchor) was a "pink" job—mine. For some reason I have a big lung capacity and can hold my breath underwater for relatively long periods. On *Another Horizon* we divided jobs according to skill and talent (those were usually Stephen jobs) or physical attributes (sometimes mine) or natural faculties (like swimming underwater without breathing much).

I went below and put on a swimsuit, and then a shortie wet suit—this was September in the North Atlantic, and I expected the water to be cold. I jumped into the water with my snorkel mask in place, and was surprised by how warm the water was. Perhaps I had so much adrenaline pumping through me that my system did not register the real temperature. I had one end of a tether tied around my waist, with the other end tied to the boat.

Although tied to the boat, I had some misgivings about being in the water, far from land, in what was virtually open ocean. There was a swell running (about five feet), and the twelve tons of *Another Horizon* were heaving up and down, up and down. I had to be careful that the twelve tons didn't land on my head.

Under the boat, I could see immediately that the net was folded around the prop. After a couple of free dives I could tell that with the tension of a twelve-ton boat on the net, I could not separate the net from the boat by pulling or twisting.

By this time the fishing boat whose net had snared us had come alongside, watching. I came out of the water and shrugged my shoulders, hoping to indicate that we could not free ourselves from the net. One of the fishermen made a cutting motion with his hand, which greatly relieved me. Cutting ourselves free appeared to be our only option now, and we were glad that the fisherman made the suggestion first. We had his permission to proceed.

So back into the water I went, with a knife in hand. About this time the net broke about a half-mile up the line, under the tremendous pressure of our intrusion. This brought acres of net down around our keel, rudder, prop—and me—in a great, huge, swarming mess. I was momentarily a little worried about getting tangled in the thing and ending up in a tuna can. No kidding, I actually had that thought. I hacked at the net around my legs, telling myself not to panic.

Stephen told me later that *he* was panicked as he was sure I had been down too long. I have big lungs, but in truth I was very near my limit when I struggled to the surface. I clung to the tether, gasped for air, and tried to compose myself. Any free-diver will tell you that you can stay down longer if you relax your mind and stay cool. I gulped, panted, wheezed, huffed, puffed, trying to get air into my lungs and calm into my mind. Stephen was collected, now that I had surfaced. He didn't push, he wasn't panicky—he was pragmatic. He asked if there was anything else I needed. "No," I inhaled, and dove below.

As I began slashing at the net tangled around the propeller, I felt ever-so-slightly bad for the fishermen. This fiasco was going to cost them their night's catch; and it would be days before they could put that net back together.

It took nearly two hours from the moment we ran into the net until we were free of it. In that two hours the sun had set and it had gotten quite dark. Stephen brought out the spotlight, shining it into the water to give me a last look at the propeller. I had to make sure there was no more line or net wound around it. The wind had died and we were going to have to turn on the engine to move away from the stringy remains. Finally back on deck, I sat panting while Stephen started the engine—and then we looked around us.

Too busy with our little drama, we had not seen the dozens of other fishing boats laying nets. They used little strobe lights on the flagsticks, every couple of hundred feet or so, to show where the nets were, and there were *hundreds* of strobe lights in every direction. We assumed the nets were laid in the same north/south lines as "our" net, so we motored up and down looking for a passage through to the west. We could find no way to proceed safely without endangering ourselves again. Stephen, more focused than I was by then, concentrated on the lights until he was able to isolate a single line, which he began following north. He was hoping, as I was earlier, to find the end of the line and go around it. But a fishing boat came up behind us, waving its spotlight in a sort of wagging motion. They seemed to be saying, "Go away." So we did— back south. In that direction another boat came alongside, wagging its spotlight. We were flummoxed! How on earth were we going to escape this maze of nets?

Suddenly it dawned on us that the fishing boats were showing us which way *to go,* not which way *not to go.* We zigged and zagged for a few minutes trying to follow the spotlights' path. At last Stephen saw, between the spotlights, what looked like a gap in the strobes. Very slowly we made our way through a space between two nets—a narrow hole of barely 100 feet. For another two hours we watched the tiny strobe lights bob and blink around us. Slowly but surely, we pulled away from the area.

After this nightmarish experience we were both exhausted and wired, a result of the intense activity and the adrenaline that was slowly draining out of our systems. It was not a great way to start a long passage, I thought darkly. In our state of nervous exhaustion, we were not in good shape for the four days ahead of us on the open ocean. On my early morning watch, however, when the dawn lit the east, I felt infinitely better. The wind was good, and the horrors of the previous night were dissipating. I had had a few hours of deep sleep, and I was adjusting to being at sea again.

We had not been in the open ocean for a long time. I had forgotten how it can be, riding to the top of eight- or ten-foot swells, sliding into the troughs, losing sight of the horizon, floundering ever so slightly, waiting nervously for the next high swell to carry us back to the top. Periodically the swell picked up our twelve tons like a matchstick, gently bearing us toward the sky. And glory! I could see forever. That morning, conditions were about as good as they can be. When things are good, they are really good.

* * * * *

We landed at Porto Santo, the easternmost island of Madeira. The Madeira archipelago was part of the territory of fifteenth-century explorers. The first to land there could have been Spanish, or Italian, or English, or even French, but they happened to be Portuguese, and they happened to land first at Porto Santo. This dry, undistinguished-looking island has little to offer modern travelers other than the fact that Christopher Columbus once lived here, and his father-in-law was the first governor.

The main island, Madeira Grande, was more interesting. But it didn't have a decent harbor, so we boarded a ferry bound for Funchal, the capital of the island group. Madeira Grande is mountainous and fertile, with a fascinating system of channels to bring water from high in the cloud-enshrouded mountains to the agricultural terraces and homes on the lower slopes. There are over 1,300 miles of these channels, on an island only 30 miles long!

But what did we really come to Funchal for? To taste the wine, of course. Madeira wine traveled well in the holds of ships in days of old. Its distinctive flavor was enhanced by the warmth of the storage as the ships crossed the Atlantic. Although this "heating" is artificially induced now, we purchased several bottles to try in our bilge.

When we returned to Porto Santo we found the tiny harbor crammed with cruising yachts. Everyone was heading south to the Canary Islands, where we would all wait for the right weather to cross the Atlantic. This was 1999, and the year-of-the-millennium business had hit the yachting community as well as every other aspect of our lives. Everyone thought that crossing the Atlantic would be a wonderful end-of-the-millennium thing to do. Europeans were banding together in rallies of a dozen to as many as forty and fifty yachts. Americans were flying to Europe and buying boats to cross, or joining as crew for boats already in position. The biggest rally, organized by Americans, had more than 250 boats registered. There were some East Coast sailors who had sailed across the Atlantic earlier in the year, only to turn around and sail back with the millennium pack. Fanatics, we mused, but who were we to talk? Plenty of folks thought we were nuts to be sailing around the world.

We told everyone in Porto Santo about the fun things to see in Madeira—getting them on the ferry—while we dashed south to find a spot in the Canaries before the fleets arrived. We landed at Santa Cruz de Tenerife.

It was October, and we had about a month ahead of us before we could begin to venture across the Atlantic. Hurricanes were still making their way into the Caribbean, and tropical "waves" were scurrying across the south Atlantic regularly. These waves are weather patterns that have the potential for turning into hurricanes, and as long as they kept popping up off the African coast, we would stay put in the Canaries.

To all the British, Swedes, French, Germans, Norwegians, and Italians that we met here, salivating at the prospect of an ocean crossing, we appeared superior. We'd been three-quarters around and had crossed oceans already. But we were just as apprehensive as they were about the Atlantic crossing. You can never be blasé about nature's whims—especially hurricanes.

When we arrived at Tenerife we were given a berth at a brand-new pontoon, but with the stipulation that we could stay only three days because the pontoon was reserved for rally boats. They were expecting four rallies to come through Tenerife. And sure enough, within a week we were surrounded by a small French contingent. No one asked us to leave, so we kept a low profile and *bonjour*ed and *bonsoir*ed as needed. The French left and the British arrived. We turned on our Oxbridge accents and smiled. A month later we were *still* encamped on the pontoon. We were fortunate that the marina management was a little disorganized, so our long tenure on the pontoon wasn't noticed for some time.

One day, however, the marina manager did come knocking to ask when we planned to leave. We were ready with our excuses: I had been suffering from an ear infection, brought on by a head cold combined with my in-the-water adventure outside Gibraltar. I was "under a doctor's care." We had hospital slips and drug orders, which we waved as evidence. We didn't think we could leave until we knew I was well.

"Yes, yes, oh, well, well, that's fine. Just let us know when you will leave," the manager acquiesced.

We were *not* lying—no we were not. I had gone to the hospital in Madeira, where a doctor had prescribed antibiotics, but after two weeks I still couldn't hear well in my left ear, and the dull ache had become a throbbing ache. Although in many places I would rather have self-diagnosed and medicated than venture into the local health facilities, the earache was beyond my medical expertise. In Tenerife it was time to look for help again. I tried my luck at the Santa Cruz hospital and was given another antibiotic. Another two weeks and I still could not hear well, and I felt "under the weather." (That could be a pun in our circles, but feeling as badly as I did, I didn't think it was funny.)

Finally, our friend John, an Australian physician, showed up in our harbor on his boat. "Do you make boat calls, John?"

He did. "Looks just like the ears of our surfers in Australia," said John.

"So what do I do?"

"Try erythromycin. I can't guarantee anything, but it might work."

In five days, I suddenly felt well for the first time since leaving Gibraltar—more than six weeks earlier. This was doubly fortunate, because now we had to leave on our Atlantic crossing. Our friend Daniel had arrived on board to help us with the passage, and he had only four weeks off from work.

We had debated long and hard about having crew for this crossing. Stephen was very wary about his heart condition. He was too new with his stent, and just too nervous with this change in his health. What if he had a heart attack? he argued. Despite these risks, I was against an extra person on board. With guests on board—even if they were good friends, even if they were just crew—I felt I had to perform. For instance, when it was just the two of us and I didn't feel much like cooking, I could produce any kind of slop for Stephen, and he would eat it. With guests, I felt I had to produce decent meals, if not good ones; at sea that can take care and energy that I might not always have.

And with other people on board, I had to be *nice* all the time.

So we argued. As usual, Stephen argued well, and we took the offer of a home-town friend to crew for us. Daniel flew into Tenerife on the 15th. On the 17th, we went to the marina manager and told him we were leaving. I kept my eyes averted from his face hoping he wouldn't say "At last!"

The Atlantic crossing is supposed to be easy. Columbus had figured it out centuries ago: run south before the prevailing northeasterlies down to the tropics, pick up the easterly trade winds, and sail downwind to the Caribbean. According to friends who had crossed in previous years, it would be a pleasant passage.

It looked good for us too, until Hurricane Lenny turned up.

We were supremely confident that this very late-season storm would take its usual course northwest and be out of the way before we were even halfway across the Atlantic. But for the first time ever in history, this hurricane tracked due *east*—toward us. We still weren't especially worried, but it did make us edgy that a hurricane had been spawned that late in the year (mid-November).

Our radio net was going strong during this time. Boats crossing the Atlantic were anxious to have their positions recorded—just in case. And Stephen's weather forecasts had their usual following. All the rallies had their own nets running too, and we listened to each other's broadcasts for information. And anyway, there wasn't much other entertainment during those long days at sea.

For the first week out of the Canaries we pushed south and a little west toward a point about 20 degrees south and 30 degrees west. Conditions were ideal for several days, just as we had been told to expect. But as we reached this corner, where we expected to pick up the easterly trades and begin the more westerly course, a low-pressure system developed in our path. That system quickly grew into a gale. Like Lenny, this storm should have moved northwest, but instead it headed southwest—on a converging course with us. If we were to head for the Caribbean as planned we would plow right into it, so we left our course and continued due south for 300 miles, with the hope that the storm would pass us by. We were annoyed with this detour, which would make our passage significantly longer than expected. We were nervous about getting Daniel back to the States on time.

Fortunately, we had planned to make landfall in the southeastern corner of the Caribbean. This meant that our track for crossing the Atlantic was already farther south than most other yachts. The large 250-boat rally, for instance, was heading for Antigua, in the middle of the eastern Caribbean chain, and the course of those boats was much farther north. They couldn't help but run into this weird storm. Several of them reported frightening conditions as they sailed through the system. One yacht, a regular on our net, reported one morning that they had sailed through a "tempest" during the night. Harry indicated that they had sustained considerable damage during a period of 60-knot winds. Were they all right? I asked. Able to continue?

"Yes," he replied, "the damage is nothing critical. We're doing okay."

It turned out the boat was fine, but Harry was not. At some point during the night his heart had started beating erratically. After his transmission to us in the morning, he began to feel poorly.

His condition worsened as the day went on, and by late afternoon he was incapacitated. (It was later surmised that somewhere along in there he had a heart attack.) In the late afternoon his wife, Ann, put out a distress call. She was the only other person on the boat, and she was frantic, trying to tend to her husband and keep the boat sailing.

The next morning during the radio net, the airwaves were abuzz with boats all over the Atlantic putting together a plan to get Ann some relief. Fortunately, because they were part of a rally, there were other vessels within a few hours' sailing time. By nightfall, three of them had reached her and had put extra crew on board, one of whom was a nurse. The following morning Ann reported that Harry was doing better. She estimated they had four more days to reach Antigua. We all held our breath for those four days. Harry was immediately airlifted from Antigua to Martinique, where there were better facilities to deal with his problems. We met them weeks later in Marin, on the south side of Martinique. Harry was still ill, but getting medical attention daily.

Stephen never said, "It could have been me," but he knew, and I knew, that it could have been. When Stephen announced at the end of the Atlantic crossing that he did not wish to do any more long passages, he got no argument from me. We had reached a critical juncture in our voyaging.

In the meantime, we had at last turned Columbus's corner, found the easterly trades, and made good time in the right direction. On the twenty-third day from our Canaries departure, we sighted land again. We had done our navigation well; it was Barbados, as planned.

In the Wake of Columbus

Eastern Caribbean

Christopher Columbus began most of his Atlantic crossings from the Canaries (just as we did), and his four explorations of the New World ranged over the entire Caribbean. Although the Spanish, British, French, and Portuguese were all nosing around in these waters in the seventeenth century, it was Columbus who left the legacy. Just the place names he left behind are enough to give him honor. The label "West Indies" is perhaps the most prominent and, of course, the most erroneous. Between 1493 and 1504, the years of his voyages, Columbus touched eighteen to twenty Caribbean islands. It is interesting to me that he never found Barbados. What would my future have been if he had!

Barbados, you see, is the land of my forebears. My grandfather was born there, but at sixteen he left for the States. In fact, there was a mass exodus of Oltons during the late nineteenth century, as the sugar industry went sour on the island and plantations folded—including the Olton plantation. Barbados was mostly forgotten as my grandfather's family put together a new life in New Jersey.

But in the early 1970s, the "roots" thing got to my father and he decided to visit Barbados. To the best of our knowledge he was the first Olton to return to their homeland. On my parents' arrival, after settling into their hotel, my father phoned to make reservations at a restaurant for dinner that night. The woman who answered, taking his reservation, giggled when Pop gave his name. "My name is Olton too," she said. My father was ecstatic. Not two hours had passed on the island and he had talked to an Olton. He would look forward to meeting her at dinner, he said.

They arrived at the restaurant, the woman presented herself, and in the words of my mother, "she was as black as black as black could be." She was, they surmised together, a descendant of the plantation workers that were attached to our family sugar plantations. She confirmed that there were no white Oltons left on the island. She and my parents enjoyed the evening together. I regretted not knowing her full name. I would have liked to call her, too.

Instead, I headed for the Barbados Archives on the north side of Bridgetown, the island's capital. Inside the Archives, which looked like an old town hall, I found young Ephraim, who said he would be pleased to help me. He led me to a microfiche reader in which he put the records of marriages and christenings, as gathered by the census of the Church of the Latter-day Saints. As I ran through pages and pages of Oltons, I began to realize that there were Oltons on Barbados almost from the beginning of British colonization in 1639, and that there were scads of Oltons living everywhere on the island over the centuries. "I'm trying to find my grandfather," I told Ephraim, "and I'm not finding anything in these records."

"Do you know his religion?" Ephraim asked. This seemed a silly question to me, as I thought it unlikely in the days of my grandfather that there was any church other than the Anglican Church—the Church of England. But I replied hopefully, "Anglican," to which he smiled and said, "Good." Out came another microfilm of christenings and marriages, as recorded in the seven parish churches of the island. I wasn't sure of my Gramp's birth year, so I started wandering back and forth from 1870. And before long, there it was: "Percy Trafford Olton," baptized in St. Michael's church on October 18, 1874.

"I found him!" I yelled. "My grandfather," I exclaimed. "He's here," I broadcast to all who could hear—the cleaning lady and young Ephraim. They had probably heard it all before, a thousand times, but they smiled for me.

"Sit down," Ephraim commanded, "and start writing." I did as he instructed, and in a very few minutes I had found the christenings and marriages of Percy Trafford's brother, parents, grandparents, and great-grandparents. Here were my roots.

* * * * *

There is plenty of conjecture about where Columbus did and did not land in the Caribbean. Every island would love to say "Columbus slept here," but the truth of the matter is that in many cases it is hard to know for sure. Some say he landed at St. Martin. Others believe the references (in his writings) for that island are really for Nevis, much farther south. In some cases he may have just "sighted and named" the island, as may be the case with Dominica, for example. Most of the maps delineating the voyages show him sailing on the third voyage from Trinidad directly to Hispaniola. Many texts make no mention of his lesser discoveries—*perhaps* St. Vincent, St. Kitts, Dominica, St. Martin, and on the west side, the Bay Islands of Honduras.

Okay, so he didn't see Barbados. How about our next Caribbean stop, Bequia? There is some speculation as to whether he put into Bequia or St.

Vincent, but I can't imagine his sailing on by these two lush, palm-strewn, white-sand-encircled beauties. He surely couldn't have missed seeing St. Vincent, whose mountainous terrain reaches above 4,000 feet.

On our trek north from Bequia, we stepped up the island chain to the Windwards, then the Leewards, then the Virgins, in a manner very similar to that of Columbus. In the twentieth century most of these islands have been released from their colonial ties, and each has tried in its own way to be an independent nation. The result for us was an accumulation of twelve countries in six months (including two French *departements* and a state of the Netherlands Antilles)—an unequaled record on our voyage.

The islands are so close together that the next stop could be reached with a short day passage, and as time permitted, we stayed for some days to get the flavor of each island … each country. We wanted to capture a little history, a little of the current character, a little of the spirit of the people—and yes, to sample the food. St. Vincent was flower-scented, St. Lucia was the venue of our New Millennium celebration, and Martinique had its "head" in the clouds, but in Dominica (not to be confused with the Dominican Republic, which we visited later), *our* heads were turned.

Dominica was allegedly Columbus's "land-ho" on his second voyage in 1493. Although he sighted this piece of land first, he apparently did not actually land there. He named the island for the day of the week he first saw it—Sunday (*Domenica* in Italian).

A desperately poor island today, Dominica seemed to be barely managing on its own: a little tourism, a little agriculture, but the infrastructure was sad, the economy flagging. The island itself is spectacularly beautiful, most of it a rain forest and much of it virtually unexplored, let alone developed, because the jungle is so dense. The largest remaining concentration of the Caribbean's Carib Indians lives on the east coast—just 3,000 beings left of a huge tribe that swarmed the eastern Caribbean in the seventeenth and eighteenth centuries. The fate of the Caribs was much the same as other indigenous peoples in the New World—death by disease and warfare.

Dominica had an election coming up, and the political parties were out in full color—literally. Each of the three parties was represented by a single color, the very elementary blue, red, and green. If you favored a particular party, you had a flag or pennant of that color flying from your house. And there were flags on storefronts, schools, community centers, telephone poles, trees, and bridges. Political haranguing was the major activity in the villages in the evening, and trucks blaring political messages through loudspeakers coursed the roads all around the island. It was all very noisy, but, well, very colorful too.

From Dominica we came to Guadaloupe, the butterfly of the Caribbean, so called because the shape of the island has a vague butterfly look to it. Columbus called the island *Karukera,* "Island of Beautiful Waters."

The French islands (Guadaloupe, Martinique, and St. Martin) all had good food (of course) and a more sophisticated infrastructure. The economy (subsidized by the French) was booming by comparison with the other islands. Except for the food, we enjoyed them less.

We had known that St. Kitts (Columbus, almost for sure, 1493) was badly damaged by Hurricane Lenny a few months earlier, but we weren't prepared for the extent of the damage. A beautiful cruise ship facility (if cruise ship facilities can be called beautiful), completed just recently, was totally destroyed in the hurricane. Only the outer walls and a few piers of the marina behind it remained. Basseterre, the capital, was a dispirited little town.

We paid a short visit to St. Martin (Columbus, maybe, 1493), and we crossed the Anegada Channel to the Virgin Islands (Columbus in the British Virgins, definitely, 1493). We had felt the United States creeping up on us the farther north we sailed, and in the Virgins we were suddenly "there." Every yacht carried a U.S. flag, and every voice spoke U.S. English, mostly in what seemed to be those "harsh" East Coast accents. And it was crowded. At the caves on Virgin Gorda we were overwhelmed by charter boat people, yelling at their kids and racing around in big dinghies and jet skis. And the New York accents ... it could have been Coney Island!

While the United States crept up on us, island culture slipped away. Tourism, most especially the cruise ship business, was homogenizing these islands. We had cruised in the island chain for our honeymoon, and ten years later for our anniversary. Another seventeen years later, at St. John's Bay on Antigua, Stephen remembered a nice anchorage and friendly town. We decided to revisit. As we approached the harbor we couldn't see anything except three behemoth cruise ships. *Three* of them, so large they obliterated the whole island behind them from view.

On St. Thomas we pulled into the first anchorage of our honeymoon. It had been the ideal honeymoon cove then—empty, except for us. This time there were seventeen other sailboats and a half-dozen day-tripper excursion boats coming and going until sunset. Not quite the peaceful anchorage I remembered, but we let the nostalgia outweigh the changes. We walked the beach.

"Twenty-seven years is a long time," Stephen mused.

"And who wouldn't expect changes," I laughed. "Look at us!"

*   *   *   *   *

Across the Mona Channel we came to Puerto Rico (Columbus, definitely, 1493). Here, I thought, would be the 51st state, but it seemed as foreign as Cuba or the Dominican Republic. True, the countryside was plastered with Penneys, Wal-Marts, Ace Hardwares, and every fast-food joint known to anyone in the upper 48, but everything else was pure Spanish-American. We were floored to find almost no English spoken in the interior towns—not even at some of the tourist attractions in San Juan. I don't know why I was surprised to discover that the schools teach in Spanish, and that English is a "foreign" language. Yet they send a delegation to our political conventions.

Sailing along the south side of the island we passed a U.S. Naval base, there in our almost-51st state, Puerto Rico. We had just passed the channel to the base when I heard five short, sharp, and loud blasts of a ship's horn. This is a recognized danger signal. It usually means that two ships are on a collision course, and the one with the right of way wishes the other to get out of the way. So I looked around, carefully, but I could see no ship. Perhaps in the base harbor there was some maneuvering going on. A few minutes later the blasts sounded again, and this time they were really close. I looked around again. Still no ship. Then I saw it—the tip of a conning tower whizzing through the water right for us. Jiminy! The adrenaline got me up, taking us off autopilot and grabbing the wheel to steer out of the way. It looked like a Disney cartoon, that tower, scurrying along through the water at an amazing speed. As it passed under our stern the top of the sub's hull was visible, but only just. I hoped that the horn blasts were just to make us aware of its presence, but if they were intended to scare me out of my socks, they did a fine job.

We came next to Hispaniola, the most significant landing of Columbus' first voyage. He called it the most beautiful island he'd ever seen, and he returned to the island on all four voyages. Although Christopher's nephew established a Spanish colony on the east end, the French settled in other parts of the island. After centuries of discontent, battles, and wars, the country of Haiti was established on the west end and the Dominican Republic on the east end.

Not even French sailors were venturing to Haiti the year we sailed over the top of the island. But the Dominican Republic had rid itself of the iron hand of Trujillo in the early sixties, and it was a relatively stable country we felt comfortable visiting. We anchored off the town of Luperon, on the north coast near the border with Haiti.

Luperon was a small, dusty place whose economy was fed mostly by the cruising yachts that call there—a considerable number in the course of a year. After we were sure our anchor was well set, we packed a bag and set off for Santo Domingo, the capital of the Dominican Republic and just about the oldest city in the New World.

We took the "express" bus—which seemed to mean it stopped for anyone who "expressed" an interest in getting on. It took four and a half hours to travel the 150 miles or so from Luperon on the north coast to Santo Domingo on the south coast.

The bus reminded us of buses in Mexico—everything came on board with the passengers, including chickens. We heard them clucking, but I said to Stephen, "I bet they're cocks." Cock fighting is second only to baseball as the Dominican Republic's national sport. Stephen said that they couldn't be cocks, they were just clucking, whereupon one of them let loose with a deafening crow. Which is when we discovered how many *more* cocks there were on board.

The whole trip was noisy. The driver honked the horn at every excuse. "Here I come" (in case you want to express your desire to get on); "here I go, hello, good-bye" (as people on the road waved); "have a good day, passing ... passed." The radio was blaring their favorite merengue music, which sounds like a cross between salsa and mariachi. If the bus driver and his assistant weren't yelling at each other over the music, the driver was whistling to the music with an amazingly piercing sound. And then we would pass a truckload of chickens, and the cocks would let loose!

The countryside that we traveled through was agricultural. Sugarcane fields lined the road, bananas if not sugarcane, tobacco if not cane or bananas. The locals' homes were insubstantial buildings—shacks, really—of wood or cement block. There were some very wealthy people in this country, but mostly the Dominicans seemed to be operating in a subsistence economy. One of our guides said that the unemployment rate was close to 50 percent. Well, I'm sure that had to do with "real" jobs and did not count the bevy of vendors at the bus stations who were ready to sell you everything from Planter's Cheez Pops to toothbrushes. It was the little boys in the bus stations that turned my head. They were selling ice sticks, a sickeningly sweet ice confection, that instead of alleviating the heat induced thirst. The kids were cute, dancing to the bus music, smiling, and rolling their eyes. But why weren't they in school?

There was an election imminent here too; the political posters were every-where. Like Dominica, every party had its specific color. Instead of flags, how-ever, the DR parties painted everything in sight: telephone poles, bridges, tree trunks, sidewalks. If the election were based on the amount of paint expended, the purple party was going to win.

We had booked a hotel in the Zona Colonial, in the heart of Santo Domingo. We had a room on the second floor, with a balcony overlooking the cathedral square. The locale and the view from the balcony couldn't have been better. Then I read this notice on the back of our door: "If you don't confirm any extra company in the formulary of register of the hotel, the administration reserv [sic] the right won't allow you to bring any extras company in your whitout [sic] confirmation." "What kind of hotel is this?" I yelled at Stephen.

While Stephen took a shower I enjoyed leaning on the rail of our balcony and surveying the scene below. There was a charming aggressiveness about the taxi drivers and tourist "guides," who tried to solicit business from me while I was on the balcony and they were down on the street. They blew kisses, proffered calling cards, and made propositions which I couldn't quite hear. "*Mas tarde* (later)," I called, smiling. The attention was flattering, but then I seemed to be the only tourist (or whatever they expected in this hotel) around.

The high ceiling and scalloped wall of our room suggested that the hotel had been something more than a traveler's hostel some time ago, and more elegant than the sign on the back of the door suggested. It certainly couldn't have been better situated for our visit. Our walk about the town the next day went from one "first" in the Americas to another. The first monastery, the first fort, the first paved street—how did they know that?

At every tourist sight, guides offered to tell us everything we needed to know. They were at our side making their spiel before we could say "no, thank you." So we had a guide. And the cost? "Whatever you think is a good tip." Oh boy ... we were unprepared for this. It turned out that the guides were good. In the historical museum especially, José was well worth the exorbitant tip we offered—all of five dollars, which was twice the museum entrance fee. José was very pleased and took us to some "special" exhibits.

There was constant, although muted, reference to Trujillo's reign here. The locals spoke of him with contempt, even hatred. But he was a factor in this country's current well-being. It was for his benefit at the time, granted, but much of the country's surprising infrastucture—amazingly good roads, for instance—is due to that evil man.

*   *   *   *   *

From the Dominican Republic we sailed through the outer Bahamas, past the island said to be Columbus's very first landfall in the New World (1492). He continued due west, sailing *through* the Bahamas, while we went straight north, up the chain to Grand Bahama and from there west to Florida.

Although it is pretty easy to see how Columbus could have missed Barbados (tiny piece of land), it is less obvious how he came so close to the American mainland a number of times over his four voyages, yet didn't put a foot—or anchor—down there.

Are We Home Yet?

To the United States

At the West End of Grand Bahama we looked into the sunset. Florida was there, just 60 miles away. It wouldn't be long now. Our home country, just over the horizon.

It was an all-day run, so it wasn't until late in the afternoon, peering into the western haze along the horizon, that Stephen yelled, "Buildings ho!"

"What are you talking about?" I asked. Squinting into the sun, I saw for myself: no land, just a long row of high-rises shimmering in the heat ahead of us. "Must be Florida," I said, "one huge hotel after another." The east coast of Florida is so flat that we did not see actual land until we were practically on it. We put into Fort Pierce, a smallish city just north of West Palm Beach. The next day we began our trek along the Intracoastal Waterway (ICW).

As we made our way up the coast to visit family and friends we hadn't seen in seven, eight, ten or more years, I was conflicted about where we were. I wasn't sure how we viewed this return to the United States, or whether we were ready for a reentry into home territory. For two and a half months we pushed north through the ICW, all the way to Cape May, just south of New York City.

* * * * *

I woke at first light and came on watch. Stephen slipped below and flaked out on the bunk. He was tired. This was one of those one-night passages that we both hated. We were quickly sleep-deprived from the four hours on/four hours off schedule. But this time my juices were flowing enough to keep me keen. This passage was different. We were heading for The Big Apple.

After accepting the watch from Stephen—when we exchanged the usual how's it going, good, okay, no traffic, good, okay, sleep, yeah (yawn)—I picked up a banana in the galley and settled into the cockpit, looking around and fixing my sense of position. Water aft, water port, water starboard, two square buildings dead ahead. That was odd. The Jersey shore, perhaps. For three hours I watched these two square buildings stay directly ahead and grow, ever so slowly, as we drew nearer. By the time Stephen roused himself again, we were seeing scraps of shoreline to the left and right. And those buildings, growing ever taller, kept their position off our bow, in the path of our destination. By 8 AM I realized that these were the twin towers of the World Trade Center.

The towers had first appeared to us *twenty-five miles* at sea. They had appeared to us from *below* the horizon. These buildings were so tall that they came up over the horizon, like the clouds in the tropics. They were talismans of the round-earth theory. There could be no question that the earth curved, gently, to their feet. They were magnificent.

Although I have never lived in New York City, this arrival was like a coming home. It was better than Barbados, better than Florida. I mean, look at that Lady, look at that skyline, look at that harbor. Geez, Stephen, that ferry is going to run us *down*. The tanker on the right ... where in gawd's name does that container ship think it's going? (Nowhere—it was at anchor.)

The glorious, if busy, harbor panorama ahead of us was favored with a crystal-clear day such as New York experiences only about five times a year. The buildings of lower Manhattan leapt out at us. The crown of the Liberty Lady burned in the sun. I felt as if I could touch the very shores of Ellis Island with my fingertips. Everything had a vibrancy that added to our excitement.

New York was a place both Stephen and I had visited innumerable times before. How was it that this morning stirred up so much emotion? At first blush it was on a par with Venice, Istanbul, Barcelona—sailing into a major city on our own bottom—with all of the awe we had experienced at those early landings. But sailing into New York harbor was different, in part because it was ours, a part of us. It was the port that brought others of our families onto this country's shores. By coming into New York harbor we had really returned to the United States. Lady Liberty held her guiding light for us too.

✳   ✳   ✳   ✳   ✳

From the moment we landed in Barbados, I had begun to feel the *homeness* of this part of the journey. And I was conflicted about that feeling. For years we had been special, foreign, gringos, white monkeys, Swedish-looking in the olive Mediterranean, with our American flag eliciting broken-English comments ("far," "a long way," "the earth around?"). Now it was beginning to look as if we belonged—the flag was not unusual; the language (accents notwithstanding) was familiar. We were blending in. All this familiarity brought forth thoughts about what constitutes "home." Is it the country? The state? The common history? The land? The structure we live in? New York City clearly had a status that the Florida coast did not. Watching the Stars and Stripes on Fort McKinley and the Fourth of July fireworks in Annapolis had an exciting feel to them. But did any of this give us a sense of *being home* again? Not really. It was familiar, like the language, but it didn't seem to constitute "home" to me. We yakked about the boat being our home. But that didn't exactly ring true, either. I was getting confused.

∗   ∗   ∗   ∗   ∗

As summer passed into fall, we sailed back down the Intracoastal to Florida again. On the radio we had been in touch with friends. So many of the Americans were packing it in. West Coast folks were selling out, or shipping their boats back overland. Stephen liked the sounds of these ideas. He was tired. He didn't want to continue the fuss of keeping *Another Horizon* fit. There were brokers for Valiant yachts in Florida, he reminded me. It was easy to sell boats in Florida, he said. One of our West Coast friends said, "We've been around. We left the States, we returned to the States. Who cares if it was a different coast? States to States, we've been around. We're home." Stephen was listening closely. This was serious business, and I didn't know what to think.

One morning over toast and coffee I said, "It's not like getting your college degree. You can't come back and finish up later. We set out to circumnavigate the world. If we stop now, it's over. In five years, I guarantee you will regret that we didn't finish what we started out to do. You're not a quitter."

A week later we were waiting in Florida—waiting for something, I don't know what—and Stephen let it slip that he thought I was right. We would finish what we started. "So, he said, "we'd better get going. We have a long way to go to reach home."

At that moment I knew at last what constituted "home," and indeed, we still had a long way to go.

In the Wake of Columbus (2)

Western Caribbean

In early December we left Florida to continue the Caribbean tour, this time concentrating on the Western Caribbean. In the countries that outline this area we met dozens of peoples—Black Caribs, Black Africans, Spanish, Haitians, Jamaicans, Mayans and other Central American Indians, mestizos, mulattoes—all with a claim to the Caribbean. This was not the "hey, mon" Caribbean, but a beautiful, serious, sometimes risky part of the Caribbean that surprised us with the lushness of its rain forests, the richness of its history, and the diversity of its culture.

* * * * *

In Cuba the faces were surprisingly bright. The man on the street was more often than not perplexed to hear we were from the States. We, in turn, were astonished that they were so friendly toward us; they had every reason not to be. But it seemed that for every Cuban in Cuba, there was an uncle, sister, son, or cousin in the States (and not just Miami), so although our governments may not see eye-to-eye, once again we found that people do care about people.

We had collected as much information and as many first-hand stories about visiting Cuba as we could. Coming on our own yacht, however, we had special rules to follow. To do it "right" we had to obtain a permit from the U.S. Coast Guard to enter the twelve-mile security limit around Cuba. I thought it peculiar that the United States was issuing a permit to enter Cuban waters, but the process of obtaining this permit did make it possible for U.S. authorities to tell us what we could and couldn't do while we were there.

We chose the Hemingway Marina, some ten miles west of Havana, as the easiest place to make port. All of the usual authorities (immigration, customs, etc.) were there, the marina provided excellent shelter from any bad weather, and transportation to Havana was available.

Many people had commented to us about the beauty of Cuba, but what struck us was the beauty lost. Almost all of the buildings had signs not just of age, but also of neglect. Thankfully, since Old Havana has been designated a World Heritage Site by UNESCO, there is a concerted effort to restore some of the most historic and architecturally significant areas. For some, however, it was clearly too late. The once-grand homes looked like tenements, with broken windows, cracked marble, rotting doors, and the paint worn to bare stucco. Every year in Havana, hundreds of people must be relocated because their housing simply falls down.

We had read that Cuba appears to be in a time warp, around 1950. Most of this impression comes from the huge number of old American cars from the '40s and '50s. They were a remarkable sight—streetloads of them.

The effects of the U.S. embargo were evident everywhere. There were shortages of even such basics as soap and toilet paper. It was difficult for us to look at the results of our hypocritical policy without feeling sad, and even angry. But Cubans are survivors, making the outmoded, outdated, old and crumbling, old and rusting, old and falling apart somehow work. The cars were an example. There can't be spare parts departments for those old cars, so I expected on side streets to see shells of cars stripped of parts to keep others going. But there were no dead cars. There were (apparently) no tow trucks either, so the mechanics went to the broken-down cars. We saw hoods up all over town—but not a single abandoned, given-up-for-lost car anywhere. One Cuban said to us, "We are the best mechanics." I believed it.

After some days of looking at Havana, we took a bus trip to Trinidad on the south coast. About halfway there an alarm went off, indicating that the engine had overheated, and the bus pulled over to the side of the road—in the middle of nowhere. Standing at the rear of the bus with the engine hood up, the driver and the "conductor" had a long discussion about the problem. It was determined that the reservoir for the radiator was empty, and they did not have enough water on the bus to refill it. So off went the driver down the road, half a mile or so, with a couple of buckets. He found a farm up a side road and eventually came back with water and the farmer, who joined the discussion about what was wrong. It seemed clear to all of us passengers gathered around the back of the bus: the reservoir had a substantial leak. It appeared that it had been "fixed" once before with a patch, and the patch was coming unglued. No matter now. The tank was refilled, we all boarded the bus again, and off we went, reservoir dripping.

Trinidad is a small colonial city founded in 1514, even older than Havana. Like Havana it was crumbling, although most of the buildings were one story tall, and collapse didn't seem so imminent. Our favorite time in this town was in the evening, after dinner, when we ventured out into the streets. They were full of people chatting with others in doorways or open windows, or going somewhere. One evening we went to a bar off the main square, where we were told there was live music every night.

We arrived at 7:30 PM to find we were the first patrons. We were serenaded by a young chap with a good voice and an out-of-tune guitar. He was accompanied by a tall, thin old man with maracas. Maximo did not much fit his name as he danced languidly to some of the tunes, while his hands kept shaking the maracas.

After the bar filled up a little more, a group of five young men came out—two guitars (including a curious, small folk guitar called a *tres*), two rhythm guys, and a bass fiddle. This was the Buena Vista Social Club in their twenties. It was that kind of music, what one of the guitarists described to me as "*musica nationale.*" They were good—not great, but good, enjoying their music and their audience, which was about half tourists and half locals.

In Trinidad we stayed in a private home. For an exorbitant fee, an individual Cuban can acquire a permit to rent rooms in his house. It was one of several concessions to capitalism in this communist country trying to cope with a sagging economy.

Our lodging was a one-story row house that from the outside looked shabby and depressing. But inside it was neat, if not elegant, and furnished sparingly with good, but old furniture. Like the other homes in the neighborhood, it had a large door on the street side and one large window (barred) that could be left open for the breeze. A long corridor led from the entrance doorway to the back of the house, with bedrooms off the corridor. The back of the house opened to a yard, where we could hear a cacophony of neighbors' children, chickens, a parrot, and a goat.

Our hosts were a charming couple who spoke no English. Our Spanish was still rather elementary, but somehow we managed to learn that they had one child (a doctor) and one grandchild. They showed us their house with pride. And they cooked us delicious, simple meals.

A few days later, at the appointed time, we returned to the Trinidad bus stop and boarded the bus for our return to Havana. It was quickly evident by the buckets of water loaded on board that this was the same bus we had come down on days before, and that the situation hadn't changed much. Predictably, the engine overheated, but this time the bus driver was ready.

We stopped on innumerable occasions to pick up and let off the occasional passenger, take on some packages from people waiting by the roadside, and once while the bus driver bought some lettuce from a farmer. Still, we arrived back in Havana almost on time.

Stephen went outside the bus station to engage a taxi, while I attempted to wrestle our bag away from the bus attendant. The "taxi" with which Stephen struck a bargain was probably not even an "independent," but just an ambitious young chap after a few dollars, and he probably was not supposed to be soliciting in the station. He hustled us into his car, almost pushed us in, and drove out of the station as quickly as he could. His car, an old Russian model, was held together with baling wire and a prayer. It stalled only once on the way to the marina, but going up even the slightest incline I was crossing my toes that we wouldn't have to get out and push. Ernesto, our driver, did fit his name. He was learning English. To get ahead, he said, he felt that he must speak English. At his request we added a few words to his vocabulary: sailboat, sharks, and storms.

The cab ride was another example of the changing economy in Cuba. Ernesto earned more for that ride to the marina than the average Cuban earns in a month. His fare was about four or five dollars less than the state-owned metered cab charged (whose driver receives a salary from the government) and about three dollars less than a licensed "independent" cabbie, who has to turn over a huge chunk of his earnings to the government. Cuba is recognizing tourism as a way to bolster its economy, but they don't yet have the service structure to accommodate the influx of tourists. Hence the government permits to individuals to rent rooms, to serve meals (in "paladars" with no more than twelve seats allowed), and to drive cabs.

*   *   *   *   *

The Revolution (over forty years ago) surrounded us everywhere we went: slogans on the walls, pictures of Che and Fidel everywhere, museums in every town. One was called "Museo de Banditos"—meaning us Americans. Che images and quotations far outnumbered those of Fidel. Che Geuvara is the martyr. He died, and thus is revered. We did not attempt to talk about Fidel with any locals. The subject seemed too fraught with problems for us, imperialists that we were.

The exhibits in the Museos de la Revolución housed every scrap of memorabilia left from those days, and they were all tagged, often in English as well as Spanish. "Shorts that belonged to Raul Perozo Fuentes, who took part in the actions at the Marche hardware store, Santiago de Cuba." "Hammock used by Frank Pias during the days of the meeting of the National Direction of the July 26th movement." "Cooking stove used at the headquarters of the Third Front." "Frying pan snatched from the enemy and used at the La Plata Headquarters."

Outside these museums were pieces of planes shot down, the weapons that shot them down, the truck that retrieved the pieces of the plane and the weapons. In Havana, enshrined in a huge glass memorial, was the entire 60-foot boat, *Granma,* that brought Fidel back to Cuba in 1956 to begin the Revolution.

We had an eerie feeling in these museums, something we'd not experienced before as Americans. We were the enemy here. It made us want to walk quietly through the rooms, whisper our observations, and silently slip away. But the museum attendants would not let that be: "Where are you from?" "I have a sister in Pittsburgh." Perhaps too much time had passed for them to realize who we were, or perhaps they didn't care that we were supposed to be the enemy.

Cuba's cuisine is basic Caribbean: roasted meats, rice and beans, beans and rice, and a salad of cabbage, tomato, and canned beets. The most curious menu item was *Moros y Christianos*—that is, Moors and Christians—or black beans and rice.

The taste treat in Cuba was lobster. Unlike the rest of the Caribbean, the waters around Cuba are not so overfished. Fresh seafood was readily available, and cheap. One day we purchased a bag of five lobster tails for $10. These tails, mind you, were at least eight inches long, three to four inches wide, and three inches thick at the base. We ate lobster for days.

And everywhere we went—morning, noon, and night—we caught the whiff of cigars.

*   *   *   *   *

We took four days to sail from Havana to Belize. It was good sailing, without the awful currents we had been led to expect, but with rather moderate winds behind us and seas that were mostly forgiving.

We set our last waypoint of the passage for the opening in the barrier reef (the second largest in the world) that would lead us toward Belize City, the country's principal port. We wound our way through shoals and coral patches, past Belize City, to Moho Caye, a tiny island with a tiny marina. We celebrated the successful passage with rum punch and dinner out: roasted meat, rice and beans, and cabbage salad. The exception here was not lobster (which had been fished out in those waters), but shrimp (which they "farmed"). I had a plateful.

We hadn't realized, being otherwise occupied and not paying attention, that a hurricane had come through Belize in the September just past. It was not a major storm, but it sat over the country for almost two days and poured huge amounts of rain on an already soggy land. The runoff from the rivers was tremendous. To make matters worse, in the weeks following the storm they had even more above-average rainfalls. Moho Caye had had a lovely beach, but it was no more. The buildings had patched roofs, and the erosion around the edges of the marina was significant.

The entrance to the marina had silted up badly, and we had to plow through more than a foot of mud to get the boat inside. There were long seconds when I feared we might be stuck, good and hard. And once inside, we began wondering if we would be able to get out.

*   *   *   *   *

The faces of Belize were as varied as anywhere in the Caribbean. The folks that hung out at the marina were a reflection of the country's population. Nazi, a native Belizian, ran a small boatyard at one end of the marina. He was a blond Rastafarian. Gareth from Wales and Linda from Menlo Park, California, worked for a dive operation in Belize City. Julio, the groundskeeper, and his five-year-old son Wilmer, were from neighboring Guatemala, and spoke only Spanish. Eight-months-pregnant Karime, a mestizo Belizian, was the bartender. The dockmaster, a native Belizian with the improbable name of Giovanni, thought he was named for a movie star. His father was mayor of Belize City. Francis, who looked as if he could be from anywhere in northern Europe or the States, was born here and spoke fluent Creole. His grandfather, a physician, came here from Germany; the city hospital is named for him. Philip, from Ireland, was managing director of a large international corporation in the city. On the weekend there were a couple of beautiful East Indian girls who worked in the restaurant. Earlene, who did most of the cooking in the restaurant, was Black African. Harrier, a mestizo, was a medicine man, but his salaried job was as Moho Caye's night watchman.

After the winter holidays, we began to feel some pressure to move on. We wanted to get an early start on the Panama Canal transit, because we knew there would inevitably be delays. We had heard that a small yacht could wait up to three weeks to get a "slot" to go through the Canal. So we plowed back out through the mud of Moho Caye and sailed for the "Bay Islands" of Honduras.

Although the Bay Islands are now part of Honduras, their history is quite distinct. The natives are descendants of Africans and Englishmen—slaves, buccaneers, and pirates. English is spoken a little more than Spanish.

Our memory of these islands will be singular: rain. For ten days it rained, almost nonstop, and almost always torrentially. We were told that water in the islands was plentiful and safe to drink—it was rainwater! The one advantage of the rain was that our salty home was well scoured by the downpouring, and we could forget the fact that water on tap was plentiful and free for the asking. We just opened our water intakes on deck and let it pour in. It took only twenty minutes to fill our tanks with 130 gallons of rain.

The course to our next destination, Isla de Providencia, was through some reefs where armed bandits had preyed upon sailors and had even killed one cruiser the previous year. Pirates like to attack lonely boats in out-of-the-way places, so for a small measure of protection, we traveled in the company of a German boat we had met in Guanaja.

After two days of nervous sailing we reached Providencia and anchored, thankfully, in a quiet harbor off the principal town. Providencia has a curious history too, giving it a flavor all its own. Although the island is off the Nicaraguan coast, it belongs to Colombia, more than 400 miles to the south. It was originally settled by Puritans, who came there to escape persecution in England. Many of the present-day residents are descendants of those Puritans, and English is spoken widely, especially among the older generation.

*   *   *   *   *

About midmorning one day we were preparing to leave the boat for an excursion ashore. Stephen was standing in the dinghy alongside while I tried to remember everything—shopping list, hat, money, suntan lotion, shoes. And Stephen said, "The bilge pump is on, and it's not going off, not at all." He could see the water being pumped out the overboard valve on the side of the boat. I popped back down below and pulled up a floorboard to look into the bilge. Water was *pouring* in.

We were sinking. There could be no other conclusion. Stephen came back on board and we both began tearing the boat apart to find where the water was coming through the hull. These were long minutes. What possessed me to taste the water coming in, I don't know, but I did. "It's fresh water," I reported, and we both sighed. That meant the water was coming from our freshwater tanks, and the leak was in the freshwater system. I checked the gauge for the water tanks and found we had already lost half of our water supply—pumped overboard! But at least we weren't sinking.

Just at this moment, as we ruminated about what might be wrong (a burst valve, as it turned out) and whether we could replenish this water (where was the rain now?), our German friends called us on the VHF radio to tell us we were dragging anchor, and drifting rapidly back onto a reef behind us. The wind had risen to 25 knots—not a lot, but enough to displace our apparently not-very-secure anchor.

We jumped to our dragging-anchor drill. I started the engine and took the helm. Stephen wrestled with the anchor. Once we got it aboard, we decided to reanchor in another part of the harbor. We made repeated attempts in various locations, trying to make sure the anchor was well set. Finally, a couple of young chaps from a motor vessel nearby volunteered to dive on the anchor. They assured us it was well dug in. Even so, we didn't like the "feel" of our situation, and we put out a second anchor for peace of mind. And then we collapsed. It had been two hours since "the bilge pump is on."

"That's it," I said. "Where's the 'For Sale' sign?" Stephen looked at me, trying to decide if I was kidding. Of course I was, at the moment. We had thousands of miles still to go to complete the circumnavigation, and I wasn't about to give up the ship. "Too much invested in this adventure," I said once again. But the fact that this little incident rattled us as much as it did was telling. It was a good thing we were heading home.

We picked a good weather window for the passage from Providencia to Panama, and it took only two days. It was a fast, but not unpleasant passage. We motored through the Canal "gate" (a huge breakwater with a 500-foot gap in the middle) at nine in the morning, dodging the container ships, freighters, and barges maneuvering through the same narrow opening. Then we made for the Panama Canal Yacht Club, where we turned our attention to the rather complicated procedures for checking into the country and scheduling our passage through the Canal.

Luckily, we found a local who called himself a taxi driver but spent most of his time hanging about the yacht club, helping sailors like us. Rudy took us around town to all the places we needed to visit to get checked in, get a visa, get a cruising permit, and sign up for the Canal—places that were in unmarked buildings, with unmarked staircases, at the top of which were unmarked doors—places we would have had great difficulty finding ourselves. He charged us $10 for this service. Along the way we learned about the other things Rudy could do regarding the Canal transit, and we engaged him to make these things happen for us. He lined up three professional line-handlers and had mooring lines delivered (four are required, at least 125 feet long), as well as tires (eight of them, wrapped in heavy garbage bags, to tie on either side the boat to protect us). The "admeasurer" came, made a bunch of measurements (an anachronism, since small yachts now pay a flat fee, and not according to their measurements), and gave us a bunch of forms. Rudy took us and the forms to the bank where we paid $500 for the transit plus $800 as a "buffer" (i.e., a deposit) in case we damaged the Canal(!), and with that we were ready.

We had read all the books about how the Canal was built: the unsuccessful attempts, the diseases, the lives lost in its building, and the marvel of the final design. We had studied cross-sections of the locks, aerial views of the route, and charts of the waterway. We had read innumerable accounts of yachts that had made the transit. But nothing prepared us for the sound and motion of tons of water filling the 1,000-foot-long chamber, or the sight of the huge bow of a 635-foot freighter as it pulled to within 50 feet behind us. We were not prepared for how strange it would feel to sail over the drowned ruins of twenty-nine Indian villages buried beneath Gatun Lake, or how strong the current produced by the exchange of fresh water and seawater would be in the last lock. We could not have imagined how easily the 800-ton doors (the original doors, nearly a century old, but still so precisely hung that it takes only a 40-horsepower engine to move them) would open and close to move us across the Continental Divide. Transiting the Canal was right up there on the awesome scale for this voyage.

Three locks are on the Caribbean side and three on the Pacific side of the Canal. For the first three, we were tied alongside another yacht slightly larger than ours, and we went through the locks tied together as one boat. The two of us were first positioned behind a large barge, and were tied alongside a tug that was tied to the wall of the lock. After the lock filled and the gates opened, the barge moved ahead and we disengaged ourselves from the tug. The tug moved into position in the next lock and we retied to it. Not a difficult maneuver.

The last three locks, however, are notoriously tricky. Here we were positioned in *front* of a freighter and "center chamber"—that is, the two yachts, still tied together, were positioned in the middle of the lock by our four long lines tied off at the lock sides. The worrisome aspect of these locks is a swift current that moves through the lock when the gates are opened to move to the lower lock. We had read of yachts being caught by these currents before they were tied in place in the next lock and being smashed into the lock gates (those 800-ton gates that we paid a damage deposit to protect). Even our eight tires would not save us from the damage *Another Horizon* would sustain from such an event.

The Canal Authority requires a yacht to have four line handlers on board, in addition to the captain. For us that was Rudy (the taxi driver), two of his compañeros, and me. We were also assigned an "advisor," a pilot who managed our transit. He coordinated with other vessels making the transit and instructed us when and where to move. The pilot was competent, but Rudy and his two compatriots, with innumerable transits under their belts, were our measure of safety. They knew all the pitfalls. They anticipated every move and calmed my jittery nerves, laughing when I flitted from one to the other asking what was happening now, what was going to happen, how were we going to do this or that.

I was very nervous. But they were experts, and soon had me enjoying the trip. In the last locks we were tied center-chamber quickly and efficiently. Rudy pointed to the current as it came rushing down to us. The lines strained and our knot meter flipped from zero to six knots! And thanks to Rudy and company, it appeared we would get our damage deposit back.

As the last gate opened and we passed through to the Pacific once again, we cheered. We had crossed the Continental Divide. We had passed through some kind of barrier—mental as well as physical—and we were now free to carry on. Next destination? Home—only 4,000 miles away.

* * * * *

We had done something Columbus couldn't have imagined in his wildest dreams. In fact, on his last voyage (1502–1504) Columbus actually sailed along the isthmus coast. But he couldn't have known what lay just over those mountains, a mere 50 miles away: another ocean, much bigger than the one he already knew. The world, my dear Columbus, is huge. We can tell you that much.

Purgatory

Puerto Madero

There are two ways to get to San Francisco from Panama. For the first, you head out into the Pacific, sailing west until you find some sort of wind that will take you to Hawaii. From Hawaii you can make the West Coast with reasonable ease. The second way is to work *all the way* up the west coast of Central America and California. The first option puts you at sea for weeks.

After finishing the Atlantic crossing, Stephen had said, "No more long ocean passages," and I sympathized. His heart problem worried him; he was feeling tired. Keeping the boat fit was wearing on him. And long ocean passages meant having to solve all of our boat problems without the benefit of chandleries, mechanics, or calm anchorages in which to effect repairs. I was beginning to feel tired too. To me, long ocean passages meant a lot of hard sailing and dealing with the inevitable bad weather, conditions that I knew I would no longer consider fun, let alone an "adventure." So, okay, no more long ocean passages.

The problem with the alternative—sailing up the coast—is that you are moving against the prevailing winds and currents, *all* the way. Contrary winds blow in several areas of the Americas' west coast, with potentially serious gale-type winds that could be dangerous, or at the very least, miserable. This route also has areas of calm, with no wind at all. All this suggests that having a good engine is desirable, even necessary.

And therein lay our problem.

Our engine, we all know now, had been problematic throughout the voyage: chronic oil leaks, chronic coolant leaks, chronic this, chronic that. But somehow Stephen, with the occasional help of a professional mechanic, had been able to keep it functional. More recently we were pouring oil into it constantly, and the fresh-water reservoir kept overflowing. But one way or another it had kept running, and we hoped that would continue to be the case as we turned right at the end of the Canal.

At the south end of Costa Rica, after a breather at Golfito, we headed for the north end of the country, a place called Bahía Potrero—"Peaceful Bay"—a three-day run. We were motor-sailing, as expected. In the wee hours of the second day, I was off watch, asleep, when I was awakened by the sudden quiet of the engine being turned off, and Stephen softly cursing.

"What is it?" I called out from the bunk.

"The engine has overheated," came the dispirited reply. The raw water flow was normal, so it was something in the freshwater system.

"Leave it until the morning when there's better light," I suggested. "We can just drift for a few hours." We were in one of those calm areas.

In the morning light, Stephen spent two hot, sweaty hours in the engine room, poking and prodding everything he could think of to find our problem. He finally had to admit defeat. "Well, all right, we'll just sail the rest of the way to Potrero," I conceded.

At midmorning a gentle breeze picked up off the beam, and at first we did quite well. It was even pleasant. But toward the end of the day, the wind shifted to our "nose" and gradually increased. During that night there were periods of 25-knot winds—not outrageous, but since we were hard onto it, we were stressed a little. By the next morning the wind had risen to 30 knots, and the weather forecast was plain: "More wind." We had only 20 miles to go, but it took us all day to sail those miles, tacking into 35 and 40 knots of wind and watching 6- and 7-foot waves come crashing over the deck. We had to steer by hand, tacking often to maintain a good course and plunging into waves that were like molasses, slowing us down, at times, almost to a standstill.

"Are we having fun?" I asked Stephen, mimicking good cheer I didn't feel. His eyes had a glazed look; there were no words, not even a whisper. We reached Bahía Potrero just at sunset, truly exhausted from some of the hardest sailing I can remember.

The next day Stephen tried again to find the problem with the engine, but in vain. We went in search of a mechanic. Potrero was not a yachtie haven, and the best we could do was an auto mechanic with some knowledge of diesel engines. I fretted at the waste of time and money. To his credit, the auto guy worked his way through the pieces of the engine that could be causing our problem and convinced us that the freshwater pump was not pumping. All right!

"It will take two to three days to fix," he said, because he would have to go to San José, the capital of Costa Rica, to find the parts.

"Whatever it takes," we said.

It didn't really matter if it took a few days, because the wind continued to howl. At Bahía Potrero we were on the southern edge of the first nasty-wind area—the Golfo de Papagayo. Our winds on the approach to Potrero were just a precursor of the days to come. The "Papagayos" blew up to 40 knots night and day, and that was just in the harbor. These winds are affected by weather on the Caribbean side of Central America, and they can be difficult to predict. They often seem whimsical, turning on and off as you work your way north along the coast.

After ten days of constant gales, the locals were telling us that this was the hardest and longest Papagayo that they could remember. Why was I was not surprised? The wind was so strong it raised standing waves in the harbor, blew spray through our open ports, and kept us awake at night. When it occasionally fell below 25 knots, the "quiet" was remarkable.

One morning, friends on another boat in the harbor felt the winds had moderated sufficiently to venture up the coast. Later in the day they reported over the radio that winds were in the 50-knot range, with gusts to 70 knots—hurricane force. The seas were white; they had never experienced anything like it. If their engine had quit, they said, they would have lost their boat on the rocky shore in a flash. We decided we could be happy with 40-knot winds at anchor.

We had long since had our freshwater pump reinstalled, and a test in the harbor was encouraging, so we were ready if the wind ever abated. After 12 days of blowing, there appeared to be a lessening. The weather forecasts were not conclusive. Maybe, maybe not. But in the harbor the wind was so light we couldn't stand it. How could this not be a window for us?

We dashed around, making ready to carry on. We would follow the strategy suggested by veterans of Papagayo crossings: set a reefed sail appropriate for 40 knots, and supplement with the motor if more power were needed when the wind was light. In this way we would not be constantly going through the energy-sapping exercise of reefing and unreefing the sails every other hour. Off we went, motoring in 10 knots of wind. We were feeling optimistic, even elated. We were on our way home again.

An hour later the engine overheated. We turned around just as the wind sprang to 30 knots. Our hearts sank and our muscles quivered at the task of tacking back into Potrero—again.

We found another mechanic.

One of our problems in all of this business was language. Our Spanish was adequate in the markets, in restaurants, and on the street. But the intricacies of exhaust elbows, heat exchangers, and freshwater pumps were quite beyond our linguistic capabilities. Nevertheless, our newfound friend was good at understanding hand gestures and drawings, and he soon had us up and running one more time, at a fine, cool temperature.

Another weather window presented itself a few days later and we were off—again. The Papagayos were reasonably mellow, only piping up now and then to 30 knots. We were content to plow through the waves of these wind surges. Our engine chugged along just fine in the calmer moments ... until the second day, when it overheated—yet again.

We shrugged. "We are being tested here," I said to Stephen. "Some god of engines is taking us to task. Why didn't we sell the boat in Florida like all our friends?"

We were heading now for El Salvador, hoping to find refuge up a river at a new marina that had been recommended to us. We called ahead to the marina on the radio. We had engine problems. Could they help us? But of course! They would send a *panga* in the morning to take us in tow. Through the night we continued along the coast of Nicaragua, sailing hard on the wind, tacking, tacking ...

As dawn broke we arrived at the narrow entrance to Bahía Jiquilisco, and there was the panga, two miles out to sea and heading our way. Luis threw us a line and proceeded to tow us a full thirteen miles, over the sandbar of the bay and up the river to Marina Barillas, an El Salvador phenomenon.

It had not been so many years since the El Salvador revolution was quelled. Seven years before, when we started out, no cruising yacht would have approached this coast: it was considered too dangerous. But now there were two or three places where yachts could put in and find a warm welcome. This is not to say that the country had fully recovered from its conflict. We saw armed guards everywhere we went, and at times we were accompanied by armed security personnel when we left the marina compound. The haves and have-nots (so much of what the revolution was about) were still evident. But in general, the Salvadorans were happy to see us, although many (especially young children) seemed mystified by our presence.

Coincidentally, we arrived in the country the day after a third earthquake of over 6.5 on the Richter scale in less than a month. There was no part of this small country unaffected by these quakes. When we journeyed into the nearest town (a 45-minute car ride) we saw buildings crumbled, compromised, leaning, demolished. But life continued. The market was thriving; stores were adjusting, and selling wares; schools were in session, even if outdoors—and people stared. The unasked question, I'm sure: why were we here? Gringos from the north had been venturing into this town for only a few months. The yachts in the marina were active in rehabilitation efforts, so we scoured our lockers for extra clothing to send into the hill towns, where the need was critical.

And we worked on the engine. At Barillas there were two other American yachties who had been engine mechanics in their former lives. Their advice and expertise were invaluable. They worked side by side with Stephen to conquer this demon, and with their help we soon had the engine running smoothly, and coolly, once again. We made test runs up and down the river for hours on end. We were satisfied. We had this problem licked.

Sooner than we might have wished at another time, we set off down the river and turned north once again. There were headwinds as usual, but they were light, so we ran the engine gently. But just as we approached the Guatemalan/Mexican border a hefty head wind developed. We pushed the engine a bit—and it overheated. We had no choice but to duck into the nearest harbor, Puerto Madero, the southernmost port of Mexico.

The engine problem was developing into a nightmare.

With considerable resignation we started the process of finding mechanics, gesturing and drawing diagrams of our problems. Pumps and heat exchangers were taken away, repaired, and returned, but this time there was no improvement in the condition. We decided that *new* pumps and exchangers were probably needed by now, and we called back to the San Francisco Bay Area for help. To expedite the delivery of the parts (Mexico is not an easy country into which to import things), we arranged for a mechanic from Oakland to fly down, deliver and install the parts, and check out the rest of the engine—just to be sure.

Bless his big heart, Nate, our mechanic-on-white-horse, arrived with parts in hand, and we anxiously brought him to our crippled craft. He suggested we start the engine so that he could see for himself what our problems were. Stephen set the starting-battery on, I turned the ignition key, and ... nothing. The engine would not even start.

Nate and Stephen spent two days taking the engine completely apart, cleaning, fixing, installing, and putting back together, but to no avail. The engine would not start. After careful analysis, Nate finally had to conclude that the engine was "dead," and there was nothing more for him to do. We were stunned.

*   *   *   *   *

Puerto Madero, in the state of Chiapas, is a small town engaged in fishing. In one part of the long, narrow harbor there were three dozen shrimp boats (60-foot trawler-type boats) crowded onto three concrete docks. Over 100 pangas (20-foot open dories), fishing at night for shark and dorado, ranged along the beach on the other side. A couple of swank, 140-foot tuna clippers came and went, bringing thousands of tons of tuna to the processing plant nearby. And dozens of Indians paddled by in dugout canoes, casting nets in the confines of the harbor for mullet and baitfish. This was not a sleepy fishing village, but an active, thriving, busy, smelly, dirty, oily, bloody fishing village in which we had cast our anchor. And its amenities were few.

At anchor and without an engine, we had little electrical energy, especially at night. So we turned off anything that wasn't essential—such as the refrigerator—and at night we used candles and flashlights instead of our cabin lights. We wanted to conserve our meager electric power to use the radio for e-mail, an all-important link to finding an answer to our problem.

But the most difficult aspect of this disaster was the lack of fresh water. The water of the harbor was full of blood and guts—literally. I gagged to look at it. We could not use our watermaker. And even filtering the village water seemed risky here. We ended up purchasing bottled water at great expense and hassle, trucking it from the village, carrying it down the beach to the dinghy, schlepping it out to the boat, hoisting the heavy bottles onto the deck, and pouring it into the tanks. Without adequate water, we bathed only every two to three days, and we laundered only what was absolutely necessary. We could not afford to wash the boat or to clean *anything* should it happen to get dirty—and *everything* on the boat did get dirty. We rode in our dinghy to shore, a black, gritty beach ten minutes away. Despite our care, the black and grit transferred to the dinghy, to the boat, to the floors, to the cushions, to the bed.

And it was hot. We sweated day and night. I wished I could dive overboard to cool off, as we so often did in the tropics. But with dead fish floating by and blood from the fish-processing co-ops swirling about, it was not a consideration. In a few days, sweat rashes appeared on embarrassing parts of our bodies. Although I wore a semiclean T-shirt after our infrequent but welcome showers, I quickly changed to the same old sweat-soaked shirt as soon as the day's heat emerged. There was no sense in getting another shirt sweaty when you already had one going.

*   *   *   *   *

In the dinghy, on the way back from seeing Nate to the airport, Stephen and I reviewed our options.

We could truck the boat home. But there were no facilities in Puerto Madero to lift the boat out of the water and onto a truck bed.

We could get a tow to Acapulco, the closest next port, where we could—well, do something else about the engine. But Acapulco was 500 miles away, and a tow across the Golfo de Tehuantepec (another gale-troubled gulf) would be dangerous.

We could *sail* it home. For heaven's sake, why not? Back to Plan A—that other option for getting from Panama to San Francisco. It would work just as well from southern Mexico. We thought long and hard about this one. The greatest risk was that without the engine, our energy sources were limited. During the day we had the solar panels, but one was now broken, and the farther north we traveled, the more likely we were to have cloudy days. When the wind blew, we had the wind generator. But especially at night, if there was no wind (and that could be expected), we ran some risk of not having adequate energy for navigation lights and the autopilot (essential for our short-handed crew), to say nothing of navigation equipment and radar. And then there was the matter of shipping traffic, which would also increase as we sailed north. If we were in the path of a freighter, and we had no wind, we would have no power to get out of the way. *And* we had said some time ago that long ocean passages were not a good idea—for other reasons.

We couldn't just abandon the boat there. Although, in my frame of mind at the time, pulling the plug and letting her settle into the mud had some appeal, but that was financially ridiculous, among other things.

And we couldn't spend the rest of our lives in Puerto Madero. We had to think of something else.

That evening as the sun was setting, I sat in the back of the cockpit, behind the wheel, and wept. We were only six hundred miles from completing our circumnavigation, and at the moment we couldn't see a way to get there. That seemed so sad.

The next morning we pulled up our socks, got on the phone, and got down to brass tacks about a solution. With the help of expert friends at home, it took two days to decide that the best way to extricate us from this miserable state was to install a new engine. It would be a formidable task, and a formidable expense.

It took a week of expensive phone calls to determine which engine we could install with the fewest problems. As we had been reminded by our mechanics for years, our particular (now very dead) engine was no longer manufactured ("a boon to society," said Stephen). Things such as specs on the engine bed, the v-drive transmission, and which direction our prop turned had to be taken into consideration. After hours of consultation with manufacturers, mechanics, and other Valiant owners, Stephen finally settled on an engine that would fit in our engine room and should work, with a little adjusting here and there.

The brightest moment of that week was discovering John in Puerto Vallarta, the sales agent for this engine, who would import it for us and come to Puerto Madero to install it. We were now at the end of our third week in Puerto Madero.

For three *more* weeks I lived on an emotional roller coaster, depending on the daily message from John. The engine is on its way. It's not on its way. It hasn't arrived in California yet. It has arrived in California, and they will ship it tomorrow. They did not ship it. It is on a plane this morning and will arrive in Puerto Vallarta this afternoon. They shipped it to Guadalajara instead. The engine is too tall to fit through the cargo door of the plane out of Guadalajara. I (John) am going to rent a truck and drive the engine back to Puerto Vallarta. *Three weeks.*

Each day, after our morning call to John, we were faced with what to do with the long, hot day ahead. Some days we took the two-mile walk into town to shop for food, passing a squatter's village as we went. The people, mostly Guatemalans, had settled there during the unrest in Chiapas back in 1993. Signs of the Zapatistas indicated that these folks were with the revolutionary group who had protested government repression. Although it was quiet then, it was not hard to see why these people had been upset with the feudal-like control over their existence. Even then, as we walked by their encampment, we saw makeshift scrap-wood-and-bamboo huts with dirt floors, no electricity, no plumbing, and fresh water delivered only occasionally to crude cisterns.

So who was I to be wailing about our wretched conditions? These people had no choice in the matter. If I stopped feeling sorry for myself, I knew that one day, somehow, we would escape Puerto Madero. But the people in these dusty, spare, somber tracts would most likely live here for the rest of their lives. These were sobering walks into town, where we scoured the shops for fresh vegetables.

* * * * *

One day John said he was coming. The engine was definitely on its way to the Tapachula airport (only twelve miles away). He and Fernando, his mechanic-assistant, had plane tickets for the evening flight the next day. I took this to be John's last message from afar. If they had tickets and were actually coming to this bleak haven of ours, we would be saved—finally. We sprang into action.

Stephen was off to see the port captain to arrange a place at the wharf where we could offload our dead engine and onload our salvation. The port captain said he would take care of a tow to the wharf. A spot at the shrimp-boat docks was cleared for us, and a panga came by to tow us over. This was progress. I felt almost jubilant. I almost didn't notice the even more filthy water by the docks, or the oil sludge on our pier that was instantly transferred to our hull.

My job was to get a crane to pluck the old engine out and plop the new one in. We were told that the API agency (a sort of port authority) could help us with that. I found API a good mile and a half from the shrimp docks, a hot, dusty, sweaty walk. Here I met a familiar problem in this town: few people spoke English.

After working through several folk who didn't understand what I wanted, they found a fellow from somewhere in the bowels of the building who had enough English that we could at least get the problem established. What I couldn't get across, and had no Spanish word for, was "crane." I drew a picture.

"Ahhh, *grua.*"

"Right, *grua,* that's what we need," I smiled. There was by now a small crowd gathered, with lots of chatting. After a bit, a tall fellow—looking taller next to the prevailing short height of the average Mexican—joined the group. A *grua* operator, I was told. Excellent. So, how much will this excellent *grua* and tall *grua* operator cost? There was a long discussion about this, but it was finally established that the job would probably only take one hour, and so the charge would be 370 pesos (about $38). I tried not to look as if that was the most incredible bargain I could imagine, and said very seriously, "I'll pay for that right now," to seal the deal. I explained that as soon as we had the new engine on the dock, I would come and let the crane operator know we were ready for the *grua.* They would look forward to seeing me tomorrow. They were so cordial.

The next day dawned and Stephen went off to the airport with a hired truck to meet John and our new engine. An hour later he returned—no John, no engine. John had discovered that the engine had landed in Mexico City and had not been transferred to the plane for Tapachula. He was in Mexico City to personally escort the engine, but would be delayed a day.

I was crestfallen. No, I was outraged. No, *furious.* There was uncontrollable emotion, words, shouts, and beating of fists. Tears.

With remarkable calm, Stephen said, "You'd better go tell API that we need the crane tomorrow, not today."

So off I went, stomping (if I'm not mistaken) on the long, hot, sweaty walk to API. On the cross road to the API road, as I passed several thatched huts, I was confronted suddenly by a pack of ten or eleven dogs—snarly dogs with fur raised on their backs. Having been attacked by a snarly, fur-raised-on-the-back dog a few years previously in Tonga—attacked and bitten—I was immediately frightened, and I'm sure I was emitting that I'm-scared-stiff smell that dogs apparently can detect. This time there were ten of these fang-mouthed brutes. Why? Why? Why? They pinned me against the barbed-wire fence on the opposite side of the road. Eventually a woman emerged from one of the huts (whatever took her so long?) and threw some stones at the dogs. They retreated, whimpering. Not your SPCA treatment of dogs, but effective. "*Gracias,*" I grumbled, as I stomped on my hot, dusty, sweaty way.

At the API building they all seemed to know me. But then I was dressed like no other woman within a thousand miles of this place: shorts; sweat-stained T-shirt; long, blond hair falling out the back of a baseball cap; and sunglasses hanging on leashes on my chest. And since it was a nonshower day, they probably knew who it was without even looking up.

The crane operator must have seen me coming, because he came to my side immediately. He said a long string of words. I was so upset that I couldn't concentrate on his Spanish well enough to understand, but I'm sure it was something like "time for the *grua.*" I sighed. "Where's the hombre that speaks English?" I asked resignedly, in my faulty Spanish.

The crane operator ushered me into a largish room where nine or ten old, rickety metal desks were lined up with nine or ten Mexican bureaucrats seated, shuffling papers. My English-speaking pal was in the midst of them. I explained our problem. No engine today, so we need the crane tomorrow.

"Oh, no," he said, "it's not possible. Tomorrow is Saturday, and we only work Monday to Friday."

That did it. My barely-contained emotions began to escape. My lower lip quivered, my eyes pooled. The crane operator was watching me intently, not understanding. There was a long exchange between my interpreter and the operator. Finally, the interpreter said, "Well, he says he will do it tomorrow, for you. Just especially for you."

Chivalry may be dead in the U.S. of A., but, in some cultures, a damsel in distress still counts for something. The pools in my eyes overflowed. He was too tall for me to reach his face for a kiss, so I kissed my palm and patted his cheek. There was a satisfied murmur from the people throughout the room who had been following the drama; their paper-shuffling stilled for the moment. "*Mañana,*" I said, exiting quickly before there could be any change of mind.

I had stones in both hands ready for the dogs; they were not going to humiliate me again. But they didn't appear as I expected. Instead, there was a small herd of Brahma bulls ambling unattended down the road. I pinned myself against the barbwire fence. I didn't think throwing stones at these fellows would be a good idea, and I hoped they had some goal in mind that would keep them on the road.

Finally back on the shrimp dock, I found Stephen preparing the old engine for its withdrawal. "We are being tested—further—in some way here," I told him. "If someone offered me a few bucks for this heap of fiberglass, I'd take it and go home. I'm ready to quit." Stephen didn't have to look at me this time to know I wasn't kidding. He felt the same way.

The next morning the new engine and the mechanics arrived on time. The crane operator arrived with the *grua,* and he plucked and plopped without so much as kissing the woodwork of the boat in the operation. I folded a gratuity into my *grua* friend's hand and effused my thanks. He reached down, put his arms around me, and hugged me, ever so gently. This was not just a good guy, this was a prince.

It was now two in the afternoon. John and Fernando began their installation. They worked without so much as a potty break until 10 PM. The next morning they were back at 7 and worked continuously again until 1 PM, when John turned the ignition key and the new engine sprang to life. Oh lord, what a sweet sound.

After some tuning and tightening, running and checking, we were ready to move off the shrimp dock and back to the anchorage. We cast off the lines, and Stephen backed out into the channel. He changed to forward gear, and swore. The engine was overheating!

"Go back to the dock," I shouted.

"I can't," he said, "I have no power." In a flash we both realized what was wrong. We had been sitting still in one place for six weeks, and although the water might have been particularly virulent to us, barnacles probably found it appetizing. There was little doubt that the propeller was encrusted with these creatures, impeding its operation. And equally likely, the raw-water intake was jammed with them, impeding the cooling water flow and causing the overheating. We stopped the engine and dropped anchor quickly.

Normally I would have popped on my snorkel and mask, flipped overboard, and cleaned off the offending growth in a jiffy. But just looking at the water made me want to puke.

"I can't," I said to Stephen, "I just can't." I was both furious and distraught. I resorted again to words, tears, shouts, and thumping of fists. John and Fernando were struck dumb, watching. This was not normal feminine behavior, I know. But all the frustrations of the last six weeks were now concentrated in this last agony.

Just then Domingo, our neighbor at the shrimp boat dock, called out, "My son dives. He has a compressor."

Where is this man worth his weight in gold? I wanted to know.

"He is coming to visit me tomorrow, and he'll take care of you then."

"Okay, we'll just hang out on our anchor here until he arrives," or until we sink, or we are wasted on the rocks over there, or something else happens. Dear lord, what else could happen now to test us? We waved good-bye to John and Fernando.

The next morning Domingo's son Sam came out and dove on our bottom, bringing up barnacles almost an inch in diameter. "It's a mess," he said. But within an hour he had it all clean, and we were at last motoring, in full control, back to the anchorage. We went to see the port captain, to say good-bye and get our all-important *zarpe* (the port exit paper). It took a full day to put the boat back to rights after so much messy engine work. We were both excited and anxious about our impending departure.

The next morning we were up, nervously hopping about, reeving the last of the lines, closing the hatches against an errant wave, putting away any loose articles. The moment came. We turned the key and the engine purred. Up came the anchor. We motored out of the anchorage and into the channel that led to the open sea. A swell was running, coming into the channel and breaking along the jetties. We needed some power to push against the waves, and I leaned into the throttle a little. The boat surged forward. We plowed along the channel, finally passing the navigation towers at the end of the jetties. We left Puerto Madero behind.

We were delivered.

Endings

We had argued about the matter for weeks. Where does the circumnavigation end? I said Puerto Vallarta, the spot from which we set out to cross the Pacific. Stephen said Zihuatenajo, where we would "cross our path"—that is, the first spot where we would touch some place we had been before on this voyage. A technicality. We would celebrate at both places, I declared. We had sufficient Odessa champagne still in the bilge.

We came to Zihuatenajo first. We had the exact crossing-our-path spot plugged into the GPS, so we would know. We arrived at those coordinates at 10:35 AM on April 19. We looked at each other and went "yeah." I think maybe we exchanged a kiss too.

We were about a mile off the entrance to the harbor, but we didn't bother to go in. We had decided to tie up at the marina just beyond, at Ixtapa. The marina was nearly empty. This was not the time of year for cruising yachts to be in this part of the world.

We took a taxi to Zihuatenajo for a celebratory dinner at a restaurant where we had eaten before, seven years earlier. I could only just remember it. We walked around town. I recognized one shop where we had purchased a rug for Holly's Christmas present, and the rest was a blur. There were two yachts anchored in the harbor where we remembered dozens.

It was all so anticlimactic.

We didn't linger. The next morning we were off again, pushing north. Pushing, pushing to get home. It was as though completing the circumnavigation was just another way station in a string of days. In my mind, the real goal had become San Francisco. My whole being was set on that place. That was really the journey's end.

Even Puerto Vallarta had lost its luster for me. The marina, the shops, the wonderful grocery store, the music from the restaurants surrounding the marina—none of it had the feeling of adventure of our previous visit. It felt old, worn, and listless. Or perhaps it was me—old, worn, and listless. Even the end of "my" circumnavigation did not excite me that much. Just another bottle of champagne.

Puerto Vallarta was the hometown of John and Fernando, our Puerto Madero saviors. They came to our Puerto Vallarta berth to make some adjustments to the engine; to check all the joints, lines, and pumps; and to give it a final blessing. Their clucking over the engine gave me more confidence that the thing would get us home.

John in particular seemed to have something invested in our making it. "Let me know," he said. "When you get there, I want to know."

"Have no fear, John," I said. "You'll know—one way or the other."

We did not tarry at Puerto Vallarta either. I had dreamed, months before, of spending some weeks revisiting old haunts, decompressing, reabsorbing this place of such fine memories. But once there, I couldn't have cared less. There were few people around from our time before; there was so little that was exciting.

In the early morning we departed and turned right, straight across Banderas Bay, to punch our way up to Cabo San Lucas. We had decided to go direct (northwest across the bottom of the Gulf of California), rather than sticking to the coast, via Mazatlán. There was a small risk in this idea. If the wind came up, we would take a beating. But we could reach Cabo in forty-eight hours if all went well, and the weather forecast sounded decent. There were head winds, but mostly light; some lumpy seas, but mostly benign.

It seemed cold: fifty-nine degrees (the air temperature) in the mornings. The water was an icy-looking blue-gray. But isn't this what we wanted? North! We were getting into the northern latitudes—it's twenty-one degrees (latitude) at Cabo San Lucas—so it should be cold. Only seventeen more degrees to go. Seventeen degrees—one thousand miles.

Just as we were safely tied up in the Cabo marina, the weather turned. It rained. The wind kicked up. I heard a tourist on a public phone complaining to someone farther north about the weather, "so cloudy and cool." For us? Cabo was a haven, and we were glad to have it so. We knew it was nasty, ugly, and foul at sea, but we were content to hunker down in this protected place, no matter how cloudy or cool. We were grateful to have arrived before the bad weather did, but we waited impatiently for the system to pass.

It took three days for the weather to clear before we could move on. The worst part was rounding Cabo Falso, as we swung right and north around the tip of Baja. Leftover confused and choppy seas, with gusty winds that naturally accelerate around the cape, added tension to the morning. But as we moved away from that particular land configuration, the seas smoothed, the winds abated, and we were soon plowing through the water at our usual speed. We were heading for Magdalena Bay.

While churning along, I happened into the head (the toilet), as one must now and then as the hours go by. The roll of toilet paper on the toilet paper hanger ran out. I fumbled in the cabinet under the sink for another and found I was reaching a long way back. Down on my hands and knees, I poked around to count the number of TP rolls left—and I got nervous. I had loaded up in Florida, and added to it here and there, but I hadn't counted on six weeks in Puerto Madero. Would fifteen rolls carry us to San Diego? For eight years I had been paranoid about running out of TP, and I made sure I stocked up whenever I could. How could I have been so distracted that I hadn't paid this important matter any attention lately?

The coast along this stretch of the Baja Peninsula was as dramatic as I remembered it: jagged, barren mountains falling sharply to the sea. The hills were a dull, flat brown, but in the early light of day the shadows added rifts, gullies, crags, and fissures. Anchored in Santa Maria, I looked longingly at the beach. This was where, so many years before, we had found enormous sand dollars and bright orange, blue, and purple cockleshells. Couldn't we just take a quick look, one last time?

No. For several reasons. For starters, our electric anchor windlass had conked out and needed attention. We were leaving again the next morning, and having arrived in the late afternoon, time to fix it was precious. (Stephen found a wire pulled loose, which probably happened while we were pounding our way around Cabo Falso.)

Number two: We would have to unpack the dinghy, outboard engine, and so forth, and repack when we returned. It sounded like too much work—especially after all the energy expended on the anchor windlass.

Number three: We had 40 gallons of diesel fuel to decant from our spare jerry cans on deck into the main tanks. In Puerto Vallarta we had invested in several cans to increase our fuel capacity, because we expected we would be motor-sailing all along the outside of Baja. Our fuel capacity in the regular tanks would not be sufficient to motor the whole distance, as we anticipated having to do. The 90 gallons in the main tanks was normally about 500 miles' worth of fuel. But with the new engine, we really didn't know. Cabo to Turtle Bay, the next fuel stop, was about 500 miles. As with toilet paper, we were paranoid about running out of fuel. So we would take time in this calm anchorage to keep the fuel tanks as full as possible.

Number four: We were tired. It had been one of those one-night passages that are exhausting. Six-inch sand dollars and colorful cockleshells would have to be part of my memory of this place. We were not going to have the time to search for them again.

The next morning we were off. The anchor windlass worked fine. The fuel tanks were looking good. The weather remained favorable.

Fifty miles from Turtle Bay the wind increased and the seas became abominable. For ten hours we pitched, plunged, and crashed through them. Tons of water came up over the bow, sluicing down the side decks and pouring into the cockpit. Everything was wet save one tiny square of space right in front of the companionway; it remained dry only because one or the other of us was sitting on it.

The pitching, plunging, and crashing was slowing us down, sometimes to almost a standstill. We were using huge amounts of fuel to move only one or two miles an hour. This was what we had been warned about; this was why we carried the extra fuel on deck; this was why we decanted fuel instead of going ashore in Mag Bay.

About 5 AM the wind dropped, the seas gave up their fury, and we began to feel optimistic about Turtle Bay. We anchored there at 10 AM, with just enough fuel in the tank to make us feel virtuous.

We put 110 gallons back in the tanks and the jerry cans, and were happy to think that would get us to San Diego. We had dinner on shore with other yachties who had been traveling with us since Cabo San Lucas. We were all excited by our progress, our generally favorable passage, and our various feelings about getting to San Diego. Our companions were all Californians who had sailed down to Mexico earlier in the year and were returning to various points along the California coast. They were duly impressed by our odyssey, although I pointed out to them that we were slogging along this part just like them, and it was equally distasteful to us. They laughed.

The slight difference, perhaps, was that San Diego would be another very important landmark for us. We were returning years, not months, later, and by returning to the United States on the West Coast, the journey's end would be in sight: just five hundred miles.

*   *   *   *   *

We continued the slog north along the California coast—harbor hopping, sailing overnight when the conditions were right, stopping when the wind was too strong or we were tired. It took many more days than we cared to mention. But finally the last day dawned in Half Moon Bay, 30 miles from the finish line. For days before this last one the weather had been idyllic—mild breezes, clear skies, and warm. But on that last day of the voyage we awoke to fog so thick we could not see the breakwaters at the entrance to the harbor. My stomach was churning. Wouldn't this be a treat: after eight years of storms, gunboats, reefs, and bomb squads, we run the boat up on some rocks, 30 miles from home.

It took an hour to feel our way out of the harbor, but out in the open sea the fog thinned a bit, and a nice 12-knot breeze filled in, right on the beam. We sailed all the way to the San Francisco ship channel buoys. It was cold.

At the ship channel the wind increased, and we knew without even seeing the Golden Gate Bridge that we were at San Francisco—cold, foggy, and windy! As we closed in on the Gate, the fog lifted to the top of the bridge towers, and between the bridge spans we could see a contingent of friends in their boats, loaded with more friends and family, ready to escort us home.

This at last was the moment. This was not a "yeah" (and maybe a kiss) at Zijuatenajo, or an anticlimax at Puerto Vallarta. This was the exhilarating finale. I was beaming.

We swept under the bridge. Horns tooted (our friends), horns blasted (ships heading out in the fog), horns reverberated (the bridge foghorns). We careened along on the incoming tide, riding some good wind waves, sweeping past the Marin headlands without even realizing they were there. We had blinders on, our sights straight ahead—dead ahead. The Berkeley Marina was within view.

I don't know if our friends were so kind as to let us lead the parade, or whether they were taken by surprise by our speed and single-mindedness. We were not going to hang back for photo-ops; we were not going to worry about whether we had missed anyone; we wanted to get tied up at the dock before anything else broke, or we blew out the sails, or we sank. We had only five miles to go.

How huge can the emotion be to return to the starting point so many years, so many oceans, so many countries later? There was a team from our local Channel Four TV at the dock as we tied our lines, seven years and nine months later. They wanted to tape a little of our first minutes on shore for the evening news.

"Could I just put this wire on your jacket so we can hear what you are saying?" the reporter asked.

"No need," I said, "I'm already wired!" Was I walking some inches off the ground, was my head in some cloud—was I euphoric? There is TV camera footage of me bouncing—really, *bouncing*—along the dock, embracing Stephen, grinning ear to ear, looking drunk with elation.

"Why did you do this, sail around the world?" the reporter asked.

"It's the ultimate goal for a sailor," Stephen said.

"It's probably like Mt. Everest is to mountaineers," I repeated my favorite analogy.

"It was a dream," Stephen made it clear.

Like a lightning bolt, the thought struck me. Had the dream come to an end?

Postlude

I can't remember who said, "There are two terrible things for a man: not to have fulfilled his dream, and to have fulfilled his dream." We had fulfilled our dream, that was clear, but *was* this the end?

For the last six months or so, I had been thinking about how things would be different when the voyage ended. There was no doubt about the things I wouldn't miss: pitching, plunging, and crashing through contrary seas would be one. The anxieties of anchors dragging would be high on the list. But one night off Panama I had looked into the sky and saw *all* the stars. It was brilliantly clear that night, and the stars went down to all the horizons, all the way around. I could see the stars rising and setting. Normally you have to go to a planetarium to see that happen. I would miss that.

And swimming off the boat, watching marine life swarm beneath my feet. I would miss that. Watching the sunset in the middle of the ocean—just *Another Horizon* and the sun. And greeting fleets of dolphin gamboling along our side, playing in our bow wave.

And at night: phosphorescence twinkling in our wake, running like jewels along the deck when a wave splashed on board. And meteor showers, and comets. Falling stars blasting into the atmosphere like rockets, giving off a light so bright it set my heart racing. A new moon rising in the east, a perfect cup, bloodred from the sun and atmospheric particles.

Catching sight of the first bird as we approached land, seeing land after days at sea. Rising and falling on the midocean swell, the only ship on the face of the sea, seemingly the only beings on the face of the earth.

The simplicity of our life, minimalist on the boat, just 40 by 12 feet to keep clean, dust, wipe off the salt, varnish. Oh, all right, the last two are on the "won't miss" list. But this lifestyle was very compatible to my being. Nothing on land could be quite like it.

And what about us? I asked myself, as we homed in on home. Just what had happened during these seven years, nine months? And would there be something missed?

We knew from the beginning that this voyage would test the limits of our determination and tenacity to endure hardships; of our tolerance for other people, whatever their behavior or beliefs; and of our goodwill toward each other, so long together on so small a boat. We knew that the voyage would either change our lives or bring us to our knees. In the nearly eight years we were constantly challenged as to which it would be.

In the Pacific lightning storm, we were close to our knees; at Tanna we were changed. Off the horn of India? Knees. In the port of Suakin? Changed. In Puerto Madero I was definitely *on* my knees, but that tenacity in us got the socks pulled up, and pushed our limits out a little further. Having sailed around the world … yes, our lives had changed.

This was the essence of our experience: we *were* changed. And I would miss the challenges that the voyage put upon us that caused the change.

*   *   *   *   *

This was a voyage to test the human condition—of the world's people as we met them, and of ourselves as we managed our life at sea together. The spirit of adventure, the complexities of the world, and the courage of the world's people, ourselves included, taught us how to live day by day. The sailing was the thread, the fabric was the world, and the colors were the people. The journey was everything.

Acknowledgments

The first time we took our "big" boat out the Golden Gate was the first time ever in my life I got seasick. We had been sailing the Valiant only a few weeks. We were still wrestling with the difference between a weekender and a heavy-displacement, oceangoing boat. Outside the Gate we turned unwittingly into the "potato patch" and crashed about in confused and anxious seas. I had, by then, realized how serious we were about ocean voyaging, and I was turned around by that day. I was going to have to cope with a lot of "stuff," and I was going to have to talk about it to get it out of my head and in front of me, where I could deal with it.

At the yacht club gathering that weekend, it was Carl who suggested that I write about those experiences as we prepared ourselves for the big leap, and I am grateful for that suggestion. Writing about the experiences was immediately cathartic. The yacht club monthly newsletter was my vehicle.

Tom gave me my first break in the commercial publishing world, giving some of my writing an airing in *SAIL* magazine. He made me think that I could write something others would find valuable or enjoy reading.

I have had many readers of my material over the years, but Jack takes the cake. He *always* responded to my letters home, even when I didn't write them. He was the one who said I could write this book. His faith in my writing has been unequaled.

In addition to Jack, I am grateful to Sheila and Mike for the time they took to read and critique the early chapters. Betty and Ron, who read the entire manuscript cover to cover, made the final product infinitely better. Dozens of other friends have been kind with compliments of my writing, which always gave my ego a little boost and sent me back to the keyboard. My thanks to all these supporters.

To our many fellow voyagers: if you are looking for yourselves in these pages, you are there, but for the most part not by name. Many of you were at the same places I talk about, and when we were together, some of you saw what we saw, and a few of you experienced what we experienced—some of the time. But these stories are about the people we met, the countries we visited, the trials we endured, and the wonders we experienced—not really about us. I have said that this book is not about sailing around the world, but about the world as we sailed around it. Once in a while, one or another of you figures in the stories, but I have veiled your identity. (In fact, the names of most of the people in these pages have been changed, just to be fair.)

The cruising community was one of the pleasures of the voyage, and I am grateful to have met each and every one of you. Many of you gave us critical help at critical times. All of you offered friendship, and sharing the life with you was part of joy of this experience. I thank you all for being there.

It goes without saying that this book wouldn't *be* without Stephen. He not only sailed every mile with me, but he read every word of our adventure again and again. And it helped to have someone who occasionally remembered how the story went when I became a little befuddled.

And finally, I thank our daughter Holly for letting us go at a time when we should have been more accessible to her. Not just to see her through her life at the time, but to be able to listen to her enthusiasms as well as the disappointments in her new life. It is one of my few regrets about the voyage—that we were too often too far away. But she was a trooper, and of all our friends and family, she best understood what we were doing, and why it was important to us.

To all these people I am indebted.

978-1-58348-473-9
1-58348-473-6

Printed in the United States
71849LV00003B/343-384